M

VIRTUAL VINTAGE

D0106902

VIRTUAL *Vintage*

THE INSIDER'S GUIDE TO BUYING AND SELLING FASHION ONLINE

LINDA LINDROTH AND
DEBORAH NEWELL TORNELLO

RANDOM HOUSE TRADE PAPERBACKS

NEW YORK

A Random House Trade Paperback Original

Library of Congress Cataloging-in-Publication Data

Lindroth, Linda.
Virtual vintage: the insider's guide to buying and selling fashion online / Linda Lindroth and Deborah Newell Tornello
p. cm.
Includes bibliographical references and index.
ISBN 0-8129-9200-8
1. Vintage clothing—Collectors and collecting. 2. Vintage clothing—Marketing. 3. Internet marketing. I. Tornello, Deborah Newell. II. Title.

GT596.L56 2002
391'.2'074—dc21 2002069925

Random House website address: www.atrandom.com

Printed in the United States of America

BVG 01

Book design by Casey Hampton

For Nanny and Cynthia
—D.N.T.

For C.D.N. and Z.E.N.
—L.L.

ACKNOWLEDGMENTS

I wish to thank my extraordinary husband, Robert, and our brilliant three boys; Peter and Christine Newell; Richard Newell; Sarah Martineau; *gracias y un beso muy grande a* Minie; Janet and Michael Jedlicka; my lovely models, Christine Heinen and Jennifer Thomas; Jill Cincotta; Mary Geraci; Jayne Kirse; Rich Stapleton; Amy Tan; Jill at La France and Sherry at Yesterdaze; Pane Rustica; Derek Ward; Bob Baggett Black and White Processing; and last but not least my coauthor, Linda Lindroth, and our exceptional and patient editor, Mary Bahr.   —D.N.T.

I would like to acknowledge the assistance of dear friends who wear clothes so well: Hedda Kopf and Loretta DiPietro; Jane Booth Vollers, Dick Blacher, Langdon Hammer, Jill Campbell, Barbara Ehrlich, Cynthia Beth Rubin, Frank Poole, and Bert Hamelin for their interest and support; Deborah Aiges and Mary Bahr for their midwifery; my coauthor, the indefatigable Deborah Newell Tornello, and her husband, Robert Tornello, ever ready and willing with a camera; and Craig and Zachary Newick for their patience and love.   —L.L.

CONTENTS

INTRODUCTION

$\mathcal{N}$ow, then . . .

Are you ready to go shopping for vintage clothing in cyberspace? It certainly seems ironic: searching for treasures of the past in the medium of the future, the Internet. Yet plenty of stylish sorts are busy right now doing just that—rummaging through the online vintage boutiques, resale shops, and auction web pages as effortlessly as if they were standing in their favorite neighborhood thrift store or consignment emporium, eagerly sorting away.

Today, as a well-dressed individual, you regard yourself *as* an individual. Instead of relying on the expression of a single designer, you prefer to trust your own unique influences and inspirations. And vintage clothing works beautifully in this modern context, whether your personal style asserts sophistication or quirkiness. Fabulous fashion is wherever you find it. Indeed, you've happened upon some of your favorite outfits at out-of-the-way yard sales and consignment shops, not to mention the closets, attics, and garages of relatives. Lately you've been hearing about a new source for unique chic. As it turns out, the avenue leading directly to it starts on top of your desk: in your computer.

Many brilliant books about vintage fashion have been written of late, and volumes of information on the subject are now widely available in libraries, at neighborhood bookstores, and through online booksellers. But none has truly addressed the subject of the Internet as a significant and breathtakingly inexhaustible source for sharp suits and retro ball gowns alike, as a cost-effective venue for selling one's wardrobe treasures, and as a surprisingly sociable entity in general. In fact, vintage collectors, shoe mavens, trend hunters, and stylists will often meet online over a sought-after something or other and wind up exchanging stories.

And that's exactly how we came to know each other—not just as friends and fellow vintage fanatics but as experienced shoppers and collectors who could advise each other about this exciting new marketplace. The months passed, the e-mails accumulated, and a body of information began to emerge: the strategies, the sources, the things to avoid, and the things to hunt down with due fervor.

And we decided to write this book.

For our purposes, "vintage" means fabulous fashion of the past, from the last century to the last season, as reflected in our own diverse collections. If you're like us, your Victorian jackets and 1950's dresses share wardrobe space with stylish finds from more recent eras, like Helmut Lang jeans and Vivienne Westwood suits. Wherever *your* unique sartorial interests lie, if you love wonderful clothes and can access a functioning, Internet-connected computer, *Virtual Vintage* is *the* indispensable guide to have on hand. Whether you're a novice—or simply nervous—online shopper or, alternatively, a seasoned web surfer wishing to expand a collection or downsize an overstuffed closet, we'll help you navigate the wide world of online vintage boutiques and auctions. You'll discover the wealth of resources for fashion and accessories available online and learn how to search for a specific treasure—and, when you find it, how to buy it with confidence and savvy. If you'd like to try your hand at selling online, we'll walk you through the steps involved and let you in on some pretty clever tactics without overwhelming you with technical details. There's even a chapter devoted to repairing and reworking your finds, advising you when—and how—to tackle things yourself and when to call in the professionals.

You'll delight in the comprehensive list of preworn-clothing and vintage websites—the first of its kind, with the inventory and price points of each online boutique described, making it easy to select the shops that suit your taste and budget. (Whoever imagined there were *this* many sources online?) And style mavens of every (pin)stripe are sure to enjoy the extensive list of online fashion information sources, including virtual fashion magazines and Internet addresses of numerous top designers' boutiques, fashion museum sites, and even websites where sellers may purchase display items or digital cameras.

Think of *Virtual Vintage* as a shopping companion, vintage boutique directory, fashion reference book, and online auction guide—all smartly rolled into one.

Enjoy.

THE BRAVE NEW WORLD OF FINE OLD CLOTHES

BY DEBORAH NEWELL TORNELLO

"Tell me a story," I said to my parents, though it was long past my bedtime and the sky was already thick with stars. "Well, just tell me the part where the fairy godmother waves her wand and turns the raggedy dress into a pretty gown. Pleeeeease."

They didn't give in, so I decided to read *Cinderella* to myself. I leafed through the pages, mainly looking at the illustrations, and arrived at my favorite scene: the transformation of the Dress. Not feeling sleepy at all now, I threw back the pink chenille bedspread and climbed to the floor. Where did I leave *The Illustrated Alice*? There it was, next to the easel and paint box. *Alice in Wonderland* was another favorite: I desperately wanted that blue, full-skirted dress with the clouds of lace beneath and the crisp white apron on top.

It was the 1960's, and most of the women in England didn't wear full skirts and aprons. They wore sharp, triangular little minidresses and knee-high boots. They cut their hair into geometric shapes and painted their nails frosted pink. When my mother danced around the living room with me, there was no orchestra playing waltzes but rather a TV show called *Top of the*

Pops playing the latest by the Rolling Stones, the Beatles, and the Kinks. Later, I would watch an episode of *Batman* while she made dinner, admiring Catwoman's outfit and plotting a way to duplicate her look by wearing my ballet tights with a black sweater borrowed from my little brother.

Fashion has been a part of my consciousness for as long as I can remember: It was featured front and center in moments of triumph, and it was there, too, when bitter disappointments fell across my path. I can remember exactly what I wore when I was awarded first prize in the Junior Art Competition (a baby-blue empire-waisted dress with puffed sleeves). I gazed at the big screen and watched Audrey, Grace, and Liz in their splendor, in their splendid roles; on those nights, my dreams fairly glowed—movie moonlight on dark satin. And I've never forgiven my ballet teacher for casting me as one of the gray mice—gray, not even pink and white!—in *The Tailor of Gloucester,* when I would have given my eyeteeth to dance in *The Nutcracker* instead and pirouette around the stage, wearing the proper tutu of the Sugar Plum Fairy.

Like all teenagers, I wanted to fit in. In the 1970's, that meant wearing an inordinate amount of denim, gauze, and a shiny new fabric called Qiana. I spent all my pocket money on sewing patterns and fabric; from these, I made all sorts of skirts and dresses for myself, constantly striving to re-create the expensive department store clothes worn by the popular girls. All the while, a small voice in my head reminded me that I wasn't like everyone else; I was different. At thirteen, I despised these little communiqués from my subconscious, and I dismissed them, wanting nothing to do with anybody or anything that might set me apart from the crowd.

At seventeen, I spun around on my platform heels and embraced the voice like a neglected teddy bear.

It happened when I was studying theater in college, helping out in the costume department to earn extra credit. There was an upcoming play in the works, *Cat on a Hot Tin Roof,* and my responsibilities included the procuring and altering of some period full slips for the character Maggie. I was sent to a thrift store—some dusty old warehouse on the outskirts of town—and, like Lucy in the C. S. Lewis novel, as I stepped into the wardrobe, I entered Narnia.

Finery. There was no other word for it, and there it was. I walked through the hedgerows of abandoned uniforms and forgotten fibers, brushing aside the everyday and plucking whatever bright blooms caught my eye. Real silk slips with coffee-colored lace and hand-rolled hems! I wondered what else might be there, waiting for a new home—indeed, for a new life. My heart started pounding. Some of these slips were going home with *me.* So were those two beaded pillbox hats, and so was that red wool coat with the fitted waist and flared, paneled skirt. Those buttons . . . that lining . . . the quality of the workmanship.

Since that day when I experienced my Reversal of Costume, I've never longed for sameness and conformity: quite the opposite. My eye has become trained to seek quality over trendiness, and I've rejoiced in the limitless offerings of thrift stores, vintage boutiques, and estate sales, having become an expert at sifting through mounds of discarded clothes and unearthing an exquisite beaded cardigan or embroidered clutch. Always, I find myself musing about the garment's Other Life. I hold up a brocade sheath and wonder about its previous owner's taste in cocktails and music, movies and escorts. Since we both loved this dress, perhaps there were other things we had in common. I shake out the chiffon skirts of my favorite 1950's ball gown and study it, for a while imagining where it might have traveled, what it might have incited.

Deborah Newell Tornello—1950's floral cotton crinoline dress by Suzy Perette; rhinestone-and-bead earrings by Trifari. *Robert S. Tornello*

Why do I love vintage clothes? Perhaps the answer lies in the mystery and history floating about the garments like invisible layers. If ever I do meet the dress's original owner, one layer is peeled back, revealing the rich and fascinating details of the others. Far more often, though, I am left to fill in the details with the paintbrush of my imagination. And this I do, every time I'm able to steal a few moments and race into my favorite haunts to indulge this passion for the styles of other times. I wonder, I dream, I invent.

In reality, I'm living in the twenty-first century, but my modern jeans coexist nicely with my vintage genes. My lifestyle is that of a typically busy grown-up, and I've given in to the demands of the age and bought a computer. I'm sitting in front of it now, in fact, connected to the seemingly borderless world of the Internet. In the old days of style stalking, the term "searching" entailed transportation and time. Now it's defined as using the right words, finessing the system, as it were. I open new windows without having to step out my door. And here it is: finery. Where to begin?

I gaze at the small screen with its invitation to explore the brave new world of vintage clothes, and I feel a familiar sensation. Here is a lovely gown, there is a gorgeous skirt, and as I look at them, I think: Tell me a story.

WEARING HER MOTHER'S COAT

BY LINDA LINDROTH

$\mathscr{I}$n the evening I seek moments of serendipity. I steal away to a room where, alone, I turn on my computer. Just a brief search, I tell myself. My floor is littered with books, magazines, folders filled with tear sheets. These days, pictures of vintage designer clothing dominate the farrago. I am looking for something gorgeous from another time and place, some garment loved and preserved for its beauty, its timeless elegance, its superior craftsmanship. I type "C-H-R-I-S-T-I-A-N-D-I-O-R." On Amazon.com, I enter a favorite keyword phrase. I begin my search with limited expectations but genuine hope of finding something to own and wear that I could never have afforded when new.

A single line pops across the screen before me: "Opera Coat." I react with measured precision. A click. A double click. The screen displays still images, most of which typically disappear in a flash as I move through this virtual bazaar. But not tonight. In a blink, I am wide-eyed facing my Technicolor dream coat.

I am the only one to see this. I am convinced of it. I am the only one who knows what this is. A seller has listed her mother's

Christian Dior opera coat. It seems to me that I am alone with the coat. I am all but holding my breath as I read, "My father, David Nemerov, purchased this coat from Christian Dior himself in 1946 for my mother, Gertrude. He was the chairman of the board of Russek's Fifth Avenue." I feel the electricity of instant recognition. I know this name. I look for the "Ask Seller a Question" link and consider briefly. "Hello," I type, "I am an artist and teach art at a university. I recognize your name. Are you related to Diane Arbus?" I click again to send. Eager for a response, I wonder how long will it take.

While waiting, I muse back to when I started collecting vintage clothing. In art school I accompanied my boyfriend to the Salvation Army thrift store in New Brunswick, New Jersey. Instead of stretched canvases, he was working on paintings that used overcoats as their substrate. On any given day he would select a heavy garment with ample size and scale so that when he covered it with his recipe of modeling paste and gesso, its batlike form would create unexpected shapes on the wall. Attacked with abstract color patterns of fantastic highways and arteries, they hung from their tails like so many brightly colored carcasses skimming the vertical surface. As he browsed the racks contemplating a purchase, I strolled the store, pausing to stroke cashmere beaded sweaters and three-piece tailored suits from the 1940's with labels from Jay Thorpe or Best & Company, now-defunct stores in New York City.

As I gravitated toward photography, my personal heroes became three artists who created black-and-white documents of America: Lee Friedlander, Garry Winogrand, and a mesmerizing woman named Diane Arbus. Arbus shocked me with her remarkable and unexpected portraits of nudists in their living room watching TV, a grimacing boy gripping a toy hand grenade, triplets on a bed wearing identical white blouses and headbands, a Jewish giant at home with his parents, two men dancing together at a drag ball. The young Diane Nemerov Arbus, working collaboratively with her husband, Allan—who is remembered for his TV role as a psychiatrist on *M*A*S*H*—did commercial work as well: fashion photography for that very same Russek's department store ensconced in a Stanford White building at the intersection of Thirty-fifth Street and Fifth Avenue, and for many magazines, including *Vogue*. Diane and Allan published their first photograph in the May 1, 1949, issue. In the center of the picture are a man's and woman's (wearing white gloves) clasped hands. She is dressed in black-and-white polka dots and a light-colored feathery helmet of a hat. His profile is sheared off the right side—an asymmetrical gesture that would all but disappear in her later work. By the late 1950's Russek's had closed, but Diane Arbus went on to do considerable magazine work before developing her uncompromising signature style exhibited at the Museum of Modern Art in 1967 and in a retrospective soon after her death in 1972.

I click on my e-mail. There is a message from REN. "Yes," she writes, "I am Diane Arbus's sister." E-mails fly back and forth between us, and the coat begins its journey back east from the Southwest. My excitement is uncontainable. I run to a bookshelf, grabbing monographs and biographies. I reread a chapter that even described the seller of the coat. She is an artist. I learn the date of her birthday and make a mental note to send flowers and, as requested, a picture of me wearing the coat.

FedEx delivers a box. On the outside it is clearly identified as a computer scanner. It is too light for that mechanical peripheral, and the return address hints at its true contents. I lift the coat from its bunting of bubble wrap, tissue paper, and small plastic supermarket bags. The heavy, shiny black velvet modulates between highlight and shadow as the folds fall away. I note that a large white Christian Dior label bears a couture identifying number in the upper right corner—16262—and there is a smaller black label stating Made in France below it. My hand slides across the low, smooth nap searching for the seams that connect a front to a back. Cut all in one, the front panels form dolmanlike kimono sleeves ending at three-quarter length with a deep—nearly six-inch—hem inside. There is a gusset under the arms; the bottom of the coat is unpressed, lightly rolled and stitched. I immediately and carefully remove those stitches, allowing it to fall unmarked to its true length (thirty-nine inches). Gertrude was my size, and as I slip the coat on and look at myself in the mirror, it seems to have been tailored for me. Gleaming jet beads—flat, round, and faceted—encircle the collarless neckline embraced in passementerie. It is likely an example of the superb embroidery technique of Maison Lesage, working with couturiers in Paris since the 1930's. With an over-the-shoulder glance to the Victorian tradition of black beading and soutache, everything Dior designed in the late 1940's influenced American style for the next decade. The great swinging skirt foreshadows the A-line, balloon, and trapeze styles to come.

As deep and black as the velvet exterior, a lining of brilliant emerald green silk shantung peeks out and glows like a beacon on a starless night. The coat is crinkly thick, stiff even, as if there were another layer of lining between the velvet blackness and the shimmering green interior. It swooshes around my knees. Warm, it is heavy enough for a northern winter evening on the town.

I feel enveloped in a mantle of magic and mystery as this glorious velvet cloak once handed to the department store magnate

Linda Lindroth—c. 1946 Christian Dior opera coat purchased from Dior himself by David Nemerov for his wife, Gertrude. *Frank Poole*

Nemerov by Christian Dior now covers me. And I notice there is something else on this coat. Something other than the three bobby pins in the pocket. There are a few—not many, perhaps four—delicate, hardly visible strokes of oil paint on the edge of a sleeve—white, beige, and, coincidentally, that fabulous green.

I imagine that the artist, who would eventually sell this coat, brushed by a wet canvas or, returning from a reception for an art exhibit, passed through her studio and could not resist an adjustment to the canvas on an easel. As exquisite as this coat is, what makes my heart race is not that it is an example of Christian Dior's astounding and influential 1946–47 collection. It

may have been touched or even hugged by Diane, her poet lau-
reate brother, Howard, and their younger sister, the artist Renée
Brown. A coat with a past—of provenance from a family so pro-
foundly talented as to provide a wellspring of inspiration—rests
on my shoulders as I pass through the doors of a gallery to an exhibition of my own.

Part One

FIVE A.M., NOON,
NINE-THIRTY P.M., MIDNIGHT

Select One and Let's Go Shopping

BASICS ABOUT BUYING ONLINE

How much would *you* pay for an old pair of jeans? Ten bucks?

Let's say these are a pair of vintage Levi Strauss jeans from the nineteenth century. Would you pay $150? Consider that nearly everything belonging to the San Francisco–based Levi Strauss Company—designs, records, and drawings—was destroyed in the 1906 earthquake and fire. Could these jeans be the only pair from the late 1880's in existence?

If these jeans were to appear in an Internet auction, would you bid $46,000? If you did, you'd lose.

Several bidders who participated in an eBay auction on May 24, 2001, registered their interest, during the final hours, in what can only be described as damaged goods: There was a fifteen-inch tear in the fly area—ouch!—and holes in the right knee, not to mention a lost buckle and label. But—whoa, Nellie—we are talking about the very fabric of American fashion history, not just any pair of indigo vegetable-dyed denim jeans with mounted metal rivets stamped L.S. & CO. PAT MAY 1873. These may in fact be the earliest example of the only article of clothing turned out by mass production in the nineteenth century. The pants were found during the excavation of a Nevada mining town and given to the consignor who reproduces historical clothing. Perhaps coincidentally, Jacob Davis, the tailor who shared that patent with Strauss for a pair of trousers with copper rivets at its stress points, was himself from Carson City, Nevada. The Levi Strauss Company, whose $46,532 bid ultimately claimed these jeans in the final moments of the auction, authenticated the garment. The auction, conceived of as a promotion by the History Channel and Butterfields auction house in San Francisco, became a powerful marketing tool for each party. The jeans were probably worth the unusually high winning bid.

After the auction, the Levi Strauss Company displayed the jeans in their flagship store in San Francisco. This extraordinary auction clearly established the significance of vintage fashion items as worthwhile purchases.

While most of us might not be able to match this level of expenditure when acquiring our personal collections, our passion for the prize is just as great. We fall in love with things and buy them or bid on them with care and genuine enthusiasm.

THE ROMANCE OF IT ALL

Vintage clothes take us back to times past, perhaps to younger, wilder days when we wore miniskirts and hot pants, or to imagined evenings of an elegant era when beaded flapper dresses were all the rage. Vintage garments have a power to comfort us and elevate our moods on a gray day when we are feeling what Holly Golightly described as the "mean reds" in *Breakfast at Tiffany's*.

FIRST STEPS: SHOPPING AT THE WORLD'S ONLINE MARKETPLACE

If you're like us, you've shopped at tag sales and flea markets, going through racks of used clothing looking for treasures. You may have favorite consignment or vintage clothing stores with names like My Secret, Second Hand Rose, or Consignment Originals. You've browsed charity bazaars, the Salvation Army, and Goodwill looking for cashmere sweaters and great coats among the donated clothing. You're no novice, to be sure, but shopping the Internet for vintage clothing is an altogether new experience.

EBay is by far the largest online auction site and an excellent place to start; there are riches galore, and it is relatively easy to learn the ropes. We'll use eBay as an example, since most auction sites use a similar process.

Log on to www.ebay.com, click on the Register Now button, follow the steps, and select a user name. We recommend you go for one that's easy to remember and not too long, as you will want to type it in quickly when you're ready to start shopping. Also, you should avoid using your own name—or anything easily recognizable—in order to protect your privacy when bidding and buying.

Once you've registered, you will receive a beginner's badge: the number of transactions for which you've earned feedback. For a new member, it's always zero, and it appears in parentheses; alongside, you'll see a pair of dark glasses. You will have those newcomer's sunglasses next to your user name for thirty days. The eBay feedback system is based on the members' recommendations of one another as responsible trading partners. As you would imagine, your first few transactions are very important because they will reflect how well you communicated with a seller and how quickly you paid for that sweater, skirt, or coat.

After thirty days the sunglasses disappear, whether or not you bought anything. Once you accumulate ten positive-feedback transactions, you will receive a yellow star next to your user name that identifies you as a conscientious, enthusiastic member—in short, someone with whom other eBayers can confidently do business. Different colored stars indicate ever-higher amounts of feedback. As you will begin to see, there are some eBay sellers—some of whom are called power sellers—who have thousands of transactions to their names; these businesses generate hundreds of thousands of dollars in sales.

Once you've registered your eBay name you may be asked to submit a credit card number to secure your identity, depending on the type of e-mail address you have. If you are concerned about using a credit card on the Internet, you should know that you do not have to *pay* by credit card at any time in order to bid on items. Should you choose to use an electronic payment service to pay for your purchase at the end of an auction, you can make those arrangements then. (For details about these services, see "Pay the Piper," page 30.)

My eBay: Your Own Custom-Made Shopping Assistant

Everyone should set up a My eBay page. The website claims that it's one of their best features, and we have to agree. Most of the work involved in doing this—if you could call it work—is already done for you by way of handy little sections entitled "Items I'm Watching," "Items I'm Bidding On," and "Items I've Won." These lists are compiled automatically. If you save the eBay sign-in page—either as a link or as a Favorite/Bookmark, you can designate, via the Preferences menu, that the "Items I'm Bidding On/Watching" page be your default screen after you log on.

Items on which you are bidding will be color-coded: green means you're currently the high bidder, and red alerts you that you've been outbid for that item. Clicking on the link will allow you to review any active bids or to raise your numbers if need be. A quick glance at the "Items I'm Watching" section shows the current high bid and the time remaining before the auction closes. If you're no longer interested in an item, you can easily delete it from your watch list by checking the box next to it and clicking the Delete button at the bottom of the page. Since you can watch only twenty items at a time, it's a good idea to restrict this list to your must-haves.

And as if all that weren't enough, the My eBay page also allows you to check on any items you are selling, read your own feedback, and specify preferences for eBay notification services. The category called "Items I've Won" lists everything that you have purchased in the last thirty days.

SEARCH AND YE SHALL FIND

After registering on eBay, you can either search through everything listed on the site or go to a specific category—like "Vintage Clothing"—which you can find through eBay's category link "Collectibles" on its home page. Once you are on the vintage clothing category page, it's fun to browse through the first few pages, as these are the auctions that are due to end soon, and bidding activity can be frenetic and exciting. However, several thousand vintage clothing auctions are generally listed on any given day, and searching through them will soon exhaust you. If you see red type that reads "ends in three minutes," your competitive nature may get the best of you, and before you know it, you'll have purchased a pair of Art Deco rhinestone shoe clips. Won't they look striking attached to your flip-flops or loafers?

Keywords: Unlocking the Language of Listings

We like to search for items by using specific keywords—words or phrases you enter in the eBay search engine. The items it then retrieves will contain that word or words in their titles or, if you've requested, in their descriptions. Some examples might be "sequin," "ball gown," "ankle boot," and "Dolce & Gabbana sequined bustier." The more general the keywords—"blue dress," say—the lengthier and wider-ranging the retrieved list of auction items will be.

The first order of business, then, is to create a keyword list; this will include every variant name of each garment on your wish list. Incorporate the names of designers, the eras, and the items themselves. If you check the auction listings, you will see how your objects of desire are most commonly titled and notice some interesting points that may assist you in your search. For example, the majority of 1950's garments are listed as "50's," to save space in the title. However, at least half as many listings leave off the apostrophe (50s), while some sellers use a full "1950" in their titles. Furthermore, while many designers are well known in the world of vintage clothing—Christian Dior, Lilli Ann, Chanel, Norell, and Halston, for example—others are more obscure, and the seller may well choose to leave the name out of the title and concentrate instead on the assets of the garment itself. So, entering "Jerry Gilden"—a well-regarded but little-known maker of cotton 1950's frocks—into your search box may not yield very many listings, despite the fact that several such dresses are indeed out there, described more generically as "floral full-skirted dress" or similar. In this case, typing "50's dress," "50s dress," or "1950 dress" into the search box and using the "show all items, including gallery preview" option will allow you to easily see the dresses—or, at least, read the titles thereof—and spot the one you're after. Alternatively, you can look for obscurely named items by checking the little box that reads "Search title *and* description." That way, if the name "Jerry Gilden" shows up in the description—but not the title—that item will be included in the resulting list. Avoid including these descriptions searches for extremely common names, however, because the results can go on for pages.

Of course, the number of auction listings for clothing and accessories has increased dramatically in the past couple of years. Not that we're complaining, but this often means your search results can indeed go on for pages, regardless of your keyword selection. The technical directors at eBay are continuously streamlining the website's search methods. One such improvement is the highlighted "Matching Categories" box that appears to the left of your screen. Whether you're searching for something with an extremely well-known name—Calvin Klein or Chanel, say—or trying to unearth a piece by someone less famous, you'll enjoy trying out this alternative sleuthing method.

Here's how it works: Suppose you'd love to own a vintage Valentino gown. Before, if you wanted to cover all the bases, your keyword search would involve numerous variants like "gown," "dress," and "ball gown," not to mention lead you through several categories—women's clothing, evening wear, collectibles/vintage clothing—and even then, it was entirely possible that you could miss a listing if the seller hadn't placed the designer's name in the title. With this new feature, you can simply type "Valentino" into the first search box you see on the eBay home page, also selecting the "Search title *and* description" option. Voilà, you've retrieved a daunting eight hundred listings. But now look at the highlighted "Matching Categories" box on the left and note all the subgroups in which something *Valentino* appears—either in the title or description. There are listings in "Movies and Television," "Antiques and Art," "Dolls and Bears," and perhaps even "eBay Motors." Next to each category, the number of *Valentino* listings therein will appear in parentheses. Of course the ones you're after are probably going to fall within "Clothing and Accessories/Women" or "Collectibles/Vintage Clothing," so you'll click on one of those category titles, and your selection is automatically narrowed for you. Immensely. Once you've browsed "Clothing and Accessories/Women," click your Back button, return to the original lengthy and unwieldy "pan-eBay" Valentino listings page, and select another category, such as "Collectibles/Vintage Clothing."

If after all this you haven't found the Valentino of your dreams—and the gown hasn't made an appearance either—you may well feel it's time to let the website itself look for the elusive thing, which leads us nicely to yet another approach.

When setting up your My eBay page you should take advantage of the Favorite Searches function. This is a sort of personal shopper program into which you enter up to three keywords—or sets of keywords—so eBay will notify you via e-mail whenever an auction title containing these words gets posted. We find the best use for this function is to spot those items that rarely appear on eBay. You don't want to keep typing "Nettie Rosenstein dress" over and over daily, only to be met with "Sorry . . . ," but if one of her dresses *should* wind up on eBay, you certainly want to know. So, decide which three items meet these two criteria—they rarely make an appearance and when they do, you definitely want to be advised—and pare them down to the fewest number of keywords that will still eliminate unsuitable items. You might go with "Nettie dress," since "Rosenstein" is more likely to be misspelled, and "Nettie Rosenstein" alone will include listings of her costume jewelry and handbags as well as magazines containing photos of her designs.

Incidentally, this clever keyword technique—using as few words as possible in order to target your item but enough so as to eliminate unwanted listings—is applicable to *all* types of keyword searches, including your regular quests, not just to the Favorite Searches function. And an added bonus is that you'll often catch the misspellings: If you type in "Armani," as opposed to "Giorgio Armani," you'll still see the listing for the "George O. Armani Evening Coat w/ Sequence, No Reserve" that seems to be mysteriously—oh joy—devoid of competing bidders. Misspellings are endemic on eBay, so try to imagine all the permutations of a name and add these to your keyword list: La Perla, laperla, la pearla. And don't say we didn't warn you.

Here is a sample list of keywords that you might use for eBay:

vintage silk velvet
Kelly bag
Prada
Chloé

Sometimes your search will yield items that say "Prada-like." These items were probably not designed by Miuccia Prada at all, but the seller desires your attention and has chosen to do it this way. It can be annoying and disappointing to retrieve these misleading listings; eBay frowns upon sellers who use them, and often sends warning notices to repeat offenders. Occasionally, however, you'll make a terrific discovery.

Searches and keywords help you find things efficiently. If you don't want to go through thousands of auctions with the words "New Look" in their titles, you can type in "Dior New Look." If you are looking for size 8 black shoes, you can add "SZ 8," or, better still, just "8," since many sellers will spell out "size" as opposed to abbreviating it. Perhaps you are looking for something very specific, like black ankle boots by the French shoe designer Stephane Kélian, in size 8. A seller might not be this specific in her title. She might have not added "Stephane"—or perhaps she mistakenly spelled it "Stephanie." The word "ankle" may have been omitted, and if an auction simply titled "Kélian black boot" was listed, well, you would have missed it. So, just search for "Kélian," and perhaps you'll discover a gorgeous pair of brown suede ankle boots size 39—which is the European equivalent of a U.S. size 8. Do try variations on the spelling of your designer favorites: YSL for Yves Saint Laurent, as well as Yves St. Laurent, or why not, Eve St. Laurent! The rule of thumb is to identify the critical word or two to narrow your search without being so specific that you unintentionally eliminate possibilities.

Killer Keyword Searches

Two final suggestions for keyword sleuthing: synonyms and wild cards. Synonyms—think back to grade-school grammar—are words with similar meanings. In the context of fashion, this means a person seeking a vintage bustier should also consider searching for corsets, merry widows, and waist cinchers. Don't assume that every seller out there knows the difference between a 1950's skirt, a swing skirt, a rockabilly skirt, a crinoline skirt, and a circle skirt—if indeed there *is* a difference. Rather, add all these synonyms to your searches, and you'll be far more likely to find exactly what you're seeking.

Ebay's wild-card feature is little known, but you'll find it extremely useful. Wild cards are asterisks used to signify "any letters." You follow a group of letters, like "rose," with an asterisk to retrieve every item beginning with those letters. For example, narrow your category to "Vintage Clothing, Accessories/Women" and enter "rose*." You'll be rewarded with a list that includes rose-covered hats, skirts with roses, rose-printed cashmere sweaters, Nettie Rosenstein handbags, and Joseph La Rose shoes. The wild-card feature broadens your search results and allows you to find the variants "rose," "roses," "Rosenstein," and "La Rose"—in fact, anything containing a keyword that begins "r-o-s-e"—in a single search.

In addition to the keyword list in your Favorite Searches section, consider keeping a list in a notebook near the computer. Making a personal keyword list is great fun: You might want to read a book about fashion and select designers you admire. Auction catalogs can also introduce you to specific styles of clothes, for example Chinese cheongsams or early-twentieth-century one-piece bathing suits. Japanese kimonos, quilted fisherman coats, Charles Rennie Mackintosh Art Nouveau fabric swatches, and handwoven Mennonite garments have all turned up on eBay from time to time, as we discovered upon entering keywords from our lists. And by all means, bookmark those sellers who seem to have large lists of items you like and check back with them frequently.

Saving Your Favorite Categories and Item Groups

When setting up their My eBay pages, expert shoppers tell the site which favorite categories they most like to peruse; these can be as narrow or as broad as you wish. To get a feel for this process, go to the home page and find the long list of general categories (on the left of the screen); click on "Collectibles." Now select "Vintage Clothing, Accessories." You can continue to narrow this by selecting, for example, "Clothing," then "Women," then an era like "1940–59," then "Dresses" (or jackets or shoes). We recommend doing this type of search a few times in order to determine exactly which parameters you want to use for your own favorite searches—the ones through which you'll most often be searching and from which you'll most frequently be buying. Some important things to remember: The more tightly restricted the search, the shorter the list of results. And bear in mind that by selecting from the master list of categories found on the eBay home page, any category can be searched—or further narrowed—at any time: It does not necessarily have to be saved as a favorite search. Furthermore, consider that many people do not categorize items the same way you might. It would perhaps seem obvious that a 1940's smoking jacket belongs in the category "Vintage Clothing, Accessories/Men," but a seller may list it otherwise for any number of reasons. If you want a comprehensive list of smoking jacket auctions, we recommend searching all of eBay.

Category searches are also practical when you're collecting a theme or motif, as opposed to a specific item. Let's say you're passionate about cherries and want to build a collection of vintage garments that feature the fruit in their print—and it matters not if the item is a dress, skirt, or pair of pants; by going through the category "Vintage Clothing, Accessories/Women" and *then* entering "cherries" or "cherry," you'll avoid retrieving hundreds of listings for recipe books, wallpaper, little girls' hair ornaments, and lipsticks *in addition* to the cherry-festooned 1940's dresses and 1950's skirts you're actually seeking.

Finally, once you've set up a few Favorite Categories within your My eBay page, notice how each one is further broken down into "Current," "New Today," "Ending Today," and "Going, Going, Gone." Click on one of these self-explanatory subdivisions to see the latest listings within your category, the ones that are about to close, or the ones for which you're too late.

PREPARING TO BID

Once you have decided to jump in, we recommend that you do so carefully—in other words, start by getting your feet wet. Bid only on that which you really want and don't bid higher than you are willing or able to pay. Do your homework: Look at similar items and see what sorts of final prices apply to them. And bear in mind that most eBay sellers do not accept returns simply because the garment doesn't fit. If you ask enough questions beforehand, you're less likely to be disappointed.

Seasoned Shoppers Will Pepper Sellers with Questions

There are times when you needn't ask any questions of a seller. When the description is thorough and you're familiar with the item—which is being sold by a high-feedback seller—you may not feel the need to probe further.

However, if you are in any doubt, ask a question or two to get a sense of the garment's condition and to establish friendly contact with the seller. You needn't be abrupt, and you shouldn't fire off a round of detailed interrogatories. Be polite and show that you're sincerely interested. The majority of sellers want you to be satisfied; certainly no one wants to intentionally disappoint a customer. Posing questions to sellers is easy: Just click on the link that says "Ask Seller a Question" and type your query into the box. If you haven't signed in, you'll now be asked to do so. The message will be sent to her via eBay, but you will receive a response from her directly, after which point you may reply with any further requests.

Here are several different questions you should consider asking—that is, if the item's description doesn't already contain the information—before deciding whether to bid on that seemingly fabulous suit or dress.

Condition of the garment:

Does this dress come from a smoke-free home?

Are there any olfactory issues like mothball odor or mustiness?

Are there any flaws, for example, moth holes, snags, pulls, or noticeable repairs?

Are there creases caused by hangers?

Are there areas of this dress that are missing beads (or sequins)?

Are there any loose beads (or sequins)? (Buying online prevents you from shaking the garment to see if any fall.)

Since leather and suede problems can be difficult to resolve, are there any soiled or abraded areas?

Is this wool sweater pilling anywhere?

Are there any marks on the velvet from using hangers with clips?

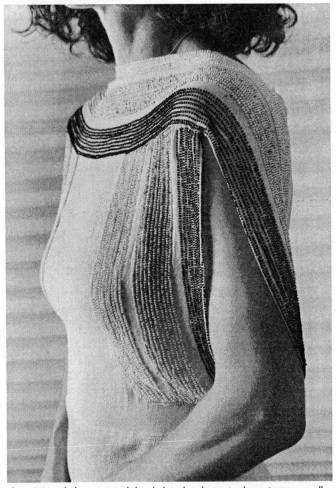

This 1940's slinky gown with lovely beadwork required repairs to a small seam and replacement of the snap closure. The beadwork itself was in pretty good shape. *Linda Lindroth*

Did this cotton garment shrink from its original size after washing?

How was this cashmere sweater laundered: by hand washing or dry-cleaning?

How was the linen blouse cleaned?

Now for Some Fitting Questions

If they haven't been provided in the item's description—and unfortunately, many sellers omit this vital information for reasons unknown—you should *definitely* ask for a garment's measurements. We've provided a size chart as a guide but recommend that you make assessments based on *your* size. Of course, knowing your own vital statistics is important, too. Buy a tape measure, choose a few garments that fit you perfectly, and make a note of these dimensions: waist, shoulder width, bust, hips, sleeve length, bodice length, inseam or skirt length (as applicable), and total length of garment from shoulder to hem (for a dress or coat). Deborah always asks for the sleeve length and inseam measurements because she has long limbs; Linda always asks for the overall length of the garment because she's petite and usually spends a lot of time at the dressmaker.

It makes sense to take your own measurements periodically. We all gain and lose weight from time to time. Regardless of your size, you'll always look polished and chic if your clothes fit you beautifully. Also remember that garments made in the 1930's, 1940's, and 1950's are *quite* different from their modern counterparts in that the sizes run far smaller today: a dress from the 1950's with a size tag that reads "12" will often best fit a woman who's a contemporary size 4 or 6. When buying vintage clothes from decades past, it's always a good idea to ask for measurements as opposed to relying on the numerical size.

INTERNATIONAL CLOTHING AND SHOE SIZE EQUIVALENTS

MEN'S SUIT/JACKET SIZES

UK/US	32	34	36	38	40	42	44
Europe	42	44	46	48	50	52	54

MEN'S SHIRT/COLLAR SIZES

UK/US	15	15.5	16	16.5	17	17.5
Europe	38	39	41	42	43	44

WOMEN'S CLOTHES SIZES

UK	8	10	12	14	16	18	20
US	6	8	10	12	14	16	18
Europe	38	40	42	44	46	48	50

WOMEN'S SHOE SIZES

UK	2.5	3	3.5	4	4.5	5	5.5	6	6.5	7	7.5	8
Europe	35	35.5	36	37	37.5	38	39	39.5	40	40.5	41	42
US	5	5.5	6	6.5	7	7.5	8	8.5	9	9.5	10	10.5
Japan	22	22.5	23	23.5	24	24.5	25	25.5	26	26.5	27	27.5

MEN'S SHOE SIZES

UK	6.5	7	7.5	8	8.5	9	9.5	10	10.5	11	11.5	12
Europe	40	40.5	41	42	42.5	43	44	44.5	45	46	46.5	47
US	7	7.5	8	8.5	9	9.5	10	10.5	11	11.5	12	12.5
Japan	25	25.5	26	26.5	27	27.5	28	28.5	29	29.5	30	30.5

GIRLS' SHOE SIZES

UK	10	10.5	11	11.5	12	12.5	13	13.5	1	1.5	2	2.5
Europe	28	28.5	29	30	30.5	31	31.5	32.5	33	33.5	34	35
US	11.5	12	12.5	13	13.5	1	1.5	2	2.5	3	3.5	4

BOYS' SHOE SIZES

UK	11.5	12	12.5	13	13.5	1	1.5	2	2.5	3	3.5	4
Europe	29.7	30.5	31	31.5	33	33.5	34	34.7	35	35.5	36	37
US	12	12.5	13	13.5	1	1.5	2	2.5	3	3.5	4	4.5

And do ask if the garment has been altered in any way: for example, hemmed with stitches, permanently shortened, or taken in or let out at the waist. You might also want to inquire about whether there are replacement buttons available and if the zipper is in good working condition. What about the sleeves and the hem—can these be shortened without altering the appearance of the garment? Sleeves may have working buttonholes and a hem may be trimmed with handmade, asymmetrical lace, meaning, in effect, that neither can be taken up.

If the Shoe Fits and the Style Befits . . .

It's smart to familiarize yourself with footwear designers and brands before you buy shoes online. Know which shoe offers the size you require and the level of comfort you demand. Many women find that the high-end European designers' wares—for example, pointy-toed Manolo Blahnik or Dolce & Gabbana pumps—tend to run small, and they'll buy a half-size larger. Other women prefer the support and comfort of Arche shoes. Some avoid high heels altogether.

Beyond matters of comfort, there are some other important concerns, such as, Are the shoes black or navy? Ask the seller to double-check the color of your potential purchase against something black. What about the size—are the left and right shoe both a 7½? Odd-sized pairs might work if your feet are correspondingly asymmetrical, but always ask.

Note that buying used shoes online, unlike buying used or vintage clothes, tends to be fraught with difficulties and should be approached with caution. We'll quickly add to our watch lists a pair of brand-new Chanel pumps that come with their box or sleeper bags. But experience tells us to proceed with caution when a seller's description states "barely worn." Then, we'll definitely ask questions about the shoes' condition: Are there nicks, stains, or gouges? Do the soles show a great deal of wear? Are there any deep creases in the leather?

Follow the Signs: Designer Labels, Care Tags, Size Tags, and Fiber Content Disclosure

Labels usually offer several clues to the vintage and condition of a garment. The typeface or color used on a designer label can indicate the period in which the garment was made. Unfortunately, the tags may have been cut out, perhaps because they were scratchy. The garment might have been purchased at a discount store—like Loehmann's—that regularly removes brand-name tags. Some labels have colored X marks, indicating they were bought at reduced prices. A care label that's wrinkled and barely legible often tells you the garment has been frequently washed. (If you'd still like to read the print, however, try this trick: Make a copy of the label with a photocopier set to the darkest setting. Sometimes the invisible text will magically appear.)

If your search methods employ general keywords like "60's flower power minidress," you may forget to ask about the label. If none is mentioned by the seller, by all means pose that question. Otherwise, you could end up buying a homemade dress cobbled together by someone less skilled at sewing than you. This may not concern you if the garment is exactly the right style and color you need for the *Bye Bye Birdie* costume you are assembling. But if, instead, you are hoping that your find hails from Biba in London or Best & Company in New York, be sure to ask about that all-important label.

NWT and N w/o T

An antique dealer does not always find everything that is for sale in his shop himself. He might enlist the services of "pickers," people who shop the flea markets and estate sales looking for valuable objects to sell to dealers. Vintage fashion works in a similar way. Dealers might also find their wares at the Salvation Army, Goodwill, or any number of other charity stores, like the Greenwich Hospital Auxiliary Thrift Shop in tony Greenwich, Connecticut.

And as for the recent vintage items from last season or last year that are listed as "new with tags," they are most likely items from last season that, having been placed on sale in the department stores and boutiques, are marked down during the months following their debuts. They are eventually sent to outlet stores like Off Fifth (Saks Fifth Avenue) and Last Call (Neiman Marcus). Collectors of "recent vintage" who live many miles from such a store can now buy discounted Dior bags and marked-down Issey Miyake tops from eBay. They might sometimes be a little shopworn, but their original manufacturers' swing tags are usually intact, as are their original store price tags. Then there are those items marked "new without tags," which are probably all too familiar to us shoppers who can't resist a bargain, even if it's three sizes too big and the color is regrettably unflattering.

Questions About Accessories

If the information isn't obvious, ask about the length of a necklace and the width and circumference of a bracelet.

Chain-style bracelets are easy to make smaller by removing links. If your wrists are small, ask the seller how difficult it would be to accomplish.

When considering bidding on a pair of earrings check to see

if they're for pierced ears; if not, assess the weight of a clip earring versus the pain quotient of a screw-on. If you find one or the other is uncomfortable, pass it by. (Remember, pierced ears were uncommon in the mid-twentieth century.)

Unlike silver or gold cuffs that may bend to fit your wrist, Bakelite bracelets are rigid and are usually about 7.5 inches around. Ask about this crucial measurement.

Pins and brooches should have working clasps and intact hinges. Ask if they are bent.

A Final Word About Asking Questions

If you ask a question and don't get an answer, try rewording your question and resending it. Again, remember your manners and be polite. If there is still no reply, consider this your red flag and pass the item by.

BIDDING: GOING, GOING . . . GONE

How does online bidding differ from a live auction? In a live auction, you can look around the room and see the faces and assess the style of your competitors. Not so in online auctions. In a live auction, everyone is able to bid until the other bidders drop out and the highest uncontested bid is offered, and this may happen within seconds, minutes, or even hours of the opening bid's placement. Online bidding ends with a flurry of activity that can only really be appreciated by continually clicking the Refresh/Reload button. This way, you'll see—more or less—each new high bidder taking the momentary lead. Another distinction: The online auction, unlike its real-life counterpart, is over when the specified ending time arrives.

You can choose to drop out of the bidding, if you wish, at any point after another person outbids you; or you can continue pursuing the jeweled handbag of your dreams, bidding a higher amount and resuming your lead. Disappointing though it may be, don't be discouraged if you are ultimately outbid—often by a measly dollar or two and sometimes even a handful of pennies—at the very last moment. After participating in a few auctions, you will find yourself less vulnerable to being outbid. You'll develop a knack for the process: knowing what magic numbers to use—we like using odd amounts, like $78.64, rather than round figures—and, most important, intuitively knowing the most opportune times at which to place bids.

Proxy Bidding Explained

EBay's system of proxy bidding attempts to duplicate, as closely as possible, the experiences of live bidding. Early in the auction, a bidder can state a price limit that represents the highest amount she is willing to pay for something. Let's say there is a wonderful and rare Gucci Victorian-style lace jacket currently listed for auction. Its original retail price was $2,500—or perhaps it was never offered for sale but rather was an exquisite sample piece that never made it to the production stage. A prospective buyer—a magazine editor, perhaps—saw it during a private showing, and the jacket is a must-have for her. She registers her proxy bid with eBay: $2,500. She is willing to pay that price for that particular garment, although at the moment, the opening bid sits at $99.

Other bidders who've seen this jacket listed have different budgets. One might enter the bidding with her own maximum bid of $199. This merely results in our editor's bid getting pushed upward, to one increment over that amount: $201.50. Any subsequent bids placed by competitors will do likewise, and the jacket will go to madam editor for $576.05—just five dollars more than the next-highest bid, the last one to attempt to knock her out of the lead before the auction closed. That "runner-up" bidder, however, did not, in reality, lose the Gucci jacket auction by a couple of bucks but rather by the difference that the winner was ultimately willing to pay at the end. Remember: The editor's maximum bid was $2,500.

Perhaps you want to bid on a Kate Spade bag that once retailed for $200. Ideally, you would like to pay about $86 for it. Here is what you should do: Place a proxy bid that is as high as you are willing to spend and still be content with your "used" handbag. Your proxy bid, $126, is still 30 percent less than the price of a brand-new version of this bag in a department store. The system will only bid the amount needed to keep you as the high bidder; eBay never divulges the whole amount to the seller—or anyone else, for that matter. Thus, it is entirely possible that you'll win the bag for even less than you imagined, though your ideal price was $86, and your maximum bid was $126.

We provide more detailed information on proxy bidding and last-minute bidding ("sniping") procedures and software in the "Seasoned Dressing" chapter.

What About Reserve Price Auctions?

No seller wants to take a loss on an item. If the evening gown she wants to list is of recent vintage—say, five years old—and it originally cost $1,000, she will undoubtedly have a market value in her head; anything less will be unacceptable. Perhaps that number is $500. The seller may not, however, want to start the auction with such a high opening bid. Thus, the price begins at $75 with a secret or hidden reserve set at $500.

Sometimes a seller will tell you her reserve, and other times she'll let you know, in the item description, what she actually paid for it—or what its value was—when it was new: "The gown originally sold for $2,000. My reserve is less than half that."

Often, this amount will be higher than you imagined and your bid might still not have made the reserve at $800. It is disappointing to be a high bidder who offered a substantial sum for something but who still did not win the auction. At that point, you might e-mail the seller: "Hello. I was the high bidder in your auction and I really loved the dress. What is the price you hoped to get?" Sometimes it is better not to ask outright what the reserve was, because the seller might be rethinking that one. It was obviously too high for the market that week. Maybe, instead of the $850 reserve, she was planning to relist the item with a $750 reserve. If a prospective buyer were to make an offer, she might accept $650. You should know that eBay really frowns on this "ex-eBay" type of selling and has made it harder to contact another member in order to work deals this way.

Reserve prices are usually round numbers. If there is no indication of what the reserve might be, you could guess and bid $50 or $100 more, just to see. If it's really high, though, you might not want to fish around thusly only to discover an ultrahigh reserve—unless, of course, you're willing to make that sort of high offer.

When your maximum high bid meets or exceeds the seller's reserve, eBay automatically enters the reserve amount of that bid, even though the high bid prior to yours may be much lower. For example, a pair of Manolo Blahnik stiletto heels has an opening bid of $9.99 with a hidden reserve—which hasn't been met—of $150. Someone opens with $9.99, after which point you enter a bid of $250. EBay will automatically accept your bid and make you the high bidder at "$150 (Reserve Met)," and you'll have an additional $100 to spare in your proxy. Having discovered that the reserve for the fabulous red snakeskin Manolos is relatively low, other bidders may now start bidding against you: $160 won't do it, however, because eBay will continue to increase your bid; a bid of $175 will be similarly unsuccessful. But then someone bids $327.48, and she becomes the high bidder at $252.50, one bid increment more than your original maximum, which, as you remember, was $250. At this point, you'll have to reassess your budget and decide whether to place another higher bid.

Sometimes, a seller will use "NR" or "No Reserve" in a title to attract bidders to his auction page from a keyword search. Since many people find reserves discouraging, the lack thereof will be enticing, especially if similar items listed all carry reserves. And you will join the bidding because even though the opening bid may be high—say, $200—you prefer knowing where you stand, with the price out in the open for all to see without a hidden reserve.

Counters

At the bottom of the auction site is a counter that tells you how many people have viewed the item. You can assume quite a lot from these numbers: A high number of viewers—into the hundreds—indicates that there is a fair amount of interest in that Matsuda jacket, and you can expect to see lots of competitive bidding. A number of less than a hundred—especially if it's just before the close of an auction—might work in your favor. However, some sellers opt for "invisible counters," and only they will know what kind of traffic their auction site is getting; others may elect to omit the counter altogether.

Time for a Background Check

Once you have assessed the competition and decided on the worthiness and quality of the leather trench coat or embroidered shawl, it's time to take a good look at the seller before you start bidding. The eBay and Amazon feedback systems make it easy for you to do this. Next to the name of the seller you'll see a number in parentheses; on eBay, a corresponding star—the color of which depends on the number of feedback comments (for example, blue for 100–500)—also appears. These numbers indicate how many transactions have been judged positively via the feedback of the buyer (or seller) after an auction. The number doesn't reflect the total of all transactions, since not everyone chooses to leave feedback. While there are "praise," "neutral," and "negative" categories of feedback, some eBayers choose to express their dissatisfaction with an item by not saying anything at all (remember the advice from your mother?).

One eBay seller might have feedback comments numbering into the hundreds, while another has thousands of positively rated transactions to his name. You are welcome—and encouraged—to read as many as you like in order to determine how comfortable you'll feel spending your hard-earned money on an eBay-listed Jean Paul Gaultier coat—especially considering you'll be doing so without the benefit of a dressing-room try-on. Regardless of a seller's sterling reputation, be sure to ask her some questions. And don't be surprised to find that a seller with several hundred positive transactions might have a couple of negative ones as well. Try to locate the negative remarks—on eBay, they appear in red, preceded by the word "complaint"— that lie within their feedback archives and read them carefully; they could indeed be a factor in your bidding. In general, mean-spirited comments should not be taken as seriously as constructive, rational complaints.

How High Should I Jump?

Once you are established as a vintage clothing aficionado, you will undoubtedly develop friendships and might sometimes find yourself trading advice about—not to mention predictions on— the closing prices of various auction items. One way to estimate the final cost of a much-wanted dress is to use the search form. Click on "completed items" and type in your keyword phrase, say "Dolce Gabbana dress" (notice how we left off the "and," since some listings will use the "&"). A list of final bids will be revealed, and you can evaluate what people have been willing to pay for Dolce & Gabbana dresses within the last thirty days at auctions similar to the one in which you're thinking about participating.

To Buy Now or Not to Buy Now

If you aren't particularly looking for a bargain, and you'd rather not wait—as much as ten days—for an auction to end, you can take advantage of an eBay feature that many sellers include with their listings: a "Buy It Now" option. Here is how Buy It Now works: Two prices are listed—the customary opening bid and, next to it, a number that's usually considerably higher alongside a Buy It Now logo. If you're willing to pay that amount, you can end the auction.

The opening bid might be $9.99, but the Buy It Now price could be as high as $100—instant gratification isn't cheap! Further, this option is available only to the first bidder (buyer, actually) who participates in the auction. If you are unsure about this amount—do you really want to go that high?—or if you simply want to think about it and not lose the chance to buy the garment, you may bid the lower, opening amount, and if there is no reserve, this will cancel the Buy It Now option for you and everyone else (with reserve auctions, Buy It Now gets canceled only when the reserve is met). This can backfire, however, as Linda once discovered when she did just that and ended up paying more for a Dries van Noten top than she would have if she'd taken advantage of the original Buy It Now price.

EBay stores also offer merchandise on a nonauction, selling-outright basis. Some vintage dealers prefer to list their items in the eBay store category rather than have an individual website because their traffic is greater on eBay, and there are numerous benefits to being part of the vaunted eBay community.

PAY THE PIPER

The auction is over and—drumroll—you won. What a relief! And how very exciting, too, since you've spent nowhere near the king's ransom charged for this garment in department stores. Within a short while, you and the seller will contact each other, at which point names and addresses will be revealed. This exchange is always fun: You may recognize a familiar name from high school or college, or perhaps the seller is related to your best friend's mother. You may have assumed the seller was a female when in fact he is a gentleman who owns a vintage clothing store in the neighboring town.

The seller will inform you of his payment terms and the cost of shipping and insurance. As you'll see, there are a variety of ways to pay. We've outlined the pros and cons of each so that you can choose the method that best suits your needs and the requirements of the seller.

Money Orders

Considered the all-around best method of payment by sellers and buyers alike.

Pros—They're available at any U.S. post office and most banks; they're like cash in that they can be deposited and drawn against immediately; and they're unlike cash in that they are safe to send in the mail and traceable (save your receipt or carbon). Further, they're relatively inexpensive.

Cons—To buy a money order requires a visit to a post office or bank, which might be inconvenient for some buyers.

Cashier's Checks

Also an excellent method of payment; however, beware counterfeit cashier's checks from phony banks.

Pros—As above. Cashier's checks, however, are not available at a post office.

Cons—As above, to buy one requires a trip to a bank.

Personal Checks

Widely used by auction buyers, but resistance to them is on the rise.

Pros—They are extremely convenient for buyers, many—if not most—of whom have checking accounts. More people may bid on your item if you accept personal checks.

Cons—Accepting checks requires that the seller keep track of the funds' clearance in order to know when to ship the item; this, in turn, necessitates a longer wait for the buyer, too. When a buyer's personal check is returned for insufficient funds, which will surely result in the buyer being charged by his bank, the seller's own bank may also impose steep fees simply because he deposited it in good faith into his account. Another consideration for the buyer is that sending personal checks to strangers means providing one's bank account information to an unknown entity—these are Internet sellers, not the electric company, the cable-TV provider, or American Express. The majority of sellers are honest, but check writers should keep these security issues in mind.

BidPay (www.bidpay.com)

BidPay is an online service that for a fee charges your credit card and sends the seller a money order. This is a good solution for buyers who want to use credit cards in transactions with sellers who only accept money orders.

Pros—BidPay is very convenient. It's all arranged online, meaning no trip to a post office or bank is needed.

Cons—The fee, which is based on the amount of the money order, can be high. The BidPay site requires that you submit detailed information about the auction, including the item number, title, winning bid, and seller's information. (BidPay can be used only for specific auctions—not for other types of purchases). Bear in mind that it's also disturbingly easy to run up your credit card balance using this method of payment. BidPay does take about a week to process money order requests, although the service notifies the seller immediately that a money order is forthcoming, and many sellers choose to ship at that time, based on the payment confirmation.

PayPal (www.paypal.com)

An online payment service that allows buyers to use credit cards or authorize payment transfers from a checking account that is extremely popular and relatively efficient.

Pros—PayPal's biggest plus is its undeniable convenience and ease of use. It's free or low cost (depending on whether a bank account or credit card is used), and it offers sellers the ability to accept immediate payment and confirmation thereof, so an item can be shipped promptly. PayPal provides its "Premier Member" sellers with protection against charge backs (in which a buyer claims, for example, that the item never arrived, and tells his credit card company to deny payment), as long as the seller ships to a buyer's confirmed address and maintains proof of shipping.

Cons—PayPal requires registration of bank account and/or credit card information online, which some buyers may find disagreeable (although all such transactions take place via secure servers). With bank-account-funded transactions, one must remember to enter the debit into one's checkbook register, and with credit-card-funded transactions, one must consider the bill that will arrive at the end of the month, the balance of which will incur interest charges if not paid in full. Another problem may occur if you use the PayPal message box to send special instructions to the seller. These PayPal communiqués don't always reach the seller promptly. If you need to send a message regarding shipping, contact the seller directly.

Billpoint (www.billpoint.com)

This eBay-affiliated credit card payment service, also known as eBay Payments, is convenient for sellers and buyers alike.

Pros—Billpoint offers an automated invoice system and allows payment via credit cards. All billing and payments are arranged online, and goods may be shipped almost immediately.

Cons—Some buyers may not wish to submit credit card information online. For sellers, there is also a small risk that they will experience costly charge backs by unhappy or unscrupulous buyers. As of this writing, Billpoint does not offer seller protection. And as always, excessive credit card debt may easily be incurred.

Cash

We strongly recommend against mailing or accepting cash payments.

Pros—Cash is king in many people's minds, and it's widely available (although some might argue otherwise!). Cash also means one can avoid divulging personal banking or credit card information.

Cons—Unfortunately, cash comes with no receipt or proof, either of having sent it or received it, and there is no paper trail. A cash transaction conducted online assumes both buyer and seller are honest, which is, unfortunately, not always the case. Finally, even if both seller and buyer live in the safest neighborhoods imaginable, sending cash in the mail is a risky endeavor.

Overseas sellers often suggest cash as an alternative to otherwise costly international banking fees. You might consider sending cash via registered insured mail in these circumstances, though the United States postal service discourages this and so do we.

Credit Cards (Direct Acceptance)

High-volume sellers may want to consider setting up a merchant account; for more details on this procedure, please see the chapter "Setting Your Sights on a Site: Advanced Selling."

Pros—Credit cards are convenient for a buyer, especially if she is temporarily short on funds but wishes to take advantage of a high-ticket bargain. Often, the seller will take the account information over the telephone as well as online, which is reassuring for many buyers. We recommend you submit your credit card information online only if the site is clearly defined as secure; call the seller if there are questions. Most credit cards protect buyers against fraud by withdrawing the payment if the item is never shipped or if it was seriously and provably misrepresented by a seller who refuses to accept returns.

Cons—It can be extremely expensive for a seller to set up a merchant account—especially if one wishes to accept American Express—unless the attendant costs are amortized over a large number of items sold regularly. There is also a small risk that a seller will experience fraudulent charge backs. For buyers, credit cards make it all too easy to incur excessive debt.

Escrow Services

For big-ticket items, such as couture evening gowns or rare antique jewelry, an escrow service can act as a middleman of sorts. The buyer pays the service, and the seller—once notified—ships the item to the buyer; upon receipt and inspection of the item, the funds are remitted to the seller. For more on this, as well as some escrow service websites, please see the chapter "Setting Your Sights on a Site: Advanced Selling."

Pros—A buyer can feel confident about his purchase, since the seller will get paid only upon his inspection and approval of the item. This is a big plus if the item belongs to that category of goods known as expensive and frequently knocked off, for example Hermès bags, Vuitton luggage, and Rolex watches. Uncertain buyers can also protect themselves by using an escrow service with sellers who have ambiguous feedback. Credit cards can be used for a purchase, even if the seller doesn't accept credit card payments directly (see page 35 for the pros of paying with a credit card). These services are generally convenient to use and allow sellers to avoid payment hassles such as returned checks (the service deals with the issue of payment). Shipping insurance is usually provided with the service, too.

Cons—There are fees involved, meaning the seller must charge more (unless she is willing to share this cost with the buyer). Fees also mean that this service makes less sense when the item is inexpensive.

FOREIGN AFFAIRS: AMERICAN BUYER MEETS INTERNATIONAL SELLER

You've probably encountered several interesting items offered by sellers located outside the United States and wondered if the process of importing a vintage suit or rhinestone bracelet would be daunting or complicated. Between us, we've bought garments from merchants in England, Canada, Japan, New Zealand, and Australia, and we can report that in most cases, the two distinctions we noted between a domestically shipped dress and one that came from abroad were these: Shipping for the imported dress generally cost a little more, and it took longer for the dress to arrive at our doorstep. We'll point to two exceptions. In the first, Linda bought a coat from a vintage shop in England. Thinking it would fortify the insurance coverage, the seller inaccurately declared the garment as new and costly; as a result, the duty charged Stateside was disproportionately high. In the second, Deborah bought a silk floral 1950's dress from a seller in Tokyo; when she saw how little he charged for shipping—less than $10—she assumed the dress would be sent by the slowest, least-expensive method. Instead, to her pleasant surprise, the dress arrived in just three days. When you're considering buying something that will be shipped from a foreign country, we've learned, it makes sense to ask for a shipping quote (and an estimated day of arrival) before you make any commitments, and when you actually *do* buy that vintage piece, remind the seller to declare it as a *used* item intended for personal—not commercial—use (this is very important).

For the most up-to-date information on importing goods you've bought online, go straight to the source: the U.S. Customs Service website (www.customs.ustreas.gov). Click on "Importing and Exporting"; then, under the heading "Information for the Infrequent Importer/Traveler," locate "Internet Purchases," and click on that. We recommend you read this section carefully—especially if you've never previously purchased goods from abroad—and check back with the site regularly, since government regulations and guidelines are subject to change, and the U.S. Customs Service policy is no exception. The following statement, quoted directly from the site, is in place at the time of this writing: "The duty rate for many items typically bought in an online auction is zero; however, Customs may charge a small processing fee for mail imports that do require the payment of duty." So there you have it. One more caveat: Notice they've used the words "many items" (as opposed to all items); if you have any questions about the embroidered 1950's dirndl skirt you're considering buying from a Swiss seller, by all means contact your local U.S. Customs Service office.

Payments for foreign-based items can sometimes, but not always, involve a few more steps than usual. If the seller requests an international money order, you should know that there are two types, both of which are available at the post office: standard international money orders and direct international money orders. The former costs $8.50 per money order and can be any amount up to USD$700; it is transmitted—through a batch process that originates in St. Louis, Missouri—to the post office of the participating country (for a list of these, visit www.uspsglobal.com/info/faq/infopost.htm). International money orders of the direct type are issued as an MP1 form that can be purchased at the post office window (cost: $3 each, with a maximum amount of USD$700); you will then send it directly to the recipient, who can cash it at most banks worldwide, as well as at many participating post offices (see the USPS website for a complete list).

Alternatively, the seller might have a PayPal account—lucky you!—in which case you're able to remit payment in your usual manner, that is, if you already use this service. Some foreign sellers request you use BidPay to send them money orders in the currency of their homeland (see the section "Pay the Piper" on page 30 for more details about BidPay). And, finally, there are international sellers who accept credit cards directly, either over the telephone or through a secure site. If you choose to use a credit card to pay for items hailing from offshore locations, be aware that some or all of the policies pertaining to that card could be affected. Some credit card companies do not extend their fraud-protection programs, for example, beyond U.S. borders. So, contact your card's issuing bank if you need to clarify the policies that apply to your account.

THE GRAND FINALE

If you have been sitting on pins and needles for weeks—and your cashmere sweater or dinner jacket *still* hasn't arrived—you might send a polite inquiry to the seller: Have you received my payment? When might you be shipping my skirt—I can't wait to see it! You could get an immediate reply that the check had indeed arrived this morning, and she expects that it will clear in seven to ten business days. Which means more waiting.

On the other hand, your credit-card-funded Chloé dress has arrived with dazzling speed, and you are delighted that the seller used not only a sturdy priority-mail box but also sheets of delicate pink tissue paper, from which the loveliest floral silk dress now spills. And look—she has included a little note card, complete with her eBay seller name, thanking you for your purchase in gold ink. How fabulous!

Troubleshooting

From time to time, you may receive an item that is not what you expected. Perhaps it was seriously misrepresented. You'd certainly never have knowingly bid on *this*. Sometimes a seller will offer to take the item back; she might, alternatively, refund some of your money to cover the cost of repair or dry-cleaning. We recommend you always contact her and remain polite: Be willing to accept a compromise. Are you truly disappointed or just mildly annoyed? As careful as one might be, a small percentage of purchases will not turn out perfectly, and this applies to things bought offline, too.

Perhaps, in a worst-case scenario, your jacket arrived stuffed in a Tyvek envelope that's far too small. The wrinkled mass smells of cigarette smoke, and what's this? Oh, no. A small hole has been clumsily repaired. *Sigh.* You e-mail a letter explaining that there appears to be some stitching in part of the sleeve; there also appears to be something resembling masking tape on the inside of the lining—it's left a sticky residue, too. Still, it's a fabulous jacket: gray pin-striped Yohji Yamamoto with seven buttons, boning, and a peplum pleat, and it fits like it was tailored for no other body but yours. Hey, the tape residue and smoke odor will disappear in the dry-cleaning. "I have a good dry cleaner," you write. "My seamstress can improve the repair with small white stitches. Will you consider reimbursing my mending and cleaning expenses?" A deal is made, and a refund check—along with an apology—is sent.

Deborah writes the most amazing disappointment letters. I am always in admiration of her British gentility. How could you not be persuaded to compromise after receiving this?

Dear Ayn:

I just returned from my trip this week, and the Chanel suit was waiting at the post office. It is a lovely suit, but I have to tell you that the condition is considerably more troubling than was described in your eBay auction site: "It needs to be dry-cleaned. There are no stains." In reality, there *are* some stains. One in particular is on the right front pocket: a three-quarter-inch orange streak. There are a few similar marks on other areas of the suit.

However, worse than the stains—which I feel the cleaners can probably tackle—are the myriad tiny hairs and particles of debris that are apparently "woven in" throughout the wool of the suit, both on the jacket and the skirt. They are more profuse in some areas than others. I started to remove many of them with a pair of tweezers, but my eyes are getting crossed.

The various sources of these hairs would appear to be human, dog, and striped cat. And as if that weren't bad enough—and I'm sorry to be indelicate—I found a half dozen tiny spider legs trapped in the wool. Now, I feel this constitutes more than just "needs to be dry-cleaned." What this *really* constitutes is unpleasant work, and lots of it, before I even take this to the cleaners to see if the stains can be removed.

I know you are a responsible seller and that these things were no doubt overlooked. But I would never have bid so high had I known about the unorthodox fiber-content flourishes. Rather than sending the suit back and demanding a refund, I thought we could perhaps work something out, say, your contributing something toward the cleaning and altering of this suit. This would defray at least some of the time I will spend engaged in the unappealing task of hair removal. Please advise.

Kind regards,
Deborah

Making the Most of a Less-Than-Perfect Transaction

What happens when you've bought something and, despite having asked all the right questions, it absolutely does not fit? We do suggest many tips and tricks for simple alterations and repairs in "Fitting, Fixing, and Flaunting"; one of them might make that gorgeous Dolce & Gabbana beaded camisole wearable. But failing such possible fixes, you could resell your purchase online. Be sure to mention the size discrepancies or other issues in your item description, as prospective bidders—not to mention the new owner—will appreciate your thoroughness and candor.

Other After-Auction Issues

Few eBay aficionados have not received an e-mail from a successful bidder who's now suffering from buyer's remorse—or perhaps her garment didn't fit. She might ask you, the second-highest bidder, if you would like to purchase the item from her. Many people do participate in this after-market purchase. Proceed with caution, however, since eBay does not offer you any recourse if you are dissatisfied: no insurance, no mediation through Square Deal (eBay's online dispute resolution), and no opportunity to leave feedback, which is a powerful disincentive to shady selling.

FEEDBACK: NOW IT'S YOUR TURN

It was important to you in determining whether you wanted to buy from the seller, and now you can evaluate each other based on this transaction. Feedback is generally given after the sale is complete: You paid, she shipped, and the item arrived as promised. When writing your feedback remarks, remember that you have only a few characters in which to relate your appreciation and give the feedback that is appropriate: Did the seller answer your question completely and in a prompt fashion? (Good communication.) Were you pleased with what arrived? (Item as described.) Was the item folded and nicely wrapped, then shipped in a box? (Good packaging.) Did she go the extra mile, in your opinion? (Great eBay seller, A+, or, Would buy from seller again!) You get the idea.

THE PAPER CHASE OF CYBERSPACE

Even though your transaction was conducted online, you should keep a paper record. Print out the auction pages after it is over. This will serve as your receipt, and you may need the pertinent data in the event that the package is lost or never sent to you. Keep a copy of any e-mails that tell you the total cost of the item including shipping and insurance (and we do recommend you purchase the insurance, in most cases) as well as the seller's name and address. And, of course, hang on to your money order stub or carbon. If you store everything in a loose-leaf binder it will be simple to keep track of your vintage collection. You may decide to resell something later and, if you wish to procure insurance for your collection, you'll need to know its value.

BEYOND EBAY

Vintage clothing sites can be found through a variety of search engines, including AltaVista (www.altavista.com), Ask Jeeves

(www.ask.com), Dogpile (www.dogpile.com), Excite (www
.excite.com), Go.com (www.go.com), Google (www.google
.com), Overture (www.overture.com), Hotbot (www.hotbot
.lycos.com), LookSmart (www.looksmart.com), Lycos (www
.lycos.com), Netscape (www.netscape.com), and Yahoo! (www
.yahoo.com), as well as search engines on AT&T's websites
(www.att.com and www.att.net). Within these search engines,
you'll find web rings—groups of users who have similar interests—including numerous ones geared toward sellers of vintage clothing. Whether you use search engines, like Yahoo! or
Google, or rummage through eBay using keywords and categories instead, you will find that keeping a notebook of keywords and planning your time are important considerations.

SEASONED DRESSING: SMART TECHNIQUES
FOR THE EXPERT BUYER

*O*nce you've tried your hand—and mouse—at buying fashion online, it won't be long before you find yourself thinking about how to develop sharper shopping skills. Perhaps you've lost a few auctions at the last minute—one-of-a-kind antique gowns you really needed for your theater company's next production, say— or maybe you'd like to cut down on the amount of time you must spend searching through the labyrinthine auction listings in order to unearth that specific something.

In the actual world of antique hunting and clothes shopping—where stores are of the bricks-and-mortar variety—the seasoned buyer is an extraordinary animal: She operates on a unique schedule, exhibits distinctive behavior, and reaps rewards of exceptional quality and quantity. She's someone we'd all love to bring along on a shopping trip—someone whose brain we shamelessly pick for insider information: which neighborhoods have the best estate sales, when the new shipments of coats will arrive at the designer outlet store, and where to find the best selection of vintage alligator briefcases.

An eBay keyword search brought two coordinating separates together from across the Canadian provinces. This stunning Dries van Noten wool and brocade wrap top along with the matching brocade skirt were won in two separate online auctions from two sellers within four months of each other.
Linda Lindroth

And so it is with online buying—the seasoned virtual shopper is a similarly talented individual who develops a knack for tracking down the gems and avoiding the disappointments. She consistently walks away with the trophies and leaves the less experienced marveling about her techniques.

Let's observe her.

The experienced buyer will often—but not always—have more funds at her disposal; in the case of a costume designer or personal shopper, the desired piece will go to a movie set or fashionable client, and the budget involved may be high. However, we're always hearing stories about clever collectors who've snapped up rare treasures for a song (as well as countless tales about the ones that got away).

HOW DO I SEARCH? LET ME COUNT THE WAYS . . .

The simplest, most obvious way to find a specific item online is also the most overlooked method: by using a good search engine, like AltaVista, Yahoo!, or Google. Let's say you're a personal shopper who must somehow find a Hattie Carnegie ball gown for a client who collects this designer's work. If time is no object, you can certainly visit every single online boutique in cyberspace. Alternatively, you can let the efficient, superpowered search engines do this for you. Go to Google's site, for example, and type "Hattie Carnegie" into the Search box. Within nanoseconds, you'll have a comprehensive listing of all web pages that include these keywords in their text. Granted, many of these mentions relate to the designer's costume jewelry or offer historical background about her, but there will also be many clothing items—sweaters, suits, and dresses—sorted and easily viewed by clicking on the accompanying links. Don't forget to make a note of the online boutiques that appear to stock Ms. Carnegie's designs; you may even wish to contact those shops and ask to be notified when more pieces arrive.

Searching the auction pages for specific items is a little trickier, but it can also be lots of fun. By and large, the eBay search techniques discussed in the previous chapter may also be applied at other auction sites.

When it comes to browsing a massive site like eBay, there are almost as many ways to search for items as there are items themselves. Don't discount the other auction sites, either. If you use a search service, like AuctionWatch (www.auctionwatch.com) or Biddin.com (www.biddin.com), which are geared to search *all* the online auction sites simultaneously, you'll get the results on a single list. We conducted a search for "Schiaparelli," and, interestingly enough, every result was an eBay listing. Many of the sniping services—we'll get to sniping a little later—include searching functions, too.

Then there are the auction pages themselves. Many sellers deal in similar items, so if you love the sequined 1970's top offered by DiscoDiva77, be sure to click the "View Seller's Other Auctions" link and see if she's also listing satin jeans and platform shoes. Read the item descriptions carefully; a seller will often say something like, "I am beginning to list some wonderful pieces from the estate of a wealthy socialite with a taste for Gucci and Pucci." Consider this your cue to *pounce* on that other auctions link. If someone sells numerous items of interest, add that page to your Bookmarks/Favorites list. You can even save the really great merchants as Favorite Sellers on your My eBay page—this way, their listings can be easily and quickly accessed.

And last, but not least, we feel compelled to inform you about a truly sneaky technique, a search tactic considered by some to be too Machiavellian for their sensibilities. However, no insider's guide would be complete without full disclosure of such a deliciously devious scheme.

Essentially, you're going to let your competitors do the searching for you.

To accomplish this, you'll start making a note of the other bidders who always seem to go after the very treasures on which you set your sights. One rival may have outbid you—by two measly dollars—for a coveted Yohji Yamamoto cape. Another walked away with the very Hawaiian shirt you'd wanted for years, one you assumed you'd win—how could it have escaped your clutches? Now that you've assessed your competition, user names and all, let's have a look at what they're buying. Go to "Search," then "By Bidder," and enter a user name—say, HawaiianRival. Voilà: A list of your competitor's intended prey appears, and many of these things are very interesting indeed. You'll notice that for some of the items, HawaiianRival may have already been outbid. Never mind: Who is *that* person, and what sorts of things might he be chasing?

This little game—sometimes derisively referred to as "bid stalking"—is definitely fun to play, and it can often yield discoveries that would have otherwise slipped by unnoticed. Even so, it is not without its drawbacks. For one thing, a search by bidder will not yield any active item listings if the bidder in question is a serial sniper (we *will* get to that soon, we promise), since her bid will show up only for the last few seconds of the auctions. However, you may still check the "Include Completed Items" option, browse through *those* listings, and perhaps discover some wonderful sellers who were previously unknown to you. Or, click on the "Bid History" link, and see who else was trying for that Hawaiian shirt and how high they were willing to go; now you have a better idea how much to bid next time.

By now you've undoubtedly realized something: As you're busy spying away, checking out other bidders' would-be purchases and bidding habits, so might they be scrutinizing *your* finds. Alas, this is part of the system, that is, having records of your eBay bids and purchases laid mercilessly open for inspection by anyone: strangers or even—horrors—friends, family, and coworkers. Of course, you can avoid this sort of exposure—to the latter group, at least—by selecting an abstruse, nonidentifying user name and keeping quiet about it. Incidentally, if the bidder you are spying on happens to be German you will be out of luck. "Not possible," states an eBay message. "German privacy laws do not allow us to pass on information involving bidders from Germany. If you want to find all auctions this user has bid on, please contact the user directly by e-mail."

ON YOUR OWN WATCH: VIRTUALLY WAITING IN THE WEEDS

Have you ever noticed the little binoculars icon on the eBay auction pages? If you aren't already using this function, consider clicking on it the next time you stumble on something for which you're tempted to bid immediately. Now the item is added to your "Items I'm Watching" list (that's a part of your My eBay page); you can keep an eye on twenty items, and the Watch list will organize them for you according to their closing dates.

We recommend watching items for a number of reasons. First, you'll avoid "buyer's remorse" by giving yourself a chance to really think about something before you jump in with a bid. If you're purchasing this for someone else—a client, say, or a cos-

A vintage hat, a fan, and a Victorian coat were used by a specialty photographer to create an heirloom image for this twentieth-century woman.
Collection of Linda Lindroth

tume department—you'll be able to keep track of the item *and* have an opportunity to enlist another opinion. Should a more suitable garment come along, you're no worse off for having added the original one to your Watch list: It can now be removed without obligation. And watching items is paramount if budgetary constraints apply—and when don't they? If the price soars above a certain point, you can simply delete the thing; a similar, more affordable dress, suit, or handbag will undoubtedly be posted soon—perhaps in an even nicer color. Another great thing about item watching is that eBay notifies you via e-mail when the auction's closing time is near. It's a good idea to remove (delete) from your list those outfits and accessories that no longer interest you, as well as the ones you've won or lost. This way, you'll free up a spot on your Watch list—there's already a record of your victories and defeats under "Items I'm Bidding On."

Of course, to the really intrepid shopper or collector, twenty items will seem like a drop in the bucket. You can save, or bookmark (in Netscape), your surplus discoveries by adding them to your Favorites list (in Internet Explorer) or clicking on the little heart icons at the tops of the pages (if you use AOL). Remember to check this list frequently and note the appropriate dates, since most auction sites will not alert you to an auction's imminent close. It's a good idea to clean house periodically, too, or your Favorites (or Bookmarks) list will soon stretch for miles, making it difficult to navigate.

GOING FOR THE GOLD LAMÉ: WINNING STRATEGIES

Once you've decided to buy an item—let's say it's an Ann Demeulemeester leather miniskirt—you'll need to decide what it's worth to you and plan your approach accordingly. Straightforward buying from online boutiques and consignment shops requires no strategizing: You simply e-mail the seller, hope the item wasn't bought ten minutes beforehand, and arrange payment. Expert-level *auction* buying, on the other hand, calls for a little savoir faire.

There are two ways you may go about winning the aforementioned miniskirt: by bidding early with a high proxy bid or by sniping, either manually or via a sniping program.

Name Your Price

A high proxy bid will hopefully scare off other buyers. Sure, they'll bump up the opening bid a few times, but once they realize their lowball bids are not successful, you can expect them to back off. How do you know what numbers to use? If you've done your homework and checked out similar items as well as the seller's other auctions, you'll have a better sense of the general going rate for the Belgian designer's pieces. But let's say this is the first time you've ever seen the skirt on eBay—or anywhere, for that matter—and there's no high-end department store in your neighborhood, or you'd have gone there to get a feel for the retail prices associated with Ann Demeulemeester; well, you'll just have to rely on your sense of pricing, your budget (or that of your client), and your instincts.

As we stated in the previous chapter, try to avoid letting emotion and competitiveness guide your bidding—if you do this, you'll always wind up overpaying. Rather, set a maximum dollar amount in your head, add a dollar or two—plus several cents—to outsmart anyone who bids a round number, and place your bid whenever you like.

Now for the downside of high proxy bidding: You will probably pay dearly for the skirt, since your bid will be nudged ever upward by other bidders as they enter the game. And you may very well be outbid at the last second by a minuscule amount, especially if you're not at home, sitting by your computer when the auction ends.

Gotcha!

The alternative method is famously known as "sniping," and although it is detested by many sellers and bidders alike, it is perfectly legal—if somewhat ruthless—and it's widely used. Sniping is defined as placing a bid at the latest moment possible. There are several advantages to this type of bidding, the most obvious of which is that you'll be swooping in at the last minute, so competitors won't be able to react in time. A successful snipe also means you'll probably pay less than you would if you'd placed a high proxy bid and sat back while others dove into the bidding. Another plus: Anyone attempting to spy on your discoveries—with the intention of stealing them out from under you—will be disappointed to find no active items on your bid list.

Sniping is not without its shortcomings, however. The manual execution of this technique takes a little practice and a lot of nerve—you'll have to resist the urge to click the "Bid Now" button too early, but you can't, on the other hand, wait too long. It is also entirely possible that other latecomers will outsnipe you, so it cannot be regarded as a guaranteed way to win. And if someone has a very high proxy bid, your sniped maximum may not be enough to win the garment; all you'll succeed in doing is pushing their price higher. In this case, if the garment is something you really, really want, you might consider testing the water by bidding a medium amount about five or ten minutes before the closing. This will not affect the snipe bid you're about to enter at the last moment, but it *will* give you an idea of what you're up against, at least with this individual.

Some sellers dislike sniping because they would rather see the bidding for their Norell gown climb steadily upward throughout the duration of the auction; if there are no bids placed after a few days, a seller might close the auction early and relist the gown at some future date rather than sell it for a low price to a sniper. And, finally, the outcome of the auction may be affected by something that, unfortunately, no one can predict or control: If one's own Internet connection fails or if the eBay site goes down during the final moments, the bid won't be placed and there will be no time left to reenter it.

If you've considered the aforementioned points and still wish to try your hand at sniping, we're happy to tell you how it's done.

Manual Sniping: Adrenaline 101

Anyone can execute a manual snipe bid; it's all about preparation, timing, and technique. Allow yourself a half hour or so before you set up your bid for that beaded Galanos jacket, since it's a good idea to conduct a little research on the current high bidder. Sign in, access the jacket's auction page, and click the "Bid History" link. Did she get into the game early? Were subsequent Galanos fans unsuccessful in their attempts to outbid her? This would indicate a high proxy bid. If you enter a snipe bid, it's going to have to be high enough to top her maximum. By researching this bidder's buying habits—conducting a "Search by Bidder" that includes completed items and clicking on the bid histories for these auctions—you'll get a feel for the dollar amounts she routinely employs when placing high proxy bids. As we mentioned before, you can enter a medium-sized bid—not your high maximum—a few minutes ahead of time and see what happens.

Once you've determined how much you'll need to bid for the jacket—assuming this amount sits well with you—you can proceed with sniping. Minimize the jacket's page and open a second browser window; sign in to eBay and access the jacket page on this window, too. Click the "Bid Now" button (it's shaped like a paddle) in order to set yourself up. This will be the window where you place your bid, and the first one—the one you minimized—will serve as a control screen, to be refreshed/reloaded frequently, thus keeping you up to date on the bidding and pricing.

Most experienced manual snipers like to use a stopwatch. When the auction's close is only a few minutes away, refresh your control screen and set the watch to coincide exactly with the time remaining. Keep refreshing that page and assessing the current price; as late as possible, decide on your final, absolute maximum bid, and add a dollar or two, plus a few cents, to any round number, for example $87.32. (This tactic comes into play when another sniper bids $85.) Remember, the closing price will be just one bid increment above the next-highest bid, but if someone *else* enters a high snipe bid, the final number could be pushed beyond your budget. It's worth repeating that you should *never* place a maximum bid that's higher than you're willing—or able—to pay, whether you're last-minute sniping or placing a proxy bid. Nonetheless, this amount should definitely reflect the highest price you're prepared to spend for the Galanos jacket, because there won't be time to change it. Enter your number into the "Maximum Bid" box and click "Review Bid." The bid will not be placed yet.

Refresh the control screen again, and notice the seconds ticking away. When your stopwatch indicates you have about forty-five seconds left, restore your main screen and get ready to click the "Place Bid" button. How long you wait is really up to you. Experienced snipers can often place a bid with five seconds to spare, but the efficiency of your computer, not to mention the speed of its Internet connection and the time of day, will directly affect how quickly your bid is placed. So we recommend starting out with a minimum thirty-second buffer.

Ready? Click the "Place Bid" button and cross your fingers. Once the auction has closed, you can immediately refresh your control window and learn the final outcome. Brava! Looks like you'll be a Galanos girl this New Year's Eve.

The Seasoned Shopper's Secret Weapon: Sniping Services

If the concept of last-minute bidding is appealing, but you find the manual-sniping procedure to be onerous—and perhaps a little too nerve-racking—you'll be pleased to hear that there are several sniping services available (literally) to do your bidding. For a reasonable fee that's usually billed annually, these online companies will handle your sniping needs, archive your purchases, and sometimes even search the auction sites for you, making them invaluable for the serious online shopper. Some good ones include AuctionBlitz (www.auctionblitz.com), Auction Sniper (www.auctionsniper.com), HammerSnipe (www.hammertap.auctionstealer.com), and Snipeware/Bidmaster (www.bay-town.com).

With most services, you'll set up a name and password, and you'll also need to give them your eBay user name and password. When you've decided to bid on something, you simply enter the item number along with your maximum bid; additionally, the sniping service will need to know the point at which you'd like your bid placed—that is, how many seconds before closing. Usually, you can edit your entries up to a few minutes before the auction ends, which means you can change your mind and decide to bid higher—or even cancel your participation altogether. E-mails are usually sent to inform you that a bid has been placed, as well as one to advise you of the final outcome. Sniping services offer all the positives associated with sniping, but the method is far less stressful and time-consuming. In most cases, once a bid is set up, you need not be home to monitor things—in fact, your computer doesn't even have to be turned on.

The downside, however, is that no software is 100 percent foolproof, and even the most reliable sniping service can experience a crash right as your Big-E Levi's auction is about to close, resulting in a disheartening absence of bids from your end, not to mention the loss of a coveted pair of antique jeans. And as with manual sniping, you may lose out to someone who's placed a high proxy bid or even get outsniped—perhaps by another user of the very same sniping service!

Some detractors argue that bidders who use sniping services are employing hard-hearted, unsportsmanlike tactics; in essence, they're removing the element of healthy competition from the world of online auctions, the climate of which is supposed to reflect a hobbyist's or collector's gentle demeanor as opposed to the ruthlessness normally associated with corporate raiding, professional football, and chess. We think it's important that you're aware of these sniping services' existence in the general online marketplace, and we've simply listed their most obvious pros and cons. Whether or not to use the programs—or even try sniping at all—will remain, indisputably, your decision.

You can read more about the art of sniping—and the controversy swirling around the subject thereof—at Auction Watch (www.auctionwatch.com/awdaily/features/sniping).

HEY, BIG SPENDER: SPEND A LITTLE TIME WITH THESE

At the beginning of this chapter, we referred to the deeper pockets of the expert buyer. Although she won't always be emptying them out, she'll certainly need to replenish them after shopping at the sites we're going to discuss now. Serious collectors of antique clothing and textiles—as well as costume designers for large-budget productions and personal shoppers with wealthy clients—will appreciate the beautifully organized, well-documented, and carefully preserved inventory offered by auction houses like Sotheby's (www.sothebys.com), William Doyle Galleries (www.doylenewyork.com), and Christie's (www.christies.com). If you're the sort who isn't fazed by dresses bearing four- and five-figure price tags, by all means look into registering at these venerable auction houses and taking advantage of an opportunity to own vintage couture previously made available only to members of a small club, most of whom reside in large cities like New York or Los Angeles.

Furthermore, popular auction sites now have special departments—for example eBay Premier (its current name)—created for the collector or connoisseur and stocked with high-ticket garments, as well as pricey jewelry, art, and sculpture. The items are all guaranteed, meaning the sellers are carefully screened. In order to list a couture gown or diamond necklace the seller must provide absolute proof of an item's authenticity.

And finally, there are many wonderful haute couture and high-end designer garments, from virtually all eras, offered for sale in some of the vintage boutiques. Karen Augusta (www .antique-fashion.com), Enokiworld (www.enokiworld.com), and decades/two (www.decadestwo.com) are just a few of the online sellers who specialize in this sort of finery; please refer to Part Five for many more, with an eye toward those noted with "$$" and "$$$," indicating a high-caliber inventory.

Special concerns arise when one spends a small fortune for a dress, suit, or piece of jewelry; these worries intensify with online purchases, because you usually won't have an opportunity to meet the seller in person. While it's always prudent to ask plenty of questions of a seller, whether you're dealing with an online vintage boutique or an antique seller who lists his wares on Yahoo! auctions, it's crucial when you're buying a really expensive piece. And feel free to contact an appraiser if you'd like reassurance about the garment's worth. We list some online ones in the Resources Directory.

If the valuable piece you're considering is listed in an auction, it's now *mandatory* that you read the seller's feedback; in fact, should it turn out that a dealer or company is involved, you may wish to informally research him by running the name through a couple of search engines. Suppose your efforts turn up newspaper articles with titles like "Diamond Importer Acquitted of Fraud Charges; Now Faces Class Action Suit." Well, you may want to reconsider your purchase.

Escrow services can be of tremendous help when you're buying big-ticket items, too, and we'll further remind you to *insist* on insurance for your Worth gown when it's shipped. Every major carrier offers it, and all reputable sellers recommend it. Should you feel uneasy about any aspect of your transaction, by all means communicate your apprehension to the vendor. Although you may be doing business online, picking up the telephone and speaking to a live human being is often the best way to resolve any outstanding issues and provide yourself a little peace of mind.

If you are shopping for high-end items, or simply interested in window-shopping along the Internet's equivalent of Madison Avenue, you might want to explore the following sites.

Doyle New York (www.doylenewyork.com) introduced the couture auction category in their live auctions in 1983. This division of the William Doyle Galleries is considered by many to be the premier auction house in the world for vintage and antique clothing. The biannual couture and textile auctions and their accompanying catalogs are excellent sources of information about vintage finery. In 2001 alone, Doyle sold $3 million in couture, costume jewelry, Bakelite, and accessories.

For the Academy Awards ceremony in March 2001 the actress Renée Zellweger wore a Jean Dessès yellow strapless gown that had appeared on the front cover of Doyle New York's 1997 couture auction catalog. Dessès (1904–70) was born in Egypt of Greek parents and opened his own design atelier in Paris in 1937. His specialty, admired by European royalty and movie stars, was chiffon evening gowns inspired by the drapery of early Greek and Egyptian robes.

Doyle made the headlines again in May 2001 by setting the world auction record for an antique dress. Advertised as a gown worn by a descendant of George Washington's family, an 1888 court dress by Charles Frederick Worth (1825–95) sold for $101,500. This Worth court dress belonged to Esther Maria Lewis Chapin (1871–1959), the great-great-granddaughter of George Washington's sister, Elizabeth Washington Lewis (1733–97). The dress, which has a twenty-three-inch waist and a ten-and-a-half-foot detachable train, could hardly have a more illustrious provenance. Miss Chapin was presented to Queen Victoria in London wearing this gown when she was seventeen or eighteen years old.

By clicking on "Sale Results" on the Doyle home page you will get to a window that allows you to choose a recent couture and textile auction. Select "See All Lots" and pull down "Descriptive" (instead of "Prices Only"). Click "View" to see a list of some five hundred lots of couture clothing, jewelry, and textiles by name and their final gavel price. All told, this is an excellent way to determine the current market value of couture vintage clothing.

Sotheby's, located in New York, Chicago, Toronto, Europe, Asia, and Africa, is probably the most well-known auction house in the world dealing in high-profile live auctions of collectibles, from paintings to antique furniture. In April 1996 they auctioned the estate of Jacqueline Kennedy Onassis, and in December 2000 their "Passion for (Punk) Fashion" event included garments by Vivienne Westwood and Malcolm McClaren alongside a Diaghilev Ballet Russe costume designed by Henri Matisse. The online auction website www.sothebys.com is an excellent place to search for fine quality vintage fashion.

Registration to bid in Sotheby's auctions requires submitting a major credit card. You will then pick a log-in name and password, and you will be assigned a paddle number when you decide to participate in an auction. Sothebys.com is a well-designed website, exemplifying the Sotheby's auction style. It is easy to read and navigate, with three to four beautiful photos of each item that you can enlarge to 200 percent. Sotheby's provides a complete description with provenance and history; a condition statement; specifications that include date, garment type, material, and label information; as well as biographical information about the designer, including nationality and birth and death dates. Measurements in inches and centimeters, estimated shipping information, and all other pertinent Sotheby's disclaimers fit easily on a two-page printable form. The Sothebys .com auction duration is fourteen days. You can e-mail your questions to the seller from the auction page or send a copy to a friend. You can even go to "Bid History," although only paddle numbers are viewable.

Sothebys.com's lot search is similar to eBay's. If you want to search by seller (Sotheby's calls them associates), for example, you can type in their name in the space provided. We visited the website and discovered an associate named Cherry. Upon further investigation, we learned that Cherry is a vintage designer boutique specializing in unique designs of the twentieth century. Complete names and e-mail addresses—plus phone numbers— are available by clicking on the seller's screen name. Cherry offered twenty-nine lots, including vintage clothing designed by Valentino, Chanel, Versace, Halston, Yves Saint Laurent, Galanos, Gucci, Hermès, Pucci, and Oleg Cassini. Items listed ranged from low (an opening bid of $125 for an André Courrèges wool-blend skirt circa 1975) to high (8,000 for a Valentino "Jackie" couture evening dress from 1966–67). Some of this associate's listings were straight auctions, while others were midpriced "Buy Now" listings. Sotheby's charges a buyer's premium of 15 percent, added to your winning bid, to cover the site's expenses. This is similar to what happens at the end of a live Sotheby's auction: One's current bid will show the buyer's premium below it. Your shipping cost is additional as well.

No sniper bidding is permitted on this site. "Fair Warning" occurs when a bid is cast in the last five minutes of the auction, and the auction is then extended an additional ten minutes. The fair warning period repeats until five minutes go by without a bid. This gives bidders a chance to answer last-minute challenges.

Bid increments are higher at Sothebys.com than on eBay or Amazon.com auctions—usually 10 percent higher than the previous bid. In order to bid you must type in your user name, password, and the bid amount, which must include a bidding increment. Unlike eBay, Sothebys.com doesn't tell you the next amount to bid, so you will need to calculate the increment. Instead of your user name you are given a paddle number that identifies you as the high bidder. You receive a different paddle number for each auction, making it easy to keep track of your activity on the "Your Auctions" page.

Sothebys.com holds special auctions like "The Personal Property of Marilyn Monroe: The Berniece and Mona Miracle Collection."

Christie's Auction House (www.christies.com) has six locations worldwide, including two in New York and two in London. Costume and textile auctions are conducted in their South Kensington salesroom located at 85 Old Brompton Road, London, SW7 3LD, telephone: 44(0) 207581 7611.

Christie's South Kensington, like Doyle New York, offers excellent reference material through auction catalogs that are available for purchase online. Out-of-print catalogs can often be found at the Catalog Kid (www.catalogkid.com) or on eBay (example keyword "Christie's Fashion").

Occasionally, Christie's offers a special auction at their Christie's East salesroom. "The Couture Collection of Tina Chow" in September 1993 included some of the magnificent couture items collected by Ms. Chow, an enchanting muse and style icon who was known for her exquisite taste, beauty, and social position. The Christie's East auction not only included clothing by Balenciaga, Madeleine Vionnet, Lanvin, Schiaparelli, Yves Saint Laurent, and Karl Lagerfeld for Chanel and Fendi but also a collection of Chow's own jewelry designs, Chinese cheongsams, and extremely rare gowns by Mariano Fortuny. Some of the proceeds of the auction at Christie's East, including fashion photographs by David Seidener, were donated to Tina's House and Housing Works, two of the late Ms. Chow's favorite charities.

Skinner (www.skinnerinc.com) is an auction house with two locations in Massachusetts: Boston and Bolton. Skinner holds auctions of couture designer clothing and accessories. For example, on December 16, 1999, Skinner held an auction that included Rudi Gernreich pieces, Fortuny dresses, Judith Leiber purses, a gown worn by Princess Diana that was sold for $23,000 to benefit a homeless shelter, and an Hermès burgundy alligator Kelly bag. The catalogs for their auctions often become collector's items.

Skinner occasionally holds online auctions at www.skinner .lycos.com, but be careful to stay on the Skinner website and not to wander into the common, garden-variety Lycos clothing listings that are not generally vintage auctions.

BUYERS' RESOURCES

PUBLICATIONS

The Catalog Kid (www.catalogkid.com) sells auction and exhibition catalogs.

Two eBay sellers that we've bookmarked are edge-online and singeldad. Edge-online offers an eclectic group of fashion ephemera, including designer catalogs, memorabilia, and rare fashion monographs. Singeldad, a former art museum curator turned bookseller, specializes in out-of-print and period materials on the decorative arts of the nineteenth and twentieth centuries.

Linda Tresham's House of Magazines (www.iluvmags.com) is updated daily and caters to designers, museum curators, art galleries, and researchers.

Visionaire (www.visionaireworld.com) is the online presence of this ten-year-old avant-garde (and hugely expensive) fashion magazine that is published three to four times a year. Each issue of *Visionaire* is a mixed-media album on a particular theme or subject and is produced in a hand-numbered, limited edition.

You can view sample pictures from back issues on this very sublime site or place an order for a subscription. You will need Flash 4 to experience the visual effects.

Gallagher's Gallery & Archive (www.vintagemagazines.com) is an online source for fashion photographs, advertising, and magazine collectibles. The store, frequented by the fashion cognoscenti, is a darling of the magazine and newspaper press. Michael Gallagher's eBay seller name is maryspaper. Their retail store is located at 126 East 12 Street, New York, NY 10003, 212-473-0840.

CONVERTING FOREIGN MONEY

XE (www.xe.com) offers exchange-rate information for foreign purchases.

MOVIE PROPS, THEATRICAL WARDROBES, ANTIQUE FURNITURE, ACCESSORIES, AND VINTAGE CLOTHING

Located in Las Vegas, the Attic Vintage Clothing Company (www.atticvintage.com) claims to be the largest vintage clothing store in the world. They sell a variety of items, including bales of vintage clothing (literally, and pictured on the website), as well as wholesale, export, and wiping cloths (they don't call this the rag trade for nothing!). The store counter has over 37,000 visitors but is more a promotional site for their Las Vegas store, located at 1018 South Main Street, Las Vegas, NV 89101, 702-388-4088. Mayra and Victor Politis are multilingual.

The Family Jewels Vintage Clothing is the twenty-year-old New York landmark store owned by Lillyann Peditto. Visit their website (www.familyjewelsnyc.com) for theatrical costumes. Popular with photographers, designers, and theatrical costumers, they also have a boutique at Bergdorf Goodman.

VINTAGE DESIGNER FASHION ADVICE AND INFORMATION

Beverley Birks Couture Collection (www.camrax.com/pages/birks0.htm): This is an astounding picture archive of thousands of couture items. The database contains one thousand entries, eight hundred images of American, English, French, Italian, Spanish, and Japanese designers. Accessories are also included: boots, handbags, Lilly Daché hats. Click on thumbnails of ensembles by Charles James, Jean Patou, Pinguet, and Poiret and large, clear photographs appear. Searching the database gives a picture along with a description that is detailed enough to include comparison with other outfits in this extraordinary collection. Photographs from the site (maintained by Camrax) are available for license. Some of the garments, we're told on their home page, are for sale.

Eras of Elegance (www.erasofelegance.com): This is a comprehensive and impressive resource site for history buffs. From the "Guides" heading, select "Fashion" from their pulldown menu and spend hours exploring the links. Their "Travel" link will provide an extensive list of museums and historical sites by state. Places that do not currently have websites—like the John E. and Walter D. Webb Museum of Vintage Fashion in Island Falls, Maine—are to be found here. You can even click on an era and get a recipe!

The Paper Bag Princess (www.paperbagp.com) is the site that corresponds to the Los Angeles vintage boutique. Proprietress

Elizabeth Mason offers a wonderful assortment of vintage haute couture and designer garments that are collected and worn by numerous celebrities and the stylists who dress them. There are plenty of press clippings to view—all relating to vintage clothes—as well as photographs of a recent vintage Yves Saint Laurent fashion show. Paper Bag Princess goodies make appearances on eBay, with a portion of the proceeds from these auctions going to benefit the United Friends of the Children (UFC), a Los Angeles–based nonprofit organization. Click on the "Shop Online" button and you'll receive the following message: "Coming Soon . . . Shop The Paper Bag Princess for Vintage Couture and Designer Resale." We can't wait! Physical store address: 8700 Santa Monica Boulevard, West Hollywood, CA 90069, 310-358-1985.

Penny E. Dunlap Ladnier created the Costume Gallery (www.costumegallery.com), a "central location on the web for fashion and costume"; this is an extremely well-organized site that promises hours of exploration and a position on your Favorites/Bookmarks list. Since the bilingual site was launched in 1996 there have been seven million visitors. Information is offered on just about every aspect of the history of fashion. Study by decade and use her links to explore various fashion topics, including designers, movies, hairstyles, celebrities, and royalty; menswear and children's clothing; and books and articles. The excellent list of book suggestions is linked to Amazon .com.

To read a great-looking magazine-style website with all kinds of fashion info, including the fashion history of Vienna, the jewelry of India, and the textile museum in Heidelberg, go to www.fashion.at. If you have Flash installed on your computer you can get music and animation.

The New York Vintage Fashion & Antique Textile Show, held each September and February usually at the 69th Regiment Armory on 26 Street in New York City, is the premier vintage fashion event in the Northeast. One hundred dealers from the United States, France, and England set up displays of exceptional apparel and textiles. Collectors of vintage fashion rub shoulders with designers seeking inspiration while sniffing out the latest trends. Only a handful of the important vintage dealers participating in this show have websites; these feature only a fraction of their inventories. We would be remiss not to remind you that these events are worth seeking out. Visit the show organizer's website (www.newyorkvintagefashionshow.com) to check on the exact date of an upcoming show and to see the lists of dealers who will be exhibiting. There is also a small list of dealer links.

Although nyvintage.com (www.nyvintage.com) is really a web presence for the SoHo, New York, store What Comes Around Goes Around, as opposed to an actual, shopable site, vintage clothing aficionados will love browsing the pages at this site and seeing an impressive selection of high-end and designer clothes. Embroidered Japanese jackets, real Chanel suits from bygone eras, plentiful vintage Levi's, terrific Halston pieces, and Puccis galore make for some wistful window-shopping, if you have the time. No prices are mentioned ("If you have to ask . . ."), but interested buyers—as well as persons with desirable designer goods to sell—are invited to e-mail their inquiries. When in New York City, you can visit the shop at 351 West Broadway, New York, NY, 888-LEVISNY; 212-343-9303.

Two television shows attract a large number of collector viewers. *Antiques Roadshow* is a WGBH production televised nationwide on the PBS network. They tape their segments all over the country. *The Incurable Collector* appears on the A&E cable network. You can view the websites associated with these shows at www.pbs.org/wgbh/pages/roadshow and www.AandE.com/collector, respectively.

FABRIC CARE

Fabriclink (www.fabriclink.com) is the award-winning website that provides you with a virtual college course covering all aspects of fabric, from care and stain removal to colors, and an excellent dictionary of fabric terms and "fabric-isms." It is an invaluable and informative service provided by the authors of *The Textiles Handbook,* Rebecca Davis and Carol Tuntland, professors at California State University, and Kathy Swantko, a textile consultant and consumer advocate.

ARCHIVAL STORAGE

For over thirty years, historical societies, museums, artists, and collectors have turned to Light Impressions as a source for archival-storage supplies. Acid-free storage boxes, nonbuffered wrapping tissue in sheets and rolls, and large-sized polyethylene bags are available on their website, www.lightimpressionsdirect.com. Located in Brea, California, Light Impressions offers an unconditional guarantee. Refunds or exchanges are given on everything except custom-made or custom-cut products. Checks, money orders, Visa, MasterCard, American Express, and Discover are accepted.

FASHION SHOWS

Go to First View Collections online (www.firstview.com) to download designer photos from recent runway fashion shows. You may search by designer and season. Great browsing.

Virtual Runway (www.virtualrunway.com): "Clean and classy" is how Janet Hobby describes her website, which features the latest collections by the top designers, photos, opinions, links to online boutiques, fashion "priority pieces," and even video clips. Click on "Design House" and get an A-to-Z list of contemporary designers and their biographies with links to their collections and—if they have them—websites.

INFORMATION ON STERLING SILVER

Modern Silver (www.modernsilver.com) is an online magazine devoted to vintage modernist sterling silver jewelry and objects. This site offers a calendar of events, book reviews, original columns, articles, and interviews as well as links to online stores and dealers. Mailing address: Modern Silver, P.O. Box 139, Waveland, MS 39576.

Spratling Silver (www.spratlingsilver.com) is a jewelry reference website dedicated to the American founder of the Taxco, Mexico, silver school, William Spratling.

Part Two

THE CYBER-WARDROBE:
A GUIDED TOUR

DRAMA IN A DRESSER DRAWER: ACCESSORIES

With rings on her fingers and bells on her toes,
She shall have music wherever she goes.

In the movie *Steel Magnolias* Dolly Parton's character remarks that what separates human beings from other primates is our ability to accessorize. We couldn't agree more. And just think: Since the 1980's, when that movie was released, we've experienced the advent of Internet shopping, so there really are no excuses for limiting ourselves to cookie-cutter fashion anymore. Nor is it necessary to live in "some big town" to personalize your wardrobes with beaded purses, vintage costume jewelry, and a gorgeous pair of new, unworn shoes. We're picturing a country-dwelling glamour queen who sings "Dah-ling I love you, but give me Park Avenue" while browsing through the baubles offered by Sothebys.com. Indeed, some of the best sources for unique accessories are the online auctions, from the high-end houses to the household names like eBay. And take a look at the sellers: Many are located in small, out-of-the-way towns unlikely to be recognized by big-city residents. Once, we applauded the convenience of one-stop shopping; now we're beginning to sample the joys of one-world shopping.

Creating a look with accessories can mean wearing a bold piece that becomes the main focus: for example, pinning a huge Miriam Haskell brooch at the shoulder of a plain linen sheath dress. Or it can simply entail adding subtle interest and distinction to an outfit with the perfect—though not necessarily perfectly matched—shoes and handbag. Conventional wisdom once held that Europeans are simply more gifted in this *art décoratif;* truthfully, however, you find stylish, creative people in all parts of the world. Remember that high school cheerleader, the one with the interesting costume jewelry, who always wore her sweater backward? And how about that sales manager in your office whose fabulous vintage ties never failed to inspire conversation? These people knew how to personalize a uniform with accessories. It's extremely useful to develop this talent, even if money is no object and you have all the closet space in the world. In fact, it's practically compulsory if you travel often. Learn how to work with a few separates and some carefully chosen accessories before your next weekend getaway, and you'll be skipping through the airport terminal with a carry-on bag that—for once—doesn't require a forklift to transport.

And speaking of uniforms, aren't we all a little bored with the standard black-and-khaki costume worn by virtually everyone for the past decade or so? Undoubtedly, classic clothes in neutral shades can form the foundation of any good wardrobe. But notice how the truly stylish among us—even when they're wearing black T-shirts and khaki pants—always seem to avoid looking like the masses. Thanks to the twisted scarf threaded through the belt loops, the armful of antique sterling bangle bracelets, or the

1980's one-of-a-kind picture hat by Michael Vollbracht; Miriam Haskell marcasite-and-turquoise necklace; 1950's taffeta bustier. *Deborah Newell Tornello*

vintage bowling shirt worn as a jacket, they stand fashionably apart from the flock.

Draw inspiration from the style icons in your world and resolve to acquire some wardrobe interest of your own. What sorts of things should you look for?

HEADS UP: THE CAT IN THE HAT IS BACK

Antique hats are often works of art. And they remain surprisingly affordable, which is a function of two things: their small sizes and their preworn status. We humans are simply getting taller and bigger-boned with each passing generation, so those lovely jeweled caps and feather-trimmed berets from the 1940's will, for the most part, only work for those with smaller heads. And as for the preworn issue, few antique hats can be washed, meaning that someone who wouldn't give a second thought to snapping up a vintage dress or skirt—both of which can be cleaned—might shy away from wearing something that's spent time on another woman's head, though she might collect the hats anyway, for their beauty or perhaps for their designer label's value.

Those who don't mind too much when it comes to a hat's past life, however, and who are lucky enough to be able to fit into the vintage versions—or find larger-sized hats—can put together enviable outfits. (And there are plenty of new, vintage-inspired hats, available in modern-day sizes, to please the rest of us.)

Hats lend polish and wit to your wardrobe, flatter your face, and sometimes even protect your skin from ultraviolet rays. The styles popular during the twentieth century comprise an impressive selection. You might try a pillbox hat as a finishing touch to a 1960's suit à la Jackie O or choose a wide-brimmed 1950's straw hat covered with cabbage roses to complement your vintage floral sundress, along with faux-pearl necklaces worn as bracelets. A black felt beret, whether vintage or new, looks great—not to mention very beatnik—worn with a dark turtleneck sweater. A classy cloche, made popular by Coco Chanel in the 1920's, will charm the other wedding guests when you wear it with your dropped-waist floral silk dress; since this style of hat fits low over the face, it shows off a pretty shade of lipstick. Then there is the cotton or denim tennis-style "crusher"—think Lauren Hutton in the 1970's—which is a casual and sexy accessory that's currently offered by almost every online clothing store, like jcrew.com and bananarepublic.com, as well as in the online clothing auctions. Other fun-to-wear (if somewhat costumey) hats include the wool felt fedora; the small, veiled dress hat; and the classic Stetson cowboy hat.

And as if being fashionable, clever, and widely available weren't enough, hats offer a stylish way to cope with hair loss resulting from illness or chemotherapy. There is even an ingenious line of hats in which actual hairpieces are incorporated into the designs, thus offering the wearer many chic, comfortable alternatives to full wigs; this collection of special hats—which includes various vintage-inspired designs as well as sports-oriented and children's versions—is available online exclusively through www.hip-hat.com.

When you visualize your favorite fashion icons of the past century—whether they're actors, artists, or musicians—more often than not, they'll be wearing hats. And although not essential to the modern-day outfit, a hat certainly sets the wearer apart as a person of style and confidence. We hope you'll get in touch with your inner hat person and convince her to come out of hiding once in a while. (Note: Gentlemen's hats are discussed in the chapter on men's fashion.)

(FAUX) DIAMONDS ARE A GIRL'S BEST FRIEND: VINTAGE COSTUME JEWELRY

Volumes can be written about the exquisite subject of costume jewelry—indeed, volumes *have* been written about it—but we can't resist offering up another impassioned idea or two about the baubles and bangles we adore, since memories of costume jewelry are themselves a bunch of sparkling—if tangled—skeins packed away in the dressing-up box of childhood. The simple act of trying on a rhinestone bracelet or triple-strand glass-bead necklace transports you with the click of a clasp to another place and time. And this is the very essence of the vintage experience, distilled to handheld dimensions.

Antique costume jewelry is a wonderful thing to collect and wear. It needn't be expensive, although it certainly can be. It might be daring or demure, gaudy or genteel, and its beauty isn't necessarily dependent on its having a name, although there are some signed pieces so feverishly sought after on eBay, their auction listings regularly earn little "flaming match" icons. Jewelry doesn't consume a tremendous amount of closet space, so you can acquire it and accumulate it to your heart's content. And best of all, costume jewelry, unlike a new dress or pair of jeans, may be enjoyed here and now, regardless of any temporary "figure issues."

Having made a good case for costume jewelry, so to speak, we'll simply suggest some well-regarded designers and encourage you to log on and see all this glittering wearable art for yourself.

And, again, consider the many unsigned treasures, as they are often just as beautiful, well made, and desirable as their named cousins, and they're usually (but not always) more affordable. Bear in mind that regardless of a designer's stamp of approval or the lack thereof, broken prongs, discolored or dull stones, and missing beads and gems are problems that are difficult, if not impossible, to resolve. Heavy tarnish on a costume piece is also a no-no, unless you're specifically seeking a "worn" look; unlike sterling silver, which can be buffed with polishing creams or dipped in tarnish remover, most discolored costume metals are irredeemable. It never hurts to ask questions of your seller, especially if you're thinking about investing a bundle in a vintage bauble.

Two terrific sites that bear mentioning offer many of the different types of jewelry discussed in this section:

True Faux (www.truefaux.com/index2.html)
Morning Glory Antiques & Jewelry
    (www.morninggloryantiques.com/index.htm)

Bracelets and Bangles

Those who favor a minimalist look might go for a bangle bracelet or two; the Lucite, celluloid, and Bakelite versions are frequently carved and always clean-lined and modern. They can be purchased from numerous online boutiques, especially those that specialize in jewelry and accessories and have dedicated vintage plastics departments, such as Sparkles Vintage Costume Jewelry (www.sparklz.com/plastic); also, be sure to visit Deco Echoes (www.deco-echoes.com/bakelite.html) for fascinating information about this celebrated material. Of course, eBay and other online auctions are great sources for colorful, vintage plastic bangles, but we'd advise the Bakelite novice to educate herself about the characteristics of the real thing. At this time, no guaranteed method exists that allows a buyer to authenticate this plastic, but experienced collectors report that a faint smell of formaldehyde is given off when a real Bakelite piece is rubbed briskly with a finger or thumb—long enough to create warmth and friction. In order to avoid getting stuck with a cheap imitation for which you've paid top dollar, double-check the seller's feedback and return policy. On the other hand—or wrist, we should say—the fan of all things ornamental might consider a vintage charm bracelet, which is perhaps the most decorative, easily personalized costume piece one can buy. While it's the perfect grace note for a 1950's ensemble—and we'll thank Ms. Kelly for that lovely trend—a charm bracelet looks equally handsome when worn with an otherwise severe suit and can also enliven a casual jeans-and-T-shirt look. Costume charm bracelets by designers like Napier and Schiaparelli—who created really elaborate versions—are becoming increasingly collectible, and auction prices for flawless bracelets will continue to rise.

Stars in the Constellation: Signed Designer Vintage Costume Jewelry

Butler & Wilson—large, outrageous rhinestone pins resembling sculpture

Carolee—wonderful, affordable faux pearls in all shapes, shades, and sizes

Chanel—high-quality, costly faux pearls, gold-tone, logo, crystal, and poured-glass pieces

Christian Dior—exquisite rhinestone and crystal necklaces

Christian Lacroix—1980's glitz, especially oversized necklaces and earrings

Coro—classic pins and earrings

1980's Carolee faux-pearl necklaces; 1950's Bruce Fox aluminum banana-leaf platter. *Deborah Newell Tornello*

DeRosa—signed vermeil pins

Eisenberg—rhinestone earrings, brooches, and necklaces

Hattie Carnegie—feminine pieces that often combine metal, stones, and pearls

Hobe—rhinestone pieces with floral themes

Kenneth Jay Lane—colorful, animal-themed rhinestone pieces and oversized faux pearls

Miriam Haskell—baroque pearl and beaded filigree flowers on necklaces and earrings

Monet—classic 1970's through 80's bold "power-dressing" jewelry in gold tones

Napier—better-quality faux pearls and faux-gemstone pieces

Nettie Rosenstein—witty, collectible pins and bracelets in various metals

Reja—World War II–era vermeil pins, often with birds and animals

Schiaparelli—bold, showy jewelry, with leaves, filigree, beads, and aurora borealis gems

Trifari—feminine rhinestone or pearl earrings and delicate necklaces

Weiss—pieces made with high-quality crystals and rhinestones of every color imaginable

Yves Saint Laurent—stylized, often peasant-inspired pieces to complement the clothing line

STERLING REPUTATIONS: VINTAGE SILVER JEWELRY ONLINE

Collectors of vintage sterling silver jewelry might want to look at three eras for their online purchases. Typical Art and Crafts–style pieces are bar pins with geometric and floral forms, many with semiprecious stones in their centers like those by Hazel B. French, and delicate necklaces made of fine chain and multiple hanging elements using beads, pearls, and precious and semiprecious stones. Look for enameled silver from the Kalo Shop, paper-clip chain necklaces with bezel-set stones, or pearls from Josephine H. Shaw.

During the early- to mid-twentieth century, Modernism came into the forefront of jewelry design in Scandinavia, Mexico, and the United States. Sterling silver and copper were worked in geometric, minimalist forms that are now highly sought after and prized by collectors.

William Spratling, considered the father of contemporary Mexican silver, was born in New York, trained as an architect, and, after visiting Mexico in 1926, moved there permanently and began creating jewelry and objects for the table. Look for his extraordinary, heavy sterling cuff bracelets with bold Aztec designs, braiding, stylized crosses, wrapped links, and incised circular motifs combined with balls as the prominent design element.

Visit Aram Berberian's Ark Antiques website (www.ark -antiques.com) for Arts and Crafts silver, and Phyllis Goddard's comprehensive Spratling Silver website (www.spratlingsilver.com) for helpful information about identifying and authenticating Spratling pieces.

Bear in mind these Mexican jewelry artisans trained by Spratling:

Hector Aguilar—an assistant of Spratling's, with his own strong design sense influenced by pre-Columbian and Egyptian motifs

Los Castillo—a family of artisans known for their use of "married metals" (silver, copper mixed with brass)

Sigi (Sigfrido Pineda)—Modernist jewelry featuring boomerang and organic fish and pea-pod shapes
Victoria's floral and animal subjects in brooches and bracelets

Greenwich Village in New York City was an important location for American Modernist jewelry designers in the 1950's. Frank Rebajes, working in copper and silver, was the first Modernist jeweler to open a studio shop there in 1934. His motifs were often animals and insects. Others soon followed Rebajes to Greenwich Village, including the African-American designer Art Smith. Smith's characteristic amoeboid and biomorphic shapes reflect his interest in African tribal jewelry. Some American Modernist jewelry designers of the 1950's:

Betty Cooke—known for her simple, sleek, and elegant pins and earrings

Margaret de Patta's jewelry is characterized by intricate shapes, undulating wire earrings, extraordinary rings with quartz and jade, and pins and brooches of silver and gold with mesh, pebbles, pearls, dots, and cross-hatching techniques

Sam Kramer—a surrealist whose jewelry is often anthropomorphic and includes semiprecious stones and minerals

Ed Levin, influenced by Alexander Calder's mobiles—delicately balanced designs characterized by abstract shapes. His work remains in production

Peter Macchiarini's combination brooch/pendants and necklaces made of brass, silver, ivory, jade, and ebony reflect African and Constructivist influences

Ed Wiener, also influenced by the Cubists and their contemporaries—his sterling silver forms are reminiscent of Arp and often contain semiprecious stones

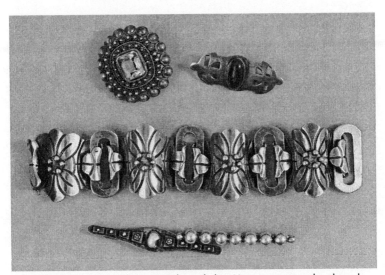

Vintage sterling silver jewelry—examples include a Victorian era amethyst brooch, Arts and Crafts bar pins, a Mexican silver bracelet by Victoria of Taxco, and a William Spratling ball pin. *Linda Lindroth*

WEB SIGHT: SPECTACLES AND SUNGLASSES ONLINE

Sometimes the most prominent accessory in our wardrobes is right in front of our eyes, resting on the bridge of a nose. For many of us, eyeglasses—vintage and designer—are the first things we put on in the morning and the last things we take off at night. Why not include these necessaries in your online searches?

Whether you are looking for the signature Lafont titanium eyeglasses worn by TV reporter Ashleigh Banfield or a pair of vintage Bausch & Lomb Ray-Ban Wayfarers, there are plenty online through which to browse. The handmade French frames of Alain Mikli, glasses by the Japanese designer Matsuda or L.A.-based Oliver Peoples, and the gorgeous Italian frames designed by

Romeo Gigli are often listed on eBay in the category called "Everything Else: Optics" or in "Women's Clothing and Accessories: Sunglasses." One of the largest suppliers is the eBay seller eyeglassfactoryoutlet, who deals in discount eyeglasses "from bank purchases of major optical chain defaults." We've seen vintage Versace, Christian Lacroix, Gianfranco Ferre, Oakley, and Giorgio Armani in these auctions. Four hundred frames were listed on the day we visited the Eyeglass Factory Outlet eBay store. Often the eyeglasses are described as new old stock; that means they are old but never worn. The photographs are excellent and easy to see. Located in south Florida, Eyeglass Factory Outlet can be reached at their toll-free number, 877-749-0907, to arrange for payment by credit card.

Other eBay sellers offer the popular Oakley sunglasses, including models in the hot Oakley Penny Family: X Metal Titanium with Ice-tinted lenses and spring-hinge mechanisms, which retail for $300. At the other end, we bought a pair of 1950's black-and-white harlequin-style sunglasses for just $2.50; the lenses were so black they turned the whitest beach sand into pitch!

Often a frame size is given, like 46-21. Compare these numbers with the ones on the earpieces of your own frames or e-mail the seller for measurements. Remember that vintage plastic glasses may be warped, discolored, or missing their shiny luster.

IT *IS* MY BAG, BABY . . .

For many of us, the ultimate quarry to bag *is* the bag, especially one with a certain name. Waiting lists for costly and coveted treasures of this sort are nothing new in the world of high-end boutiques, but these days, the amount of lead time before delivery of that bit of Hermès grace has stretched to absurdity, along with the patience of many a moneyed customer. A friend recently remarked that stock market analysts could quickly evaluate the state of the nation's economy by weighing the waiting lists at Prada, Fendi, and Hermès: Multiple pages of luxury bag–owning hopefuls would signify large numbers of profitable portfolios.

Never mind the unavailable young hunks, we say. There are plenty of handsome, mature versions that will look equally wonderful linked to your arm.

A few words of caution, starting with these: Know your source. Many disreputable sellers deal in counterfeit handbags—in fact, it's fairly well known that, at the U.S. Customs offices, counterfeit high-end designer handbags and watches are among the most frequently confiscated items. Even if one takes into account such things as workmanship and high-quality materials, a large percentage of a designer bag's retail price undeniably reflects the designer's name and attendant prestige. Therefore, much profit can be made by reproducing a high-end handbag—often using inferior leathers and cheaper techniques—and selling it as a designer piece. The auction houses are well aware of this situation and are doing their best to screen out questionable items. It became so prevalent that at one point, you could log on to eBay, for example, view a selection of Louis Vuitton auctions, and upon returning to a particular bag for a second look, find it had been mysteriously pulled by the eBay authorities. All that remained was a bewildering "Invalid Item" message.

Further, handbags are utility items, and if they've been used and loved, they will certainly show this to at least some degree. Keep an eye out for "like new," "new without tags," and, if you're really lucky, "new with tags" versions of the bag you're seeking. Expensive handbags usually come with cotton flannel drawstring bags, too, so ask if one is available; it's also a good indication that your bag was properly stored. If you can live with a few tiny dings or marks, the opportunities for finding reasonably priced high-end designer handbags increase; perhaps you'll be fine with a flaw or two if that generous-sized and (relatively) affordable Kelly bag is something you wanted to use every day in place of your decidedly unchic canvas tote. If, however, it's perfection you want, either because you will accept nothing less or the handbag is intended as a gift, you'll need to take a much more selective approach, and you might find yourself—ironically enough—waiting awhile. Not for years, let's hope!

If having a high-end designer handbag is less important than finding one with a charming, unique design, however, there are plenty of wonderful vintage pieces—classy, ornamental, or utilitarian—available online from the limitless boutiques and auction pages. Look for gorgeous beaded evening bags, the most antique of which can be as much as a century old, worked in floral patterns and adorned with sterling filigree and silk tassels, and the more modern of which were often created in the Far East and close with rhinestone clasps. Also fabulous are the metal mesh purses—from all eras—by Whiting and Davis. A see-through Lucite box purse can be a unique addition to an outfit, although the contents had better be beautiful (now is the time to take along your best jeweled compact and lipstick holder); these bags are definitely becoming more collectible, with perfect, unscratched versions regularly costing over $100. And for gaudy whimsy, nothing beats a jeweled bag by Enid Collins of Texas, who decorated purses with flower themes and American scenes, such as San Francisco cable cars, zodiac signs, insects, animals,

"Three Old Ones on a Bench": 1950's wool handbags with velvet roses, all by J. R. Florida. *Deborah Newell Tornello*

and trees. Although these bags—both the fabric and leather versions as well as the highly coveted wooden ones—were once considered commonplace and more than a little kitschy, they're now regarded by many folk as textile art forms, so prices are inching upward, as you'd imagine. Note: Be sure that the large, decorative stones are all in place; if they aren't, you can certainly visit the craft store and purchase replacements, but the bag's purchase price should be lower, naturally.

As for exotic-skin vintage handbags, there are also some incredible alligator, lizard, and snakeskin purses available in the online boutiques, with Bellestone and Lucille de Paris being two of the best names for which to search. Since the quality of digital photos can vary and dark items are particularly difficult to see in detail, ask about the condition of the skins—they should be smooth and glossy, with no raised scales—as well as the state of the handle, especially at the points where it is bent through metal hardware to attach it to the body of the purse. Look for classic shapes in the spirit of the famous Kelly bag, since these will never go out of style; also keep an eye out for easy-to-pack, slim clutches.

Finally, be sure to check out the collectible and frequently wildly expensive minaudière bags, especially the compactlike vintage mother-of-pearl versions and the gold-and-rhinestone ones designed by the famous Judith Leiber. These sparkling little purses, which are still in production today, are truly handheld jewelry for the woman who needs only a lipstick, a theater ticket, and a gold credit card to see her into the evening. Be prepared to pay dearly (or bid high)—stratospherically so for the limited-edition models—and dare to carry your minaudière to a casual function from time to time, as it will not only serve as a great conversation piece but also will provide witty contrast to a pair of jeans and strappy sandals.

We'll conclude with a comprehensive—though by no means complete—list of some fabulous fine-handbag names you'll undoubtedly encounter in your searches. Carry it with you on your next virtual shopping trip.

Cartier—exquisite leather 1950's handbags

Bonnie Cashin—the leather bags she designed for Coach are wonderful and collectible

Chanel—classic quilted bags in every color and size (watch out for counterfeits)

Roberta di Camerino—the connoisseur's vintage handbag

Christian Dior—"basket weave" quilting, gold charms, vintage logos, and unusual shapes

Enid Collins—fabric or wooden bags adorned with oversized jewels and signed "E.C."

Fendi—myriad baguette and croissant designs, vintage logos

Gucci—vintage bamboo-handled bags, vintage logos

Hermès—classic Kelly and Birkin bags in unusual colors or reptile skins

Judith Leiber—the famous minaudière evening bags; animal, flower, and shell shapes

Kate Spade—cheerful and witty fabrics; flower-strewn straw bags

Louis Vuitton—vintage logos, unusual shapes, and colors in the Epi line

Prada—ballistic nylon backpacks were early 1990's staples; also, innovative evening bags

Whiting and Davis—metal mesh bags in gold, silver, and matte colors

Willardy—very collectible Bakelite and Lucite handbags

TO WEAR AND KNOT TO WEAR: SCARVES AND SHAWLS

Reports of the pashmina's demise have been greatly exaggerated. Once upon a time, this deliciously soft cashmere-and-silk shawl could only be seen wrapped around the shoulders of wealthy so-cialites as they made their way from the limousine to the theater; the truly coldhearted status addicts in their midst wore smug-gled shawls made of shahtoosh, an even costlier fiber that was banned in the United States because harvesting the fibers in-volved killing an endangered animal.

Shortly after their arrival on the scene, the lightweight pashmina shawls seemed to be everywhere and could be purchased at any nice department store for a couple of hundred dollars at most. And this was all good, as any woman who dreaded wearing a strapless formal dress in December would tell you. Sure, pashminas aren't the latest thing anymore; such is the fickle nature of fashion. But they continue to be practical, portable, and elegant; not only are they here to stay for a while, they're also readily available online. We advise skipping past the really cheap ones, though, as the dictum "you get what you pay for" could never be more on target. Correspondingly, we wouldn't purchase a pashmina from a boutique or seller who didn't offer a money-back guarantee, since one needs to actually feel the shawl in order to determine its quality.

A holdover from the 1970's, the "granny" shawl was one of the ways a lot of us learned to crochet or knit. Yves Saint Laurent included "cossack" versions in his Ballets Russes collection. The English design firm Voyage—recalling vintage Zandra Rhodes—offers some sweet examples with mixes of velvets, satins, and beaded trims.

For many of the same reasons we are enamored of costume jewelry, we adore the fine silk scarf. It's collectible without being a closet hog; it's graceful and movie-star-like, offering a quick way to enliven a plain outfit; and, most important, it doesn't remind us of those loathsome extra five pounds whenever we wear it. Hermès, Tiffany, and Versace scarves are made of especially weighty, luxurious silk twill and are well worth the investment you'll be making. A fine scarf will last a lifetime if cared for properly. Some of the Hermès designs are passionately sought after by collectors, so don't be surprised if, after bookmarking an auction one afternoon, you check back in a day or so and discover that the price has soared beyond your budget. It's difficult to predict which patterns will incite that sort of bidding frenzy in an auction, so perhaps buying your scarf outright—from an online vintage boutique like RetroActive (www.designervintage.com)—might be the way to go.

Also, consider decorative scarves, such as early-twentieth-century men's ascots, boas, tiny bow ties (worn on high-collared Victorian shirtwaist dresses), or lovely bits of lace to tie around necklines. Furthermore, a hand-rolled, pure silk scarf makes a delightful gift for someone who collects "tourist" scarves. Look for those screened with vintage panoramas, such as Atlantic City or Coney Island.

You needn't be a flight attendant to get plenty of use out of your scarf, nor should you limit yourself to wearing it around your neck with a business outfit. Large silk squares can be folded in half diagonally and worn as strapless tops with jeans or rolled lengthwise and threaded through the belt loops of chinos; smaller scarves can be twisted and knotted around a ponytail or tied to the strap of a purse.

A QUICK GO-AROUND: BELTS

Perhaps you're not inclined to fiddle with scarves, and your taste in jewelry leans toward wearing simple bangles or pearl stud earrings. You prefer the look of black turtlenecks in the winter, white T-shirts in the summer, and pencil skirts year-round. It sounds as though you're a belt person, someone who might pack as many as four belts for a simple ski weekend. Your duffel bag might contain a silvery one, made from hundreds of individually sewn snaps, by Ann Demeulemeester; a cast sterling Navajo concha belt; a soft, pliable three-inch-wide glove-leather cinch belt sold at London's Biba in the early 1970's; and a tan harness-leather belt with shiny chrome fittings and a neat little kilty bag attached to it with straps—pure vintage Ralph Lauren.

The accessory departments of the larger vintage sites offer numerous waist-cinching and hip-slung beauties. If you like the look of links, consider the embossed aluminum linked belts from the 1940's or the plastic or Bakelite rectangles from the 1950's. Chanel belts often have dangling C's and metal or wood links with suede or leather woven through them. Beaded belts from the 1930's and 1940's may need to have a few beads replaced, but they add a touch of elegance to a simple black wool dress. And vintage belts with hand-painted designs are uniquely beautiful; look for stripes, stars, unusual dyes, and various reptile skins.

If the belt you're considering is made of leather, try to ascertain how broken in and worn it is, especially at the points where it fastens. And when you're buying a belt from an online seller, ask about the overall length and placement of the holes, for example, forty inches in length with three holes placed at thirty, thirty-two, and thirty-four inches. This way, you can check these measurements against similar belts you already own or cut some pieces of stiff paper and make a facsimile. Be sure to ask if the fittings and hardware are in good working condition. And be sure to inquire about the material. You don't want to be disappointed by "pleather," vinyl, or even bonded canvas when you expected—and paid for—a genuine leather belt.

If you like logos and initials, the double locking L's and the large gold H's of vintage Lanvin and Hermès belts, respectively, will definitely interest you. Hermès also has a great "wrist belt" that occasionally makes an appearance on eBay, priced in the $160 range.

"Bamboo with Belts": (From top) 1970's rhinestone; 1980's Karung Judith Leiber with gold chains; 1990's Escada with gold sunflower and bee; 1970's Fiorucci "comic strip" vinyl; 1980's Charles Jourdan double buckle.
Deborah Newell Tornello

Wide corset-style and peasant belts are great, especially if you have a small waist. Yves Saint Laurent created some wonderful belts for his 1976–77 Russian-inspired collection, and we've seen these silhouettes in Tom Ford's recent collections, too. As for elastic cinch belts, while they may have lost their stretch or even hardened permanently, you might find the buckle is irresistible. If your waist is less than wasplike, there are terrific hip-slung belts from which to choose.

Finally, the true belt lover might experiment with wearing several identical versions at the same time, crisscrossing them. You should also check out commemorative brass buckles embossed with advertising and trademarks, Bakelite and Czechoslovakian crystal buckles, and Japanese obis, usually beautifully embroidered, originally meant for kimonos. Here are some belt designers' names to get you started:

Ann Demeulemeester—the "shoelace" belt, sometimes offered on eBay, usually with many bidders

Gucci—the famous double G belts

Hermès—the renowned H-buckle belt, ultrachic and also perfect for those named Hillary or Hope

Barry Kieselstein-Cord—sterling silver frog- or alligator-shaped buckles

François Lesage—the embroidered "Hand" belt ca. 1986 and Fish belt, ca. 1987

Issey Miyake—the early Plantation belts

Elsa Peretti—stirrup-shaped sterling silver buckles designed for Tiffany around 1974

Prada—logos and, more recently, vintage-inspired designs

Yves Saint Laurent—wide, waist-emphasizing belts

SOLE-SEARCHING IN CYBERSPACE

A rather old-fashioned and judgmental saying goes something like this: One can learn a great deal about a man simply by looking at the watch on his wrist, the woman on his arm, and the shoes on his feet. The modern corollary might hold that if your hair incites envy and your shoes are amazing, you can get away with wearing faded jeans and a plain white T-shirt to dinner—at many restaurants, anyway—regardless of who is on your arm.

Sneakers, flip-flops, and espadrilles have their place, certainly, but a man or woman who has the confidence to wear luxurious Italian loafers with Levi's is saying something interesting before even being shown to a table. Like it or not—and the avowed fans of Nike and Birkenstock will probably dislike it immensely—shoes do matter. We aren't suggesting that anyone attempt to go power walking, or even power shopping, in four-inch stilettos. We *are* suggesting that everyone pay attention to their feet when they're dressing to impress, since stylish shoes will always be noticed and appreciated.

Hopefully, we don't have to convince you any further: Take a look at the incredible shoes—sometimes gently worn but frequently brand-new, never worn, and still in the box—that are offered for sale by Designer Exposure (www.designerexposure.com) (a high-end resale website), Piece Unique (www.pieceunique.com), and eBay. You'll feel the same rush of adrenaline you normally only experience at the end-of-year shoe sales. If you've longed for a pair of Manolo Blahnik pumps or Christian Louboutin sandals but always marched straight past the designer shoe boutique, fearing that your credit card might ignite, well, do we ever have an inside secret for you.

There are sellers on eBay, for example, who live in the major U.S. cities and buy up the end-of-season designer shoes in bulk. As their business is conducted online, and they have little or no overhead expenses to factor into the cost of the shoes, they can offer them to the world at deeply discounted prices. A pair of Jimmy Choos might cost upward of $500 in the department store, but if you don't mind shoes from the previous season, or ones that have been worn once in a fashion show—with names like Natasha or Jasmina scribbled on the soles—or a pair that consists of a size 9 right and a size 9½ left (which suits you perfectly, since your feet are oddly sized), you might be able to snap up those gorgeous Choos for well under $200.

As you'd expect, fabulous shoes at bargain prices sell like Krispy Kremes during morning rush hour when the neon HOT DOUGHNUTS NOW sign is lit. So if you've found a pair in a resale boutique, you will have to act quickly. The same goes for the "Buy It Now" auctions on eBay: She who hesitates is disappointed. And bear in mind that really pricey designer shoes are handmade, and sizes run small. Women should buy at least a half-size larger in Manolo Blahnik, Christian Louboutin, Jimmy Choo, Gucci, Prada, and Dolce & Gabbana footwear, especially if their feet tend to be a little wider or the shoes they're considering are of the closed, pointed-toe variety. Men would be well advised to familiarize themselves with the sizing peculiarities of the designer or manufacturer whose shoes they're mulling over.

If you're thinking about buying or bidding on preworn shoes, remember to ask questions about condition. Sometimes there will be a photo of the nearly pristine soles, showing the potential customer that these shoes really *were* worn just once. Un-

"La Rose Arrangement": 1950's Joseph La Rose shoes; Red Wing gladiolus vase. *Deborah Newell Tornello*

fortunately, flaws like nicks on a stiletto heel or scuffs on a toe are small and difficult to see in a digital photo; furthermore, sellers have been known to forget to mention these things. How satisfied you'll ultimately be with your purchase depends on the detailed nature of your e-mailed questions—asked *beforehand*, of course. Be sure to also ask about return policies.

Promise yourself this: Casual shoes of the athletic and beach variety excepted, you'll never again wear a pair of cheap, poorly made, or less-than-fabulous footwear. Not when there are so many delightful—and, at last, affordable—designer shoes waiting to take you dancing.

CHASING A CENTURY OF SKIRTS

*W*hen you first discover the myriad vintage clothing offerings of the Internet and begin browsing all the virtual racks, you're bound to feel a little overwhelmed. Not only are there innumerable vintage websites to visit (a wide assortment of which are reviewed in this book) and countless listings on eBay and other auction sites to browse, but every vintage garment you ever imagined yourself wearing is suddenly available at the click of a mouse. Lovely as the clothes may be, they're causing your head to spin. What if one were to buy something, only to discover it didn't fit? After all, absent the luxury of trying things on in a dressing room, there is a certain element of chance when you buy clothing online.

Unquestionably, one could test the waters by bidding on a Miriam Haskell bracelet or snapping up an Yves Saint Laurent chain belt. No real size issues there. But perhaps you'd like to discover one of those legendary Internet finds you keep hearing about. Why not set your sights on a wonderful skirt? Access to the countless styles created during the last century is now at your fingertips, and you'll have far fewer concerns about fit with a vintage skirt, which makes it a great get-your-feet-wet garment for any newcomer to the virtual vintage marketplace. With dresses and coats, one must be concerned with sleeve length, bodice measurements, and bust issues, since we tend to be taller and larger in the twenty-first century, and, unfortunately, this sometimes means one has to pass on something really intriguing. With a skirt, you need only be concerned about the waist size and, possibly, the hip measurement. If these will work and, of course, if you love the skirt's color and style, you can feel quite confident that your first online fashion purchase will be a successful one.

There were so many skirt silhouettes created in the preceding decades, it's practically guaranteed that many, if not millions, will suit your taste and flatter your figure. A vintage skirt, whether it's a funky 1960's mini or a flounced Victorian cotton petticoat, will complement your existing wardrobe and allow you to create many unique looks. Let's say you're a more "tailored" person. You might wear a 1950's hand-painted Mexican skirt with an oxford shirt knotted at the waist or a simple fitted T-shirt, perhaps one with a boat neck and three-quarter sleeves. Add a pair of Keds-type sneakers and a couple of Bakelite bangles, and you've created a fresh look that is still true to your personal style. If you think of yourself as a more of a girl's girl, you can similarly experiment with contrasts by pairing a severe, 1980's black pencil skirt or an asymmetrical style—perhaps from one of the Japanese designers—with a beaded cardigan or ruffled camisole you already own.

Vintage skirts are absolutely wonderful wardrobe enhancers; what's more, they're relatively easy to alter. Remember buttons or hooks can often be moved a little in either direction, so there is some flexibility with the waist size. When you consider the length, bear in mind that while it's usually pretty simple to shorten a skirt, lengthening one will often leave you with a fold mark where the old hem was. It's a good idea to avoid buying anything too short, even a skirt that's described as having a really generous hem. Furthermore, the older the garment is, the more set that hem crease will be, but if you are determined to have the skirt and the price is right, there *are* a few ways to lengthen a skirt and then camouflage the previous owner's hem (please see Part Four, "Fitting, Fixing, and Flaunting").

In our own ever-expanding collections, we each have countless vintage skirts, many of which we found online, that never fail to win compliments. These are the trusty garments one tends to grab when one is uninspired but needing to look and feel great in a hurry. One such item is Deborah's 1980's black Alaïa pencil skirt with the mermaid ruffle that she wears with a small white T-shirt, black stiletto pumps, and a vintage crocodile bag. And Linda owns a terrific Ann Demeulemeester hip skirt from the 1990's; whether she wears a funnel-neck sweater or a T-shirt on top—depending on the temperature outside—she always looks modern and polished. If you were to rummage through our closets, you'd find, among many other things, a 1950's circle skirt with painted poinsettias and sequins (worn to holiday functions with a fitted cardigan or sparkly tank top), a black silk-taffeta ball skirt (made from an online vintage-fabric find), several dark satin origamilike skirts by Japanese designers, asymmetrical wool skirts that Linda likes for Connecticut winter wear, and armfuls of cheap, colorful printed-cotton full skirts, mostly from the 1950's, on which Deborah relies during the insufferable Florida summers (these skirts get worn with tank tops and ballet flats—a feminine alternative to the expected uniform of shorts and logoed T-shirts).

Look to the past, and you'll find a wealth of fabulous skirts. A century's worth awaits the online vintage shopper who knows what to look for and where to find it.

WHITE COTTON VICTORIAN PETTICOATS

These former undergarments create such a romantic silhouette, they call to mind the covers of those "bodice-ripper" novels. Who could resist effecting *that* transformation? Wearing these lovely skirts might not increase the number of flowing-haired and well-muscled heroes you encounter in the course of a normal work week, but you'll definitely look the part of the desirable damsel for as long as you have them on. And although these are easier to wear—not to mention more generously and flexibly sized than the imposing taffeta bustled skirts of this era—be careful not to step on your own hem, as the fabric, as well as the lace trim, is often fragile. A great many petticoats are available through online vintage boutiques and auctions, and prices range from about $20 to well over $200. You should know that few, if any, are perfect. They're all a century old! So expect a few tiny age spots here and there, unless you're incredibly lucky, as well as an occasional mend. Since these are voluminous skirts, many of these flaws will disappear into the cumulonimbus of cotton and lace. Ask questions. Is this spot in the front? Is that hole bigger than a pinhead? How was this skirt washed? And look for embroidery, lace, and hand finishing, as these details will increase the skirt's worth (and usually its price).

What to wear with your Victorian? At the time of this writing, some of the Parisian designers, inspired by movies like

Moulin Rouge!, are showing Victorian-styled ruffled petticoat skirts with corsets and laced-up boots. Of course, you can take this costume to a more personalized (not to mention more wearable and less fashion victimy) level and dress up your genuine article with a fitted 1940's jacket, a rhinestone-studded rocker-chick T-shirt, a fitted, ruched bodysuit, a denim jean jacket over a tank top, or a sequined 1950's cardigan. And on your feet, try ballet-slipper flats, stiletto sandals, or even riding boots.

BIAS-CUT SKIRTS

These slinky 1930's or 1930's-inspired beauties are terrific finds. Often there is no waistband, and the skirt is made of silk or a similar, slithery fabric. Darker colors are obviously easier to wear (and if your tummy or hips are issues, this type of skirt might prove less than flattering). Pair a bias-cut skirt with your business jacket or go in a completely feminine direction and wear it with a lace camisole or a beaded tunic.

PENCIL, OR STRAIGHT, SKIRTS

Often the bottom half of a 1940's suit, these skirts usually have a kick pleat or slit in the back or side. The genuine vintage skirts are, more often than not, side closing with a metal zipper (be careful when trying on a tight one!). Sometimes you can have the skirt slightly pegged at the hem (see Part Four) to create a leaner, better-fitting garment. When worn with a man's-style button-front shirt with the cuffs rolled up, this simple skirt shape can pack a very sexy wallop. (Think Kathleen Turner in the 1981 movie *Body Heat:* She sits at the bar, wearing a plain white shirt and pencil skirt, and the beleaguered William Hurt makes a remark about what she is wearing. She replies that it's just a blouse and a skirt. Indeed.)

CIRCLE SKIRTS, FULL SKIRTS, AND DIRNDLS

Classic 1950's pieces, these are sometimes called "swing skirts" by online sellers. Whatever the name, they are easy to wear for curvy girl and beanpole alike, and they're comfortable to boot. Skip the cliché poodle skirt (many of which are reproductions, anyway) and check out all the other bright, original patterns of this era: geometric designs, atomic patterns reminiscent of *The Jetsons,* bright florals, story prints—like dancing ladies or jousting knights—and polka dots. If there are sequins or beads involved, be sure to ask about them before bidding or buying (please see the section on asking questions, page 15, in order to buy with confidence), as repairing beadwork is not for the fainthearted.

THE MINISKIRT

Hasn't that little scrap of fabric provoked some fierce language? We're convinced it can be worn by almost anyone, as long as she knows what she's doing silhouettewise. Keep your eyes open for examples by the fabulous designers of the 1960's, like Courrèges, and don't limit yourself to safe and boring black miniskirts but instead go for color and playfulness: zippers with big rings for pulls, interesting pocket details, witty patterns. An A-line mini is easier to wear (it will stand out from your thighs a little and make them look slimmer), but the length is going to be key: You don't want it to stop at the widest part of your leg. If you're considering buying a mini you've found online, measure one you already own and compare the numbers. Hosiery is a big consideration, too, as the 1960's dresses and skirts were often worn with wildly patterned or contrasting tights, and many of us prefer wearing a little something, colored or otherwise, on the legs. And, of course, if you love the look of a short skirt with knee-high boots and have the figure for it—or, at least, the nerve—the vintage miniskirts of the 1960's were also made for walking. Enjoy!

THE FLOWING MIDI- AND MAXISKIRTS

These were inspirations for some of the hip, pricey designs currently offered by Voyage (of London) and others. These remind us how unusual and gorgeous some of the authentic 1970's hippie skirts were (how did we forget?). Take heart: There are still plenty of originals out there in vintage cyberspace if you're disinclined to spend upwards of a thousand dollars for a skirt. Draped and ruched velvet is especially luscious to wear; and if you can find a long silk velvet skirt that's in great shape, grab it immediately (after checking the measurements and condition, of course). Your skirt will appear quite elegant—formal even—yet to you, it will feel as comfortable as a nightgown.

THE 1980'S POWER SKIRTS

This was the decade in which almost all the designers really began to draw inspiration from other eras (understandable, as there are only so many shapes with which to work). The most prevalent silhouette is the pencil skirt, which was directly inspired by the narrow skirts of the 1940's. It can be found almost everywhere. The hemlines of the 1980's, for the most part, fell somewhere around midknee, as women primarily wore these skirts incorporated into career outfits. This style doesn't utilize a great deal of fabric, and since the amount of workmanship involved in making such a skirt is minimal, compared to, say, a jacket or evening gown, the price will be surprisingly low. This means you can afford—and should buy—the very best labels, for example Donna Karan, Giorgio Armani, Escada, Thierry Mugler, Claude Montana, and, of course, Chanel. Especially Chanel, says Deborah; exclusively Yamamoto, says Linda.

At the time of this writing, we are in the midst of a 1980's revival that actually began in the late 1990's, underscoring how short these style cycles have become. This feels a little odd to those of us who began our careers in that decade and, at the very least, have one or two of the original so-called 1980's icons hiding in our closets behind all the aforementioned vintage skirts. If you come across an interesting pencil skirt online, or if one of your own buried treasures is an 1980's straight skirt—which in those days would have been paired with a wide-shouldered jacket (think *Dynasty*), a bat-wing silk blouse, or a high-necked shirt with pin tucks and French cuffs—you can give it an interesting modern look by wearing it with a sheer lace 1940's short-sleeved blouse over a contrasting camisole. Or you can draw

1950's Christian Dior tulle strapless ball gown; 1950's satin gloves. *Deborah Newell Tornello*

inspiration from the movies and accessorize your skirt with a simple white shirt and an attitude.

1980'S ASYMMETRICAL SKIRTS

The Japanese lines like Comme des Garçons, Issey Miyake, Matsuda, and—one of Linda's favorites—Yohji Yamamoto produced unique garments. These have a timeless appeal: They didn't really toe the line, trendwise, when they debuted, and more often than not one will be unable to distinguish a 1980's Japanese avant-garde skirt from a current-season piece. Measurements for many of these uniquely shaped skirts can be confusing, so check that the waist and hip will fit. For asymmetrical skirts, be sure to ask about the shortest point of the hem, as there were certain skirts that were purposely designed to be risqué and others that were meant to be layered over longer skirts. Some of the voluminous, lopsided skirts can be tricky to wear for even the most slender woman. Often it's just a matter of adjusting one's eye. On the other hand, if the skirt makes you look like a pterodactyl with a penchant for large-scale origami projects, as they say, it's a look. Fashion is supposed to be fun.

ETHNIC EMBROIDERED SKIRTS, REWORKED PIANO SHAWLS, JEAN SKIRTS, AND PATCHWORK SKIRTS

These all are offered on eBay as well as in the many online vintage collections. Some of the Guatemalan textiles are especially lovely and feature bright, geometric patterns, animals, and people that are actually woven into the fabric; often, the skirt itself is a simple shape, and the pattern makes the statement. Remember that the dyes used in these textiles may not be stable enough to withstand machine washing with all your other clothes. Hand washing separately in cold water—and then, only when needed—is the best method for laundering hand-loomed skirts.

Piano shawls from decades past are wonderful when worn as sexy, fringed skirts. You might have seen modern versions of these in the boutiques and department stores over the past couple of years, but it's unlikely that the quality of the fabric and workmanship were anything like those of a genuine silk piano shawl "re-purposed" as a skirt. We've seen these worn with everything from denim jackets to satin bustiers to T-shirts. With the really old shawls, you will undoubtedly encounter a few flaws: pulled or loose embroidery, tangled fringe, tiny holes. The more problems there are, the lower the price will be, naturally. If you're a patient sort and you don't mind combing out a matted tassel or two (hundred), you can find all sorts of antique piano shawls on eBay and in online vintage boutiques for less than what you'd pay for a modern, machine-made (and vastly inferior) version; and you'll be able to create an incredible, unique evening skirt with almost no effort. Be sure to select a shawl that's large enough to fold diagonally and tie around you like a sarong. And when you tire of *that* look, you can actually wear it as a shawl. Either way, remember the trailing fringe if you're given to making dramatic, door-slamming exits.

And as for the homemade jean skirts, versions of every length and shade can be found online. When enterprising 1970's girls ripped open their Levi's inseams and filled in the gap with a wedge of denim or other fabric, a new style was born (often to the chagrin of their parents, who were still struggling to come to terms with the shag hairdos and psychedelic outfits worn by celebrities). Lots of companies are reproducing these skirts today, and many of them appear pretty authentic with their raw edges and frayed belt loops. Vintage ones, however, are special, because peace-sign patches, embroidered declarations of love like "Spirit + Jeremy," and colorful trim that's dotted with tiny mushrooms or frogs constitute someone's heartfelt and creative expressions. That sort of karma can't be reproduced thirty years later, but fortunately, it lives on in the originals.

UNIQUE 1990'S SKIRTS

Skirts made of leather, suede, paper, pleather, and other delicate or difficult materials can be very tempting to the eye. They are recent, and they're all over the place. We recommend, however, that you proceed with caution. Think about your own experiences with these materials for a moment: How many different leather skirts did you try on before finding one that didn't flatten your derrière or stand out stiffly at the waist? In what sort of condition are your suede items, and have you had any success removing stains from them? Did your diligent searches ever turn up a craftsman (or even an auto body shop) capable of rechroming your chain-mail miniskirt? Certain materials show their age and wear—some more so than others. Since we're aiming to help you purchase a vintage skirt that you'll actually wear and enjoy (as opposed to hang on your repairs rack or, worse, hide altogether), we suggest designating all skirts from this category as "for window-shopping only," at least for the time being. Certainly, eBay has numerous listings of fabulous leather skirts, some of which may fit you perfectly. And perhaps one of the online resale shops is selling a papier-mâché skirt by your favorite

Belgian designer. No one is saying you should avoid these enticing treasures indefinitely. Rather, we're suggesting that you wait until you develop more of a feel for buying clothes online before you gamble on the delicate and the difficult; even then, keep the wear-and-tear factors in mind. Ask the seller every possible question, and for goodness' sake, don't pay an exorbitant sum for something that appears to have problems you're not sure you can fix, especially if the seller has a no-returns policy.

Looking into the future, we see you standing in front of your brimming closet, rummaging through the rainbow layers of lace, wool, and satin, and pulling out—only to stuff back—one armful of clothes after another. Every so often, you stop to check your watch: It's getting late. You alight on the perfect thing. You love this skirt, and you always look great in it, no matter what. Your reflection agrees. And, as you always do these days, you fleetingly recall how this particular garment came into your possession. It was the first vintage piece you bought online, and it's even nicer on your person.

IT'S NOT OVER TILL IT'S COVERED: COATS

$\mathcal{F}$rom the cloaks that can accommodate enormous crinoline-enhanced skirts to the now-classic military-style trench coat with epaulets, the nineteenth century launched a retinue of styles that have kept us warm and protected ever since. A sacque was a sleeveless jacket worn as a negligee, and the redingote evolved out of the English riding coat. Lined with fur, embroidered with beads, waterproofed, or created out of sheer organdy, coats provide the finishing touch for any ensemble.

We've collected coats from Biba and Bendel's, and we love our vintage additions from eBay and Amazon. Wide-lapeled and sleek coats or collarless, barrel-shaped, and bulky ones find their way into our style consciousness and closets. Balloon anoraks, ponchos, and dusters are regularly reinvented as couture's seasons hop and skip over one another.

Then there are jackets that thrill us in leather, whether they're a classic motorcycle style, vintage World War II bomber jackets, fringed-and-beaded suede from the 1960's and 1970's, or svelte and supple licorice black with Azzedine Alaïa's body-hugging silhouette.

1950's Christian Dior satin jacket; rhinestone earrings and brooch (unsigned); feather boa worn as a hat. *Deborah Newell Tornello*

There are the great fashion-history-making coats: Jacques Fath's hourglass shapes followed by Christian Dior's inventive interpretations—triangular tent shapes and his *envol* jackets that flared into wide shapes with their extended cuffs and stand-up collars. The mackintosh, before it evoked the name of a computer, might have sported a red tweed lining to match a dress and jacket if Molineux had designed it. Schiaparelli fastened jackets with buttons shaped like butterflies and cicadas; an evening coat she designed with Jean Cocteau featured Lesage embroidery with the profiles of a man and woman, a vase of roses above them. Zandra Rhodes created felt coats with pinking at the hems, while Claude Montana designed a red satin coat in the shape of a cocoon. We admire a coat—covered with great swirls of open-winged seagulls—by Jean-Charles de Castelbajac and Cristobal Balenciaga's delicious cape made of a pouf of black gazar. Trompe l'oeil motifs were captured by Marcel Rochas and in Adelle Lutz's urban camouflage suits for David Byrne and John Goodman in the 1986 film *True Stories.* We long for Yves Saint Laurent's sequined lip coat of 1971 or even his "Russian" day coat, and we would adore anything by Charles James.

You, on the other hand, might choose a yellow slicker or a safari, tuxedo, or Edwardian-style coat. A Nehru style will appeal to you one year, a mandarin style the next. You wonder if a cape might be right for you as opposed to a swing coat, then you settle on a combination of the two by Yohji Yamamoto. Whether knitted as long sweaters or fitted as dresses, well-made coats endure many seasons and return from the depths of storage with renewed vigor.

And vintage Levi's denim jackets in all sorts of faded conditions are never in short supply on the Internet.

Cowl-necked, shawl-collared, down-filled, peplum-waisted

—the designs are seemingly endless in their variations. And vintage brass-buttoned tunics, velveteens, brocades, lamés, tweeds, or quilted boxy jackets from one designer can easily be worn with pants or skirts from another. Creative combinations express a sophisticated style that is unmistakably your own.

HAWAIIANS AND GUAYABERAS, OH, MY!
COOL VINTAGE SHIRTS AND OTHER MENSWEAR

Gentlemen, start your search engines. The wired world of vintage has much to offer the stylish man: dress suits, weekend wear, and everything in between. And, best of all, you can afford to experiment—perhaps even get a little adventurous—since chest and inseam measurements will be your main concerns, as opposed to arm-and-a-leg price tags.

Even designer suits of recent vintage (meaning, last season) are frequently offered at bargain-basement prices by auction sellers and resale websites (see Part Five). Let's say you've been thinking about treating yourself to a new suit, perhaps an elegant one by Zegna, for example. All you need do is log on to eBay, enter the Z-word into the search box, and sit back and see what we mean.

The Internet has proven to be a lifesaver for the busy or shop-phobic man now that a guy's favorite basics—like jeans, khakis, and baseball caps—are just a mouse click and a mail truck away. It follows that once big retailers like Banana Republic and J. Crew started taking to the web, small vintage boutiques would also set up shop online. Add the voluminous virtual wardrobes of the auction sites, and the selection of styles and sizes is so broad, there's no excuse for dressing any way other than impressively.

Before you start style surfing, there are a few things to remember. Most important, you should know your actual measurements, especially when you're buying fashion from another era. The sizes of these clothes tend to run small, meaning you'll probably have to buy a larger 1950's bowling shirt, say. Don't be discouraged by this—put your ego in your pocket. Almost every vintage website provides detailed measurements of the garments, so if you're forearmed with your chest and waist stats, at least, you can skip over the small-sized jackets and bound-to-be-baggy shirts and focus instead on the things that will fit. So, locate or buy a tape measure and determine your true chest and waist size and write these down. It's also useful to measure the chest, sleeve length, waist, and inseam of your favorite jacket, shirt, and pair of pants (choose ones that fit you well at the moment). Since most sellers list these details in their descriptions—and if they don't, you can ask for them—it will be easy to determine if a garment will work for you by comparing its measurements against those of the baseline garments in your own closet.

Another thing to keep in mind is that fabric labels are often nonexistent in vintage clothes. If, for example, you're someone who avoids certain kinds of wool because they aggravate your allergies, you will want to pose very specific questions to the online shop or auction seller. It might be a good idea to avoid sweaters and heavy winter knits altogether, since there may not be any way of guaranteeing a garment's wool-free status. Fortunately, there were myriad linens, cottons, and synthetics used in the past century, and once you start browsing through the clothes, you'll not only be amazed at the range of colors and designs available in vintage but you'll also see the original inspirations for many of the prints and patterns showing up in current designers' collections. And the prices for these first editions will be much more attractive, we promise. Finally, remember that vintage clothing has usually been worn by another person. Oddly enough, this fact doesn't seem to bother women as much as it does men; in fact, the majority of women find the garment's previous life to be an integral part of its charm and appeal, whereas men—certainly the ones to whom we spoke, anyway—are sometimes a little squeamish about wearing someone else's shirts, ties, or jackets. We'd love to change your thinking on this, so may we offer some suggestions to the vintage neophyte?

1. Start small. An antique sterling lapel pin or a fabulous 1940's silk tie embroidered with palm trees will individualize your business suit without causing you too much anxiety.
2. Learn how to hand wash. Sure, it's a little more time-consuming than simply stuffing everything into a washing machine and pressing the Start button. Speaking from our own experience, though, we feel so much better about wearing a beautiful but really old blouse if we've soaked it in a gentle soap (like liquid Dreft, Woolite, or Ivory), rinsed it, hung it up to dry on a plastic hanger, and ironed it. Perhaps it is a psychological thing, but once the bathing ritual is performed on a garment, it not only feels clean, it feels like it's yours. (For much more on this subject, see Part Four.)
3. If you don't already know a great dry cleaner, now is the time to ask around. Everyone we know has dry-cleaning horror stories, and your friends and associates will undoubtedly be only too happy to vent their frustrations about the company that crushed all the buttons on their favorite coat or whose

stain-removal techniques burned holes in the lapels of their new jacket. These are the places to avoid, obviously. Ask about the good cleaners, since that's what you're after: the small, out-of-the-way establishment whose on-site tailor replaces lost buttons; the company that calls you on your cell phone to ask if you'd prefer medium or light starch in your shirts, since you didn't mention this.

Vintage clothing is usually well made and durable, or it wouldn't be around for you to buy. But take it from us: It's well worth paying a little extra to a wonderful dry cleaner, especially when the garment you're handing over is one-of-a-kind and special. The rewards of careful cleaning are the same as those of hand washing: Your garment looks and feels refreshed.

4. Hire, and befriend, a capable tailor or seamstress. Perhaps you were taught to thread a needle and you're perfectly capable of sewing on a button or even repairing a falling trouser hem. Bravo! Even so, a time will come when the waist of a dinner jacket will need altering, and involved procedures like this are usually best left to the pros. You will considerably increase your range of choices if you know you'll be able to have those coat sleeves professionally shortened or that jacket properly fitted to your body. And once again, the vintage garment becomes something customized, something personal.

5. Last, if you absolutely, positively cannot get past your distaste for wearing something worn by someone else, look to the shops and sellers who either deal in new old stock vintage clothing (sometimes called dead stock) or who carry new garments—frequently by high-end, sought-after designers—from recent seasons, always at prices far below current-season retail. Sellers of new old stock can be a little harder to locate,

but they are there. Look for the abbreviation "NOS" in auction titles and pay attention to the boutiques and sellers who deal in estates, as many an unworn treasure can be found in these collections. Sellers of recent collections are all over the Internet and are especially prevalent on eBay. Simply enter your chosen designer's name into the Search box, and start browsing the virtual racks.

Remember that most vintage items are one of a kind, meaning that the great shirt with the funky pattern might not be there if you wait until next week to e-mail the seller, and if it's being sold in an online auction, you'll have even less time to make up your mind. Fortunately, most sellers are quick to respond to their customers' questions, so e-mail away and snap up your fabulous finds as soon as you can.

HATS OFF: GENUINE PANAMAS, BASEBALL CAPS, AND MORE

Guys who love the graceful and dramatic looks of yesteryear have new reason to rejoice: The hard-to-find, beautifully made hats that complement a stylish outfit are now available online. If you love the tropical elegance of your ivory linen suit and have been seeking a genuine Panama hat, new and custom-made to the exacting standards of long ago—and using the identical methods, too—you must visit Montecristi Custom Hat Works (www.montecristihats.com). As you would expect, these gorgeous Panama hats are investment pieces, and their price tags reflect this: Panamas start at $300, and prices can soar into five figures. With proper care, however, the hats will last a lifetime. For casual headwear, look no further than the online auctions,

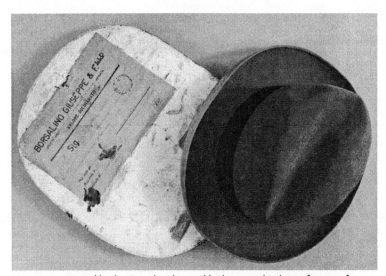

Vintage menswear like this Borsalino hat and hatbox may be the perfect item for a display or store window. *Linda Lindroth*

where new, old-style baseball caps—emblazoned with every-thing imaginable, from the logo of your hometown team to the title of your favorite childhood TV show—cowboy hats, fedoras, even vintage hatboxes can all be found in abundance.

THE ULTIMATE BACHELOR WEAR: SMOKING JACKETS AND SILK PAJAMAS

For a while, the only loungewear available to men were those awful cotton-polyester pajamas reminiscent of the outfits worn by extras in *One Flew Over the Cuckoo's Nest*. It is little wonder that so many men relied on sweatpants, T-shirts, and baggy shorts to see them through those difficult leisure hours. But the suave, stylish men of yesteryear—at least, the ones we saw in the movies—never resorted to sweatpants and tank tops when the mood called for relaxation wear. Indeed, wearing a sophisticated satin robe or smoking jacket was practically required of our martini-mixing, romantic-fire-building hero. And those very jackets can be found in several online boutiques; check out the Cats Pajamas (www.catspajamas.com) and Glorious Vintage (www.gloriousvintage.com), both of which offer nice selections. Remember that a dedicated antique-clothing buff might love a pair of vintage silk pajamas from an online boutique or auction, but many guys' "no old clothes" mandates become even more rigid when it comes to intimate apparel.

EVERYBODY LIMBO NOW: HAWAIIAN SHIRTS, CABANA JACKETS, AND GUAYABERAS

Almost every vintage clothing boutique carrying menswear offers a great selection of Hawaiian shirts. And if you're someone who already collects these witty and wonderful garments, you're well aware that some of the rare specimens can approach the stratosphere, pricewise. No matter—there is a wealth of affordable vintage Hawaiian shirts available, both in the online shops and at auction, for under $50. All-rayon Hawaiians are the most coveted and collectible, but don't pass up a great-looking cotton or silk version, especially if you love the pattern. Look for buttons made of bamboo, coconut, or shell, which generally indicate an older, and therefore more valuable, shirt. Other signs of a high-quality vintage piece include a long, pointed collar (often containing collar stays), an absence of topstitching on the collar, and a little fabric loop above the top button. Of course, other than its excellent condition and perfect size, what will attract your eye is the Hawaiian shirt's pattern and color scheme. To view a wonderful online collection of these American treasures, go to The Vintage Hawaiian Shirt: An Artistic Retrospective (www.vintagehawaiianshirt.net); to purchase one for yourself, visit one of the many vintage clothing websites, such as Neen's Vintage (www.neens.com), whose extensive inventory offers a wide range of Hawaiiana, and Aloha Vintage (www.riseuphawaii.com), a much smaller site but one that is still worth a look.

The guayabera (pronounced "gwi-a-BEAR-a") is currently enjoying a resurgence, thanks in part to the ultrahip club crowds and sun worshipers of Miami Beach. The basic guayabera is short sleeved and it buttons down the front; it has patch pockets and is worn outside one's pants or jeans. There are usually rows of vertical tucks down the front; sometimes there's decorative embroidery, either matched to the shirt or in a contrasting color. Red guayaberas with white embroidery are especially festive for holidays, and one stylish man we know likes to wear his all-black guayaberas while cooking for friends, calling them the "ultimate tropical chef's jackets." The postwar generation knew something that we younger folk are just beginning to get: Guayaberas aren't just cool, they're *cool*. They look impossibly crisp and stylish, even after one emerges from an ovenlike car, feeling medium to well-done. Still produced and enthusiastically sought after today, the guayabera calls to mind the slower pace of times past. It is the perfect uniform for daydreaming and mojito drinking on a hot summer afternoon. Vintage and new versions abound; look for them in online boutiques and, of course, in the auction listings.

As for the cabana jacket (as worn by Kramer of TV's *Seinfeld*), this short terry cloth robe, usually lined with bright, patterned cotton and frequently reversible, is worn as a swimsuit cover-up. Often, there will be patch pockets for your sunglasses and zinc oxide. Be sure to look for cabana jackets that are in excellent condition, since well-worn terry cloth can look shabby, and suntan-oil stains can be difficult to remove. In other words, ask questions.

THE SPORTING LIFE FOR ME: BOWLING SHIRTS, LETTER SWEATERS, AND VINTAGE BASEBALL JACKETS

Men can be hard on their clothes, and athletic wear usually takes more abuse than most garments. We don't mean to sound sexist, but between the two of us, we have four sons and two husbands, all of whom are active, fast-moving guys. We know from whence we speak when we tell you their sportswear is definitely the worse for wear. But vintage garments like bowling shirts, baseball jackets, and football jerseys are both appealing and valuable. If you do come across a great piece that's been gently worn—or, lucky you, never used at all—be sure to seize the day and grab the jersey.

Vintage bowling shirts, like Hawaiian shirts, are personality pieces that are great fun to wear. Often the logo of the team or its sponsor is embroidered on the back, and the bowler's name appears in chain stitch on the chest. Clothingwise, one would be hard-pressed to find a better conversation starter: Imagine a quiet, mild-mannered computer programmer showing up at the company picnic in a scarlet-and-black bowling shirt advertising Palatka Farms Champion Pit Bull Breeders, Inc. He'd be assuming an intriguing new identity for the afternoon—even if his name really *was* Jimbo. Rayon fabric, real appliqués or embroidery (as opposed to silk-screening), fine condition, and appealing color combinations and team names can all increase the desirability and price of a bowling shirt. Reproductions abound, too, and while they are certainly nice enough, you shouldn't pay vintage prices for something that isn't. Remember to ask questions, as always. For terrific new, retro-style bowling shirts on which names can be custom embroidered, check out Daddy-O's (www.daddyos.com), and be sure to visit BowlingShirt.com (www.bowlingshirt.com) and see their vast inventory of vintage-inspired bowling shirts in all styles and sizes (including children's versions).

Letter sweaters and baseball jackets are highly collectible vintage garments, if you are lucky enough to find them. We suspect many such treasures were simply passed on from father to son or from mother—who received or "borrowed" the sweater or jacket from *her* boyfriend—to daughter. And they remain at large. But once in a while, you'll spot an Old English–typeface Y on a cardigan and find yourself wishing you'd kept up your saxophone lessons. Knits are particularly susceptible to wear and tear, so be certain your find is a well-preserved, hardly worn specimen. Team jackets and jerseys were often made of silky knits or woven satin—dry-clean-only satin—and any attempts at machine washing by the previous owner may have rendered the fabric fairly wilted looking. Then there is the inevitable pilling—those patches of fuzz that plague well-worn woolens—to consider. Unless they are new or obvious collector's items, we'd recommend passing on these types of garments.

STAYING ALIVE, STAYING ALIVE . . . DISCO WEAR

It really isn't necessary to say much about disco fashion, since it's probably the most accessible and available category of vintage clothing on the market. Almost every site reviewed in this book (see Part Five) offers at least a small selection of 1970's treasures. Start with the 70s Disco Room at The Way We Wore (www.thewaywewore.net), which stocks period wigs and jewelry.

There is a saying that if you wore a style once, then you shouldn't wear it when it comes back around, but as fashion cycles shrink—so much so, in fact, that magazines have started referring to "early 1990's vintage"—that edict seems awfully harsh, not to mention joyless and limiting. If you love the look of a white suit over a black shirt, you are going to have a disco ball with all the online boutiques and auctions. Nik-Nik and Huck-a-poo shirts, ethnic dashikis, and ponchos were all big then, and they're back now. And look for bright-colored crushed-velvet tuxedo jackets, too, which you can wear with an almost straight face over an Egyptian cotton T-shirt with your modern jeans and loafers.

DAMN RIGHT, I GOT THE BLUES

For a moment, let's put aside all discourse about the innovative styles, fabrics, and concepts for which U.S. designers and textile manufacturers are responsible and focus instead on the one thing that gives Americans the right to say we know from casual wear. Wherever you may be on the big blue marble, you'll see the beloved blue jeans. Hands down, they're the buttoned or zipped-up favorites of young and old. Vintage Levi's are feverishly sought by collectors and dealers around the world, but while Levi Strauss is by far the oldest and most famous jeans manufacturer, many companies have added their own voices to the chorus of American blues. Since vintage jeans are already broken in and feel nicer than new ones—many new jeans are now sold as "vintage wash" or "distressed" in retail stores—they are well worth seeking. Know your size for the label and style you're considering, ask about any flaws that might not be visible in a digital photo, and be confident about your purchase. With very few exceptions—such as leather jeans, hand-painted jeans, and signed-by-your-favorite-rock-star jeans—denim can be safely laundered in the washing machine (turn the jeans inside out, fasten the zipper, and use a gentle detergent).

Levi's fans wishing to date and authenticate their treasured vintage jeans can visit the Levi Strauss website (www.levistrauss .com) for more information on submitting photos of the labels and stitching.

THE AMAZING TECHNOLOGY AND DREAM COATS

Let's say you want an elegant winter coat. Not a windbreaker or a puffy, down-filled ski jacket—you already have plenty of those. You want a *legendary* coat, something in cashmere or camel hair. You mean to be stylish, stylish beyond your means. You need only log on to the Internet and browse the vintage sites and auctions: Mission accomplished.

The rare, fine fibers that contribute to a modern coat's four-figure price tag at retail were used just as much in the past—perhaps even more frequently, as clothing manufacturers had not yet invented low-cost, throwaway fashion. Certainly, the caliber of workmanship in vintage clothes is appreciably higher than that of today's offerings: Buttons were sewn on by hand, seams were bound, garments were lined, and hems were sewn with real cotton thread as opposed to the loathsome synthetic monofilament used so commonly today. The fine coats of yesteryear were often

1940's pair of navy-blue pants made of heavyweight linen. The fly front
features buttons embossed "Brooks Brothers" and a label dating its manu-
facture to April 13, 1940. *Linda Lindroth*

made of cashmere, wool, camel hair, or vicuña; and they were usually beautifully lined. They were made to last—and they did.

Just remember to ask detailed questions about the coat: Don't accept that nebulous phrase "good vintage condition," but rather inquire as to the state of the lining, the absence of stains, holes, and cigarette burns, and the presence of all the topstitching, not to mention the belt, if there is supposed to be one. Is there a fiber-content label? While these are seldom present in jackets, they're often quite visible in vintage coats. Usually a large, square, satin label proclaims the garment to be 100 percent cashmere, for example, and is found about eighteen inches above the hem on one of the inside front flaps. Classic styles such as the trench coat and the overcoat with medium-width lapels will never go out of style, and nor will flattering, tasteful colors like black, navy, charcoal, and camel.

VINTAGE IS AN ACQUIRED TASTE FOR QUIET TASTE

Buying a beautiful, well-made suit shouldn't cause your paycheck to evaporate. Nor should having great personal style mean that your American Express bill makes a sickening thud every time your wife tosses it onto your desk. If you've long suspected that women are onto something with this vintage thing, there is no time like the present to start exploring the past, fashionwise. As time goes by, you'll find you've begun to develop an eye for quality that steers you away from ill-constructed mistakes. These are clothes for wining and dining in style, which is a perfectly affordable proposition now that you've discovered the fiscal logic—not to mention the charm, elegance, and wit—that is vintage fashion.

SELL-EBRITY: WOULD YOU LIKE TO SWING IN A STAR'S DRESS?

*W*hen fashion designers are asked to describe their muses—those elusive images of inspiration that help them create glorious gowns and must-have suits—their replies are filled with references to stylish ladies hailing from the rarefied worlds of entertainment, politics, and royalty. Names like Audrey, Grace, Cher, Jackie O, and Princess Diana are frequently invoked. And there are many others who possess the sort of magic that transcends whatever they're wearing, making that outfit something special, something more.

As the auction world has discovered fairly recently, people will spend large sums of money for used clothing if the owner was famous or even infamous. To wit: Superstar Wayne Gretzky's NHL All-Star Game jersey sold for an astonishing $80,500 in the online Hockey Fights Cancer auction held in February 2001. In 1997, shortly before her death, Princess Diana donated seventy-nine gowns to Christie's, asking that they be sold at auction, with the proceeds benefiting AIDS and cancer charities; over $5 million was raised, and the auction catalogs themselves became instant collector's items.

Who can forget the charming triple-strand faux-pearl necklace that Jackie Kennedy frequently wore during her White House days? Despite its costume status, that bauble sold for more than $200,000 at a Sotheby's auction in 1996. And speaking of the Kennedys, remember that amazing, sparkling, nude-silk gown that Marilyn Monroe wore when she breathed new life into the phrase "Happy Birthday, Mr. President"? It sold for over $1.2 million at a Christie's auction in 1999; also auctioned off was a collection of Ms. Monroe's furs, the proceeds of which went to benefit the World Wildlife Fund.

Clearly, stardust has a dollar value, a concept that's not lost on vintage clothing dealers. Dresses, coats, skirts, handbags, costume jewelry, and even baseball caps routinely sell—both in standard and online auctions—for far more than you'd think, simply because they once belonged to a celebrity. The proceeds don't always go to charity, either, as well-meaning bidders should note. Moreover, certain sellers merely invoke a famous name in order to market their wares—conveniently dodging the fact that said celebrity still owns the original—in auction listings with titles like "A Necklace like the One Madonna Wore" and "Liz Hurley's Favorite Jeans."

If you'd like to swing in a star's dress but would rather not spend a million dollars on a crystal-encrusted evening gown—even if it *was* worn by one of the great beauties of the twentieth century—there are sellers who specialize in everyday clothing culled from modern Hollywood closets as well as from the wardrobes of sports heroes and famous musicians. On eBay, for example, a search by seller for "Starwarescollectibles" will yield a list of interesting goods that might include Farrah Fawcett's cowboy boots, Don Johnson's leather jacket, or Cher's embroidered skirt.

Movie buffs and couch potatoes alike will enjoy the production wardrobe store It's a Wrap Production Wardrobe Sales; check out the online inventory at www.itsawrappws.com. And at Reel Clothes Studio Wardrobe (www.reelclothes.com/hotcoll .htm), you can buy dresses, boots, handbags, and even jewelry worn by actors in numerous Hollywood productions.

Finally, you must remember this: A dress is just a dress, a sigh is just a sigh. Your fundamental sense should always apply.

Part Three

SELLING YOUR WEARABLE TREASURES FOR
FUN, PROFIT, AND CLOSET SPACE

SHE SELLS RESALE ON THE INTERNET SHORE

*P*erhaps like many fashionable people, you've indulged your passion for clothes since your early teens, when your baby-sitting income had accumulated sufficiently to warrant a trip to the mall. There, you'd shop for those must-have brand-name jeans that Mom refused to include as a line item in the family back-to-school clothing budget. Consider the countless pairs of similar jeans—not to mention dresses and skirts (or suits and ties) and pairs of shoes—that have been featured in your personal wardrobe since those days. What became of them all?

The really worn-out things were discarded, turned into cleaning rags, or cut up for craft projects. Some garments were simply outgrown, either literally or emotionally. And these were given away to a church or to a charity thrift shop like the Salvation Army. Still, there have been many things in your closet over the years that just sat there, taking up space and mocking you for your poor judgment in buying them in the first place. They're new or almost-new clothes, and there is nothing wrong with them. You simply don't wear them; you're tired of looking at them (and feeling this disdain all the more acutely if you live in a city apartment with minuscule closets).

Then there are all those vintage pieces you've been collecting. You visited a thrift store here and an estate sale there, and before you knew it you had an impressive collection of antique clothing and accessories. Trouble is, many of these treasures are stashed in the "alterations corner" of your jam-packed armoire, waiting for a day of lengthening that might never come. You spent a small fortune on these various garments, and you feel guilty about dropping them in the thrift store bin. Perhaps you'd love to recoup a few of those hard-earned dollars or even put them toward one really fabulous dress for an upcoming event.

In the past, you'd have a garage sale. Maybe you'd gather the offending finery into a bundle and haul it to the nearest consignment shop, which you hoped would sell it all for you and send you your percentage at some point later in the year.

Now, thanks to the Internet, there is another alternative: selling your wayward wardrobe items online. We're going to tell you about the two primary venues for doing this: consignment or resale boutiques, which entail sending your garments to an online retailer in exchange for a percentage of the selling price, and online auctions, which require you to photograph and describe the items yourself but allow you to keep all the proceeds (less their nominal fees). Additionally, you can often sell a special vintage piece directly to an online antique clothing boutique; please refer to Part Five. Often a seller will have a "want list," allowing you to sell your garment directly to him or her.

Selling via online consignment boutiques comes with all sorts of options. An abundance of consignment websites currently exist on the Internet, many of which are reviewed in Part Five. If you decide to test-drive online consigning, we strongly suggest reading the site's policies before sending them your clothes and accessories. If the site is not clear about something, and you have questions, communicate with the person in charge of accepting or rejecting garments; many of the sites, if not most, prefer to communicate via e-mail. Here are several questions you might ask:

1. What percentage of the selling price is paid to the consignor?
2. How long, after an item is sold, does it take for a check to be issued to the consignor?
3. What is the minimum number of items one needs to consign in order to get started? What is the maximum amount of items a person may consign at any one time?
4. Which eras or designers seem to sell best on the site? Are there any particular items for which demand exceeds supply? These are especially good questions to ask, because the answers will give you some insight into not only the site's merchandise and price points but also its customers. A consignment shop that moves a lot of Puccis will be the perfect place to send that flawless white Courrèges coat you found at the opera thrift store ten years ago but never wore, whereas a shop that specializes in Victorian petticoats or 1980's career wear might not even accept such a coat for consignment.
5. What are the site's garment requirements? Usually the online consignment shops are no different from the neighborhood shops in this respect. Clothing must be clean and pressed, and items must be of salable quality (a subjective term, as clients who purchase, say, 1920's flapper dresses will necessarily tolerate a few tiny snags and discolorations, while clients who shell out for last season's Armani usually want

nothing less than perfection). Also, the Main Street type of consignment shop usually requests that the garments be brought in on hangers; with an online boutique, they'll ask you to pack the items in tissue to prevent excessive wrinkling and ship them at your expense in a large enough box.

6. What happens to the items the site deems unacceptable for consignment? Will they be shipped back to the sender? This will undoubtedly be at your expense!

7. As for those garments the site accepts, how is the price determined? Does the consignor have any input with regard to the price of an item? How long does the site keep clothes in their active inventory before reducing the price? If there is an expiration date beyond which the site will not keep an item in its inventory, what happens to it after this date passes?

8. Does the site sell globally or just within the country of origin? This is important, as boutiques who'll sell and ship worldwide can command higher prices for your consigned items.

Once you hear back from the consignment boutique, you'll have a much better idea if this establishment is right for you and whether your business relationship will be a positive experience. Ultimately, though, the true test of an online boutique's character will be when you've sent them a dress and your consignor's check eventually arrives. Either you'll be quite pleased with yourself, having turned an unwanted garment into cash with relatively little hassle, or, the worst-case scenario, you'll be annoyed that after the ironing, careful packing, and interminable waiting, your payment seems rather paltry and slow to arrive. You'll now be in a better position to decide whether to let this shop help you sell some more goodies or simply take your business elsewhere.

SOLD TO THE HIGHEST BIDDER . . . GOLD
TO THE SMARTEST SELLER

The other way to deal with the fashion surfeit occupying your limited closet space is to sell your garments via an online auction site. The largest, most popular, and most successful of these is eBay, although several others are growing in size and improving in user-friendliness and should not be ruled out. Some of these are discussed in the section on high-end auctions (see page 59). We recommend visiting all their websites and searching for items similar to the ones you're thinking about selling. You'll soon know if the site is going to be worth your while and whether it can bring your goodies to the attention of a wide enough audience to guarantee you a decent price for your effort.

And speaking of wide enough audiences, it's useful to note that one of the huge advantages of selling online in the first place is that you get to offer your wonderful navy-blue 1940's suit with the embroidered lapels to a pool of potential buyers so vast, it is virtually guaranteed that at least a few people contained therein will not only be searching for that very suit but will be all too happy to enter into a bidding war with the other vintage wearers who are just as intent on owning it. This would never happen if you held a garage sale. Even if you limit your auctions to buyers within your country (as opposed to selling to the whole planet, which isn't especially difficult, trust us), you've still expanded your market immeasurably.

Finally, selling your wearable treasures online can be surprisingly enjoyable. You will meet all sorts of new friends who share your passion for fashion, and, if you're lucky, you might even stay in touch with some of them and find you have things in common beyond your mutual love of Schiaparelli earrings or 1970's disco tuxedos. What's more, if you're enjoying yourself when you create an auction listing, your writing can't help but be infused with a positive attitude and a sense of fun, which, in turn, are magnetic to buyers.

So you're ready to try your hand at selling something online, let's say on eBay. Now what? Well, after you've chosen a user name, you'll register as a seller, which now requires placing a credit card number and banking information on file with the site via a secure server. This is also the credit card to which eBay will automatically charge your listing fees, which range from $.30 to $3.30 depending on your opening bid. You will also be charged a final value fee (determined at the end of the auction), which ranges from 1.5 percent to 5.25 percent of your item's final sale price. Once you've taken care of that, you'll be ready to choose one or two wonderful pieces from the farthest reaches of your closet (or the under-bed box or the guest room armoire) and prepare them for selling.

ITEM SELECTION: WHAT TO SELL AND WHAT TO SKIP (FOR NOW)

1. Name brands and designer labels (as well as collectible vintage clothes and accessories) sell best and bring the highest prices.

Yes, we are a big bunch of label snobs at heart. Decades of exposure to advertising, in both print and electronic media, not to mention careful product placement in movies, have rendered us a world of consumers who energetically seek out name brands, especially when it comes to clothes. Sometimes our label obsession is justified because certain designers and companies can be relied upon for quality. Equally as often, though, it's an emotional preference, a need to align oneself with a designer because his creations resonate with the type of image one wants to project. Either way, none of us is going to change the status quo, as it were, anytime in the immediate future; and as a seller, you will be reminded time and again that a rose by a designer name will always sell more sweetly.

2. Keep your items season-specific if you want to get the highest prices. For example, list red evening gowns a month or so before Christmas (or Valentine's Day) and auction a collection of 1950's cotton sundresses in the spring or early summer. Remember that people tend to shop for items they expect to wear immediately. Conversely, when you're buying vintage in online auctions, you should deliberately look for out-of-season garments—think heavy coats in July—as you'll run into *far* less competition and final prices will therefore be lower.

3. Resolve to build a reputation for selling high-quality goods. Garments should be in good to excellent (or brand-new) condition; if they aren't, the selling price won't be high enough to justify the time you've spent listing them for auction. The only possible exceptions to this would be items of extremely high antique value, for example, a 1950's beaded evening gown that, despite its torn hem and wine-stained sleeve, is outrageously beautiful and bears the hand-sewn label of a famous Hollywood costume designer.

In summary, choose a few nice designer pieces, make sure they can be worn in the near or immediate future, and do unto your auctioned garments as you would have others do unto the ones they send you. It bears repeating that dirty, wrinkled, and damaged clothes neither photograph nor sell well. And if you do manage to find a buyer, she won't be very happy when she opens the box and sees something less than wonderful. Ensure that your merchandise is always above reproach: If it needs to be dry-cleaned, ironed, or mended, you should take care of it out of respect for your customer and because you value your reputation.

We would be remiss if we didn't mention that there are plenty of sellers, on eBay and elsewhere, who list clothing that is flawed or stained and, in lieu of repairing or cleaning the garment, simply mention this in their item descriptions and leave it up to the buyer to decide if he wants to deal with the problems. And of course, when it comes to really old vintage items, a certain amount of flaws can be expected. As a seller, it's your decision: Repair the flaws or leave the healing process to the customer. In a perfect vintage world, though, every garment would be clean and mended before its image is launched into cyberspace, and every auction winner would be thrilled to pieces when she opened her package and found inside the embodiment of that image: spotless, nicely folded, and free of cigarette smoke.

A PICTURE SELLS A THOUSAND DRESSES

Now that you've decided on a piece or two with which to get started, let's discuss how you're going to show them to your customers. It *is* possible to sell online without using photos; if you

1950's cotton gloves, like these with curling decorative stitches, are in rich supply on the Internet. *Linda Lindroth*

surf through some of the online auctions, you'll notice that items are sometimes listed without pictures. Without a photo the buyer must rely on the written description when deciding whether or not to bid. Think about it: Wouldn't you rather see a suit and know immediately that the stripes are too wide for your taste? Wouldn't you prefer to look at a photo of that 1930's bias-cut silk gown described as "seafoam," given that some interpretations of the color are flattering and others make your complexion take on the pallid shade of Elmer's glue?

Fashion and accessories are, primarily, items of adornment that are visual by their very nature, and if you want to convey their essence to your customers, the best way to do this is with a good electronic visual or three. Pictures will ensure that you get a decent price for your garment. On eBay's listing pages, a little camera icon placed next to the title of an item tells shoppers that the seller has included at least one photo—an indication of how important photos are to potential buyers.

Once you understand the importance of photos, the next order of the day is to procure a digital camera of decent enough quality, or, at the very least, a scanner with which to copy photographs of the item. If you can possibly borrow or buy the former, we strongly recommend doing so, as a digital camera will produce an image directly to your computer, resulting in a clearer picture. You simply shoot the photograph of the item and load it into your computer; if an image is not quite right, you'll know immediately and be able reshoot the picture on the spot. Another option is having your film processed by a service that can transfer the images to a photo CD. Whichever method you choose, remember that a few clear, well-lit photos will go a long way toward reassuring your potential customer that the outfit you're selling is what you say it is. Use the best camera you are able to borrow or buy and take several different shots of each of your items. This way, you'll be able to choose the best ones. Perhaps your auctions will be so lucrative, you'll decide to invest in a digital camera for your next round of listings.

Picture This: Your Fashion in Its Best Light

1. Choose a suitable background. Usually, a plain, light-colored wall or curtain works best. Be sure to remove all unrelated personal belongings from the area where you'll be photographing the item, and please don't include pets in the picture (if a buyer sees your adorable puppy next to the dinner jacket, he is more likely to be concerned about hairs on the garment than charmed by Fido's photogenic smile). In the case of cer-

tain vintage garments, a piece of fabric from the same era can be used to set off the design—for example, displaying a 1950's dress in front of a flowered barkcloth curtain. In all cases, however, the background should complement the item rather than compete with it.

2. Dressmakers' dummies and mannequins are best for displaying clothes. Many dummies and mannequins—from inexpensive wire dress forms to elaborate, lifelike models—can be bought on eBay itself; you can also find reasonably priced used versions in the newspaper's classified listings under "Display Retail." Dummies and mannequins are also available from websites that offer display materials (see "Sellers' Resources," page 197), and, of course, almost all large fabric retailers sell a few different types of dressmakers' dummies. This isn't to say you can't show something on a padded hanger, but a three-dimensional prop will really demonstrate the way a garment hangs. Try to use a dummy of the appropriate size for the clothes you are selling or they will look ill-fitting. We recommend using plastic clothespins at the back to custom fit the garment, especially at the waist (dummies tend to have tiny ones); it's an old stylist's trick that is quick and effective.

3. Use a live model only if you feel it is absolutely necessary. We are going to go out on a plastic limb here, but we feel we must say that some of the auction photos of people wearing our potential purchases can be off-putting, at best, and downright distasteful, at worst. Bear in mind that very few human beings can make clothes actually appear better in pictures, and those who *are* able to do this generally command fees in the neighborhood of several thousands of dollars per day. If, however, you decide to use live human beings to dis-

play your garments, choose your models carefully and consider cropping the photos so that their faces don't show.

4. What about jeans and pants? That's easy: Lay them flat on a nice table or a (made) bed, remembering the smooth, uncluttered background rule. We don't think it's a good idea to photograph them on the carpet, though: People instinctively shy away from buying something that has been on a stranger's floor.

5. If you're fresh out of dressmakers' dummies and mannequins and want to use a hanger, choose a padded one. A rusty old wire hanger might give your buyers the impression—perish the thought—that you don't care about your clothes. Hang the garment on a screen or some other visually pleasing background. Even a simple back-of-the-door hook will work well, and the plain paint of the door won't compete with your article of clothing.

6. Lighting is important. Although we haven't seen a camera of recent vintage that didn't have a good built-in flash, it bears stating that placing your item near a window or strong light source will still help your photograph immensely. Some sellers take their items outdoors in order to ensure the photo is well lit and clear; we'll admit it, though: The comically surreal image of a vintage tulle prom dress on a headless dummy in the middle of a suburban backyard, complete with playground equipment and giant SUV bumpers in the background, can inspire one to rent every John Waters movie available.

Once you've taken your pictures—a "full-body" shot, some close-ups of important details (perhaps even the label), and a view of the back of the garment, which can often be as interesting as the front—you're almost ready to go. If you really want to maximize your photographic efforts, take a few minutes and pull up your photo-editing software. Many computers today come with at least one such photo-editing software package preloaded, and we recommend taking advantage of it. They are extremely user-friendly programs, and they'll let you crop, darken, lighten, and generally improve your pictures. Pull up each shot and crop out any unwanted background so your item is nicely centered. Black garments—actually, all dark items—don't always photograph very well for the purposes of computer screens, but you can still show the pin tucks on a navy-blue 1940's blouse, say, by lightening one of your close-ups and remembering to mention in the description that you've done this and that the other un-lightened photos depict the garment's true color. Here are a few more hints to enhance your digital photography:

1. Use an AC adapter for your digital camera when uploading photos to your computer, as this process will quickly consume your batteries.
2. Save only the best shots, the ones you will definitely use in your auctions. There's no point in taking up valuable hard drive space with outtakes that might soon number into the hundreds.
3. Use simple, easily identifiable file names for your pictures.
4. When finished with your digital camera, clear it out (delete the pictures), so it's ready to use again without having to scroll through dozens of already loaded photos.
5. When using a scanner, save the photos as JPEG (.jpg) files, as this format works best for the web.

Once you've got your photographs loaded onto your computer, choose a photo host and upload them. Many Internet service providers allow users to utilize allotted FTP-space as a photo host; refer to your members' services page for further information. The simplest way to include photographs in your auctions, when selling on eBay, is to take advantage of the photo hosting offered by the auction site itself, which is a relatively recent innovation. It's really simple to use, doesn't require any knowledge of HTML whatsoever, and is inexpensive: At press time, the first photo is posted free of charge, and subsequent images incur a $.15-each fee. Follow the on-screen instructions, browsing to locate the pictures you'll use for each auction, selecting the most important (and impressive) images to appear first.

Describe and Conquer: Words to the Wise

Now you are ready to write a description of the garment or accessory. Although it certainly isn't a mandatory requirement, we strongly recommend composing this in a word-processing program and saving it on your computer as a separate file. When you're ready to fill in the "Sell Your Item" form, you can open the word-processed document and copy and then paste it into the item description box. This way you'll have your description intact and ready to repaste—thus saving you the frustration of having to retype a paragraph filled with carefully described details, not to mention all sorts of measurements—should your Internet connection suddenly fail while you're in the middle of filling out the selling form.

Consider writing a "seller's statement" of one or two paragraphs—to be saved as a separate, single document—that outlines your policies as a seller. You should indicate the methods of payment you accept, the type of shipping you prefer and what the costs might be, the time frame in which you ship things to winning bidders, your policy on returns (many, if not most clothing items sold at auction are noted "final sale," but naturally, you are welcome to deviate), whether you will sell to international buyers, and any other points of interest as they pertain to your merchandise in general. Many sellers also thank customers for their interest and invite them to view their other auctions. Save this piece as a document entitled "Seller Statement," or something similar, and open it along with your item description documents. This way, when you're finished entering (that is, pasting) each item description, you can simply copy and then paste this general information at the end, using it every time instead of retyping the same information over and over in each description. This is a useful little trick, but be sure to update your seller statement from time to time, as not only do postage rates rise but there may be an inclination on your part to change or add something, fine-tuning as you go.

Let's begin writing about that 1960's brocade sheath with the leg-baring slit up one side and the 1950's dinner jacket that makes the wearer look like a movie star from another era. There aren't any hard-and-fast rules to writing descriptions about clothes, certainly no more than apply to all types of commercial writing. There are, however, some guidelines that will not only maximize your efforts to showcase a garment's appeal but also have the subtle and important side effect of reflecting well on you, the seller. A clear, articulate piece of writing is a pleasure for a buyer to read, it engenders his interest in the subject, and it goes a long way toward earning his trust. This is important, since you are asking complete strangers to send you money for something they haven't seen in person or held in their hands.

1. Keep it simple but don't skimp on details. Try to anticipate what your customer would want to know about the garment and go from there. Use clear, straightforward language in your description, and please take advantage of your word processor's spell-check function; it only takes a few seconds and will help you produce a legible, professional description as opposed to a sloppy and often inadvertently humorous one. We also recommend consulting a good fashion reference book like *The Thames and Hudson Dictionary of Fashion and Fashion Designers* when writing about the parts of a garment.

2. Place the most important information first. In journalism and commercial writing, this is sometimes called an "inverted pyramid," the idea being to have the critical details appear right at the beginning of the piece, so that an editor can simply cut from the bottom up and know that the crucial content will be preserved. In advertising copywriting, which is what you're doing here, you front-load the information because you're aware that your customers' attention will inevitably start to drift. Your buyers are busy people who've been conditioned to expect quick rewards; if there is any delay, they are likely to move on to something else that captures their eye. Knowing this, you should start out by describing the color, size, designer or era (as applicable), the item style and type, and the condition of the item (for example, "Cherry-red, size medium, 1950's full-skirted silk dress in excellent condition"). If someone is still interested, because she looks good in red and loves the 1950's silhouette, she'll keep reading, and that's when you can detail the exact measurements, the number of tiny buttons that climb up the spine, and the flattering portrait neckline. Avoid apologizing for the poor quality of a photograph or saying that the pic-

tures simply don't do the garment justice. A buyer might then wonder if the photo appears blurred due to the quality of the photography or, more darkly, if the out-of-focus effects are deliberate attempts to camouflage several moth holes. Do your best with what you have, and resolve to invest in a digital camera with a good flash, if you don't already own one, as soon as you get your selling ball rolling.

3. Measurements: the more the better. Potential bidders will e-mail you and ask for them anyway, especially if they've read this book, so you might as well save yourself some time and include as many as possible in your item description. Again, try to anticipate your customers' questions.

Taking the measurements is simple. First, have your tape measure and notebook handy and lay the garment on a flat surface. For the bust, measure across the widest point of the bodice, which is usually slightly below the underarm of the garment, drawing the tape straight across. Multiply the results by two: A sixteen-inch measurement means a thirty-two-inch bust. Some vintage dresses and swimsuits have attached bra cups, in which case you should try to follow the curve over the fullest part. Note that measurement, turn the garment over, and measure across the back. Now, add these two together. For the waist, measure straight across the waist seam, or where one would be—usually it's the narrowest point of the bodice—and multiply this number by two. For the hips, measure straight across the garment about seven inches below the waist, or at the widest point, and double this number. For the bodice length, place the tape end at the shoulder seam and measure straight down the front to the waist seam. Measuring from the waist seam to the hem will yield the skirt length. Sleeves are generally measured on the outside, from the seam where they join the shoulder (or where the shoulder would be, if there is no seam) to the end of the sleeve. Pants inseams are measured on the inside, from the crotch seam to the hem. The shoulder width is determined by measuring straight across the back, from one shoulder seam to the other. Of course, the overall length of any garment is generally considered to be the distance from the shoulder to the hem. And if you're selling a pair of shoes, you should include in your description both the heel height—that is, the distance from the back of the foot bed to the ground, measuring straight down—and the shoe's length from heel to toe.

Although virtually all countries have adopted the metric system, most clothing and accessories listed in online auctions, you'll notice, have measurements in inches. With all the sizing discrepancies one must navigate when shopping for clothes these days, it's nice to know that the reliable old measuring tape—for the time being, anyway—is counted upon universally to provide a true indication of fit.

4. Include additional details that make your item special. How does it fasten? Is there an extra deep hem, and are there other alterable areas? Is the lining removable? Sometimes, mentioning a tiny hidden pocket containing a ticket stub from a 1960's Broadway show will add an element of romance to an otherwise straightforward description of a simple cashmere overcoat.

5. It's so beautiful, flaws and all . . . but you respect your customer, and you're going to disclose those little problem areas now. Some examples might be snags, stains, holes, loose stitches, pilling, worn areas, fading, and fraying. You need not mention the flaws first; if that lovely Dior evening gown

is such a spectacular color—and it's a popular size—your customer will be so enamored of it that when she reads about the little stains at the hem, she'll already be mentally shortening the Dior into a tea-length dress. What's important, then, is that your buyers be sold on the wonderful piece in all its glory but, nonetheless, are fully informed of any attendant problems. Be honest but don't exaggerate: If you keep the flaws in perspective, your customer will do the same. Many sellers offer items "as-is" and flaws are understood to be the buyer's responsibility. We recommend that you put aside those items that are badly flawed and see how you fare selling things that are in good to excellent condition. Later, you may well wish to leave the damaged garments aside, as they're unlikely to bring a high price at auction, unless, of course, their attributes—rarity, provable antique value, incredible fabric, and so forth—greatly outweigh the problems. We urge you to use your best judgment when sorting through these subjective areas of the closet and jewelry box, because, once again, there aren't any hard-and-fast rules. However, an honest seller who respects her customers and whose merchandise is consistently above reproach will earn herself a sterling reputation—something that cannot be borrowed or bought and that repays, many times over, the effort one expends to gain it.

6. Finally, for the sake of those who will be browsing through your auctions and reading your descriptions, hoping to form some sort of opinion on the garment and decide whether or not to bid on it, please avoid hyperbole and overused words. You know the type of writing to which we are referring. Here's an example: "Ladies, get ready to drool over this one, 'cuz it's as SEXXXY as it gets . . . amazing, fabulous HOT

fuchsia skirt that hugs your every CURVE while making you look ten pounds thinner!! Heads will turn when you walk into the room, and you'll be sure to snag Mister Right with this SCORCHING little number . . ." et cetera, et cetera. First, if a simple pink polyester skirt could indeed deliver on all these promises, the author would have worn it, to the exclusion of everything else, throughout her dating years, and it would be threadbare. Second, there is a certain step-right-up-and-buy-my-snake-oil tenor to this sort of language, and, quite frankly, it cheapens the métier as a whole. When people first discovered the Internet's potential as a marketplace, plenty of snobbish comments were made by influential fashion writers and magazine editors who'd have one believe that the only legitimate places to purchase an antique, a designer gown, or a piece of vintage costume jewelry were the high-priced boutiques and auction houses exclusive to large, sophisticated cities. Many of those former naysayers now buy regularly from eBay, and many of those exclusive auction houses are themselves conducting business online. Still, the negative perception of online auction selling lingers, due in no small part to the hucksterlike verbiage one encounters all too frequently in the listings. So use clear, straightforward language and allow the buyer to determine whether or not your avant-garde Japanese designer suit is going to help him climb the career ladder and simultaneously impress all the babes within a ten-mile radius.

7. Having put our collective foot down in the paragraph above, we'd now like to back off slightly and state the following: If you are truly inclined to write descriptive prose, and a few individuals outside of your immediate family or employ have told you that they not only enjoy reading the words you

thread together but also find your writing funny or inspiring, then by all means extend your creativity to your auction pages. In our respective quests for the perfect vintage something or other, we've both come across sellers who are clearly moonlighting screenwriters (or practitioners of a similar vocation), and we'll admit to reading all the way through their lengthy item descriptions despite having little interest at times in the garment itself. The stories (or at least the writing) can be that good. You know who you are, you artists cum fashion collectors who can wield a pen (or keyboard) as mightily as a sword. When in doubt, though, think of Audrey and contemplate the timeless, elegant appeal of simplicity, whether pertaining to a dress or matters of address.

8. If you haven't done so in a separate paragraph that can be cut and pasted repeatedly, you'll now need to state your payment terms. Decide whether you'll accept personal checks. Some sellers prefer to say no and avoid the extra steps (of confirming with their banks that the funds cleared) before they ship. Others will accept them, reasoning that by so doing, they are likely to appeal to more buyers. We've even come across sellers who will accept personal checks only from eBay users who have earned a high-enough feedback rating (usually at least 50). You're the seller and it's your choice. Electronic payment transfers, facilitated by sites like PayPal and eBay's own Billpoint, are also popular methods of requesting payment (and sending it, for that matter). Be sure to register with them first, as each has its own requirements for setting you up to receive monies. With PayPal you can build up an account and use it for your own purchases, or transfer it to be deposited in your own bank. There is a small fee—currently $.30 plus 2.9 percent of the total—for a payment made to

you if the buyer used a credit card to fund it. You should know that electronic payment services have drawbacks, too, the most serious of which is the remote but nonetheless very real possibility that someone might use a stolen credit card and place your payment in jeopardy. Be reassured that these services have instituted programs to guard against this kind of fraud. PayPal even offers protection to its participating sellers by requiring that items be shipped only to buyers' verified addresses—those that correspond with the billing addresses of the credit cards. Lastly, the simple money order, along with the cashier's check, is welcomed by virtually every seller. It travels well and the cost to the buyer is negligible. But it is not especially convenient for the buyer. The best solution is to give your buyer a couple of payment options at the very least. And don't forget to request payment in U.S. dollars (unless, of course, you happen to be a seller based in Sydney, Australia). You wouldn't want to lose a chunk of your payment to the caprices of the currency market.

9. How will you ship, and what, if anything, will you do about returns? Answer these questions, too, and your buyer will feel far more secure. If you are stating "All sales are final," you'll have plenty of company, because the majority of sellers will not accept returns, at least not as far as we've noticed. This doesn't mean it's carved in stone, though. If you, the seller, neglect to mention a little problem, say, a loose hem that requires two hours' worth of stitching to make a circle skirt wearable, you can expect to hear from the buyer, especially if said buyer has read our section on what to do when the garment doesn't make her happy. It's important to urge your potential customers to e-mail you with any questions they might have about your garment, in light of your final sale

rule. If you've done your homework, spelling out the measurements and listing all details about the good, the bad, and the ugly in the item description, you'll find these e-mails will be fewer than you imagined.

What Kind of Shawl Am I? Categories and Titles

When you begin filling out the "Sell Your Item" form, selecting an item category is one of the first decisions you'll make. You might think that this is a minor detail: not terribly important and unworthy of much deliberation. However, as many people shop the auctions by browsing an individual category, you want to be certain to choose wisely.

Nonetheless, it's entirely possible that the piece you want to sell might legitimately fall into more than one category. For example, let's say you have a dark green wool suit from the 1940's that would fit a present-day size four. It's immaculate and timeless in its design. You could definitely call this a collectible and list it under "Collectibles/Vintage Clothing/Women's," but you could also list the suit under "Clothing & Accessories/Women/Misses & Juniors/Career/Suits." In the first category, you are pointing out the fact that it is a vintage item, and its history (or that more nebulous term "romance") becomes integral to its value. In the second one, you are presenting the suit to a wide audience that is seeking business wear, and since they're shopping an online auction to begin with, you may safely assume that these customers are bored with the current offerings of the department stores and career boutiques at the mall and might, therefore, be open to the suggestion of wearing a one-of-a-kind vintage suit to work. With a little experimentation, you'll learn which categories bring your auction page to the widest audience.

Brvty. Is the Soul of Rsn.: Writing Efficient and Effective Titles

Your item title is the single feature that has the most power to capture your customers' attention. This line is, on eBay, just forty-five characters long (and that includes spaces and punctuation), and will respond to a buyer's keyword search. Think of the title as a distillation of your item, and you're halfway home. To help you choose the best, most appropriate words and eliminate the extraneous ones, try to imagine what someone might type into the Search box if they were looking for the very thing you're about to list.

Here is a simple way to make the most of those precious forty-five characters, using as our example a lovely vintage hat that, let's say, you found in an estate sale but that isn't quite your color. First, type in the most important word, which will be the designer name and/or the era and use all capital letters for the name: "40's SCHIAPARELLI." Notice how we've abbreviated 1940's in order to conserve space. Your buyers will know what you mean. Next, decide which detail is most important, that which will draw someone's attention and entice her to click on this listing and have a look at your wonderful treasure. Is it shocking pink? Great, let's call it fuchsia for the time being, though, to save space. Another option would be "magenta." If we've got room left at the end, we can go back and change it to "shocking pink," because the designer, Elsa Schiaparelli, was actually known for her use of this color, and one of her perfumes is even called Shocking. Click in front of "40's" and type "Fuchsia." Now you have "Fuchsia 40's SCHIAPARELLI," with some space still remaining. What style hat is it? Click after "SCHIAPARELLI" and type "Pillbox Hat."

We're up to thirty-seven characters (the spaces count, unfortunately), but we've articulated the hat's most important details. To use up the eight remaining spots, you might want to change "Fuchsia" to "Shocking Pink," which is thirteen characters as opposed to seven. A better idea would be to mention the ornamentation, as in "jeweled" or "ornate" or even "w/Rose."

At this point, you might be curious as to why we didn't include the word "vintage" in the title. It's redundant, and we're aiming to maximize those forty-five characters. If your buyer is looking for a hat like this, the keywords she will most likely type in are "SCHIAPARELLI," "hat," and, possibly, "40's." If something is made by Schiaparelli, or, for that matter, any designer whose creations haven't been produced recently, one could safely assume that it's intrinsically vintage. Furthermore, you'll most likely list this hat in the Collectibles/Vintage Clothing & Accessories category, so buyers browsing by category will assume that it's vintage anyhow.

Here are a few examples of titles that anticipate a buyer's keyword choices while taking full advantage of the forty-five characters:

Blk. 80's ISSEY MIYAKE Aztec print skirt M
Floral silk SUZY PERETTE 50's swing dress L
Ivory YVES SAINT LAURENT YSL dinner jacket 42 (Note
    the addition of "YSL" despite already spelling out the designer name; this will ensure that someone entering only "YSL" as a keyword will still be directed to your jacket.)
Pastel Op-art 60's SHEATH DRESS w/sequins S

These are outstanding titles because they incorporate as many relevant details and potential keywords as possible, given the extremely limited space. As you browse the auction listings, you will see many sellers taking a different approach to writing a title. You'll notice the use of asterisks before and after the item (**60's Blk. Leather Biker Jacket**), you'll see other abbreviations and punctuation marks used in strange new ways (Great 80's Power $uit—L@@K!), and you'll occasionally come across a sentence masquerading as a title, for example: "Marilyn Would Have Loved This Dress." Asterisks and other unusual symbols are undeniably eye-catching and can often make your title stand out in a page without incurring the additional listing fees of bold lettering or highlighting. We suggest using them if and only if you're satisfied that your title contains all the potential keywords it needs and there is a little space left. And please use them judiciously: A blizzard of exclamation marks might make your title jump out at the buyer, but things jumping out at us often cause us to recoil.

Nice-If-You-Have-Room Adjectives	Space-Saving Versions and Abbreviations
crimson, scarlet, maroon, burgundy	red, wine
apricot, tangerine, red-yellow	orange, peach
primrose, marigold, custard, sunflower	yellow, lemon
emerald, chartreuse, seafoam	green, olive, lime
turquoise, ultramarine, sapphire	blue, aqua, navy, indigo, cobalt
amethyst, lavender, mulberry	purple, plum, orchid
charcoal, granite	gray, slate, ash

obsidian, pitch-black	black, jet, raven
alabaster, bleached white	white, chalk, snowy
buttercream, off-white, oatmeal	cream, ivory, bone, ecru
chocolate, espresso	brown
new, with tags	NWT
new, without tags	NWOT
new old stock (for vintage items that either still have their original store tags or were clearly never worn)	NOS
new in box	NIB
no reserve	NR
small, medium, large	S, M, L
Italian size, French size	IT size, FR size (or sz.)
full-skirted (as in 50's)	swing
attenuated, streamlined, formfitting	sleek, lean, slim
gleaming, sparkling, polished	shiny
substantial, abundant	heavy, full
sylphlike, featherweight	light, airy
authentic, bona fide	genuine, auth.

Finally, we must emphasize that if you use a brand name in your title, the garment or accessory must be something designed or produced by the named company. Otherwise, you will, at the very least, hear from the disciplinary people at eBay; at worst, you'll be contacted by the legal department of said company. Incidentally, this practice of misleading name-dropping is known as "keyword spamming," and it can involve something as seemingly innocent as comparing one brand to another, as in "Black wool AGNES. B pleated skirt, like Chanel." Keyword spamming is also a serious breach of online selling etiquette.

ON YOUR MARKS, GET SET, POST!

Now you are ready, if not anxious, to post this auction listing and start selling. Here's what you'll do next. Log on to the site—for our current purposes it's eBay since most sites employ a similar procedure—and sign in (enter your user name and password). Click on the Sell button at the top of the page; this will take you to the "Sell Your Item" form. Be sure to read all the rules, and if you have any questions or doubts, go to the Help section, which is very user-friendly: It asks you to type in a query and then offers you several interpretations of it. You'll click on the one that addresses your particular concern, and the vast database will sort and provide the information you need.

Hopefully, though, you're now feeling forewarned, forearmed, and confident. Start by choosing your category, which will probably be either "Clothing & Accessories" (for items of more recent vintage) or "Collectibles" (for vintage pieces that date back more than two decades). In both cases, you can easily select the subcategory by scrolling down in each box and clicking on the appropriate word or phrase, working from left to right. With "Collectibles," you'll need to scroll almost to the end of the list—which is a considerably long one—to arrive at "Vintage Clothing."

Once you've selected the category, you'll fill in the title box as we discussed above. Then you'll arrive at the item-description box; this is when you'll open your word-processor documents, select the appropriate one for this item, and copy and then paste the text into the box. Now open your "Seller Statement" document and copy and then paste this into the description box so it appears after your specific item description. (If you're listing more than one thing at this time, you may minimize this document so it's easily accessible for copying into the next item's description box.)

Now it's time to bring the photos into the picture, so to speak. EBay, at press time, offers a package deal for sellers who use their affiliated photo host, which, currently, is IPIX. It's one of the easiest to use of all such services, and we recommend you give it a try, if only because you won't have to spend an inordinate amount of time uploading your photographs to a host site and then typing in lengthy web addresses that tell eBay where to find your photos when someone looks at your auction page. There are a few choices you can make about how you want the pictures displayed, including giving your potential customer the option of enlarging ("supersizing") each photo or having the photos appear in succession, as with a slide show.

Here's how it works: Place the cursor next to the box for the first photo and click the button marked "Browse." Automatically, your computer's storage will become visible and accessible, and you'll locate the photo (which you've previously cropped and saved) that you want to appear first. Select this and click

"Open." The program drops the file name of this photo into the box. If you have a second, third, and fourth photo, you continue likewise. At the time of this writing, the first photo is hosted free, and subsequent pictures will incur a charge (currently $.15 apiece); there is a flat-fee option that gives the seller up to six photos, all with the ability to be enlarged, and appearance in the Gallery. We hope this economical option remains available to sellers, as it has encouraged a great number of reluctant technophobes to include wonderful pictures in their auction listings.

Next, decide if you want to have a photograph included in the Gallery. All this means is that a thumbnail (miniature) photo of your item appears—for $.25—to the left of your title, should the buyers browsing the auction pages select the option to view "All items." If buyers choose the "Gallery items only" tab, your having paid the extra quarter and providing the picture guarantees you a place on this photo-album-like page; and the thumbnail picture itself can be clicked on to link the buyer directly to your auction page. At press time, the Gallery option is included in the above flat-fee photo package, but we recommend it, even if you're not choosing the package, since a quarter won't pay for a pack of gum these days, and capturing the attention of more potential buyers will only further your interests.

Scroll down through the various sections, answering the questions and filling them in as you go. In the box marked "Location," some sellers express themselves a little humorously or remind the buyers to view their other auction offerings: "Seattle, Where the Old Man Is Snoring," "Cleveland Rocks," "Check Out My Other Fabulous Fashions," "Beverly Hills, Land of the Face-lift," and "Stranded in the Desert—Please Send Money." Of course, you may simply wish to write in "The Midwest."

Special Instructions for Apple Computer Users

When uploading images to eBay from an Apple computer, you'll need to follow these steps carefully. First, size your photo in Photoshop (or another image-editing program) to 300 × 400 pixels. Then pull down Save As and save the photo to your desktop (or a folder) in the JPEG format. The file name should not contain slashes, periods, plus signs, or ampersands. Remember to include .jpg at the end: "chanel.jpg." EBay suggests you set the JPEG option to 10 (or maximum quality). Using the eBay seller listing form, click on "Browse" and select the photo from the file in which you saved it.

A PENNY FOR YOUR THOUGHTS, A FORTUNE FOR YOUR GOODS

You will need to decide the parameters of your auction by answering some questions. Here's a tough one: At what level do you set the opening bid? And here's another tough one: Do you make this a reserve auction or not? Make these decisions before you fill in the "Sell Your Item" form. There are no hard-and-fast rules governing what price points will entice buyers or frighten them away, so you will need to rely on your familiarity with prices of similar items.

Reserve auctions are simply those in which the buyer specifies a certain price beneath which the item cannot be sold. Let's say you list a cashmere coat with an opening bid of $15 and you set a reserve of $50. As the bids are placed, a small red phrase beneath the current price indicates to buyers that the reserve has not been met. Once the bidding goes to $50, this will change to a green legend informing everyone that, yes, the reserve was met. If the price never meets or exceeds this reserve, however, the auction will close unsuccessfully: Neither the high bidder nor the seller is obligated to the other. There is a fee—from $.50 to $2—for listing items with a reserve, and it's only refunded *if* the item sells. You should keep this in mind when you establish your dollar amounts. Many sellers only use reserves with high-priced garments and accessories as a way to protect their investments. With middle-priced and low-priced pieces, they simply set the opening bids at levels that reflect the very lowest amount they'd accept for the items, should any of them receive only one bid. We think this is a sensible approach: Use reserves only when you are auctioning a high-priced item, and keep the opening price realistic. Too many sellers set reserves for every single thing they list, sometimes combining them with artificially low opening bids, a practice that smacks ever so slightly of disingenuousness. If you're a buyer who's interested in a lovely wasp-waisted 1940's suit, you're going to be very disappointed to learn that the opening bid of $7.99 is a couple of hundred dollars away from the $250 reserve price, because more often than not, you won't find this out until the auction closes unsuccessfully with the reserve unmet. You bid $150 in good faith, thinking that this amount would be more than enough to secure you a terrific suit for your cousin's upcoming wedding, and then you are unceremoniously let down. If the seller should relist the outfit, its new closing date might be too late for your needs, provided you were inclined to bid on it again anyway.

So, sellers, listen: If you're going to set a reserve, please allow the opening bid to be at least somewhat indicative of the level wherein your real asking price resides. If you want to be trusted and well regarded within the online-auction community, you'll try to be fair and reasonable with your opening prices and reserves.

Here are a few suggestions for pricing those garments in the first place. Before you start your auction, have a look at similar items that are currently listed. Are they getting plenty of bids? How are they categorized and titled? And, perhaps most important, what sort of prices are they bringing? This is probably the best way to get a reasonable ballpark figure to use as your opening bid. Click on a few listings; they will always show the bid that started it all, and they get updated regularly so the number of bids placed thus far is generally accurate. You can do this ahead of time by bookmarking an item and returning to it after the auction closes; this way, you can click on the "Bid History" link and see what sort of frenzied spending activity occurred before the gown, suit, or alligator bag was finally acquired, and you can get a feel for the prices associated with these items.

She's Gotta Have It: Using "Buy It Now" in Your Listing

Although eBay is an auction site, a listing might sometimes include an option that allows potential bidders to bypass the whole competitive scene and simply buy the item outright. Buyers usually pay a premium for this privilege; indeed, many sellers set such high "Buy It Now" prices, they frighten their customers away. When a seller sets a "Buy It Now" price in an auction listing, a buyer may still place an bid on it, eliminating the "Buy It Now" option. (In the case of a reserve auction, this will happen when the reserve is met; until then, "Buy It Now" remains available while early, below-reserve bids are placed.)

As we discussed in Part One, "Buy It Now" has drawbacks as well as benefits; it's up to you to decide if it's right for your selling approach. You may wish to try it with one or two items and see what sort of response you get. For a seller, the advantages of "Buy It Now" are fairly straightforward: Your item can sell quickly for a respectable (or even thrilling) amount, and you'll have one less auction item to track. You invoice your customer, receive your funds, and ship the item—it's a done deal. On the other hand, you might have sold that unusual Georg Jensen choker for considerably more if you'd allowed the marketplace to dictate the price. Perhaps you weren't aware that only a few such necklaces were ever made, but several sharp-eyed jewelry collectors would have feverishly bid against one another in order to get their hands on that treasure. When you set a "Buy It Now" price, you have to honor it when someone jumps on the opportunity. So, if you'd like to try out this seller's option, we strongly recommend researching your item thoroughly in order to determine its true value in today's market. As we go to press, no additional fees are charged to include a "Buy It Now" option on your listing page. But that isn't an invitation to use it indiscriminately: You shouldn't set such outrageously high "Buy It Now" prices that people are frightened away. Nor, on the other hand, should your asking price be so low that something sells within five minutes of being listed and prompts several other interested buyers to e-mail you—leaving you to wonder if you could have perhaps reaped a better reward for your efforts.

THE HOME STRETCH

Getting back to the rest of that selling form, you now will carefully read through all the options before checking them. Is this to be a five-, seven-, or ten-day auction (this will cost another

$.10)? Do you want to pay $2 extra and have bold lettering in your title or $5 for a band of highlighting? How about really shelling out and opting to be listed as a "featured category item" (about $20 at the time of this writing but worth it if you're sure the garment will sell extraordinarily well, since many more potential customers will see it)? Would you like to have eBay place a counter on your page to keep track of the number of hits your listing is receiving? We think it's a great idea, and at press time, it is a free feature. Once you're satisfied, you can also instruct eBay to remember your choices for many of these and create a sort of profile; this will save time when you fill in the "Sell Your Item" form for the next dress, jacket, or coat.

You are almost finished. At the bottom of the page, click on the button that prompts you to confirm your listing. Don't worry, this doesn't mean you're committed to whatever appears next and that you can't make any changes. Rather, you'll be shown a list of your choices: the category selection and title; the item description; the various options you checked regarding pricing, payment, shipping, and location; and, once they've uploaded, the photos. Once the page is complete, you'll go through it line by line to see if everything is in order (and if it isn't, you'll click the Back button and make corrections and changes as needed; if you do this, though, you'll need to reenter the photos). Then, when you're satisfied, click the Submit button.

The next screen will offer its congratulations—which you may well feel are thoroughly deserved—to you, the seller, for successfully listing your item. Shortly thereafter an e-mail will arrive to confirm the listing. Now don't panic if you go to the eBay home page and enter a keyword or two from your title in the Search box only to find a list of other people's Cardin jackets and not yours. The people at eBay update the listings regularly, day and night. Yours will be slated for the next update, which will occur shortly. If you want to see how your first eBay auction page looks, all you need do is click your Back button and locate the congratulatory page that popped up after you clicked Submit. There will be a link to your new auction page, right there in blue and white.

LET'S TALK SHOP: THE NOUN, NOT THE VERB

Here's an interesting thought: Now that you've got a thing or two listed for auction, you've become a sort of minibusiness, haven't you? You have a product that other people want, and you'll soon be selling it for actual money. True, you aren't taking on the mantle of responsibility, fiscal and otherwise, that every retail business owner assumes. But it wouldn't hurt to step back for a moment and reflect on the model of a successful shop. The same principles of good business that are relevant to a boutique selling two hundred dresses a month can be applied to a single proprietor who's just listed a tuxedo and three gowns on eBay.

In other words, you are about to get some customers. We've already discussed all the ways to attract their attention. Now let's talk about managing your auctions while they run and dealing with the potential customers—the serious and the "tire kickers" alike—in a polite and professional manner.

Have you ever called a store and been put on hold for fifteen minutes? Or, worse, did the automated voice mail send you to seven different departments and then inform you that the mailbox was full, please call again later? We all feel frustrated when treated with so little respect. The message, of course, is that you should respond to those "question for seller" e-mails promptly.

Timing is everything, and in the world of online auctions, the adage applies in ways you can't begin to imagine. Now, there is no need to write lengthy responses; simply address each of the buyer's questions honestly. If you don't know the answer to something, say so. And be sure to thank the person for her interest (that, and you might mention just *one* more time what a truly beautiful opera cape it is).

Sample Question for Seller

Hi, I love the yellow Versace dress and am interested in bidding. What is the measurement of the bodice from the shoulder to the waist? Is there any sort of hem that would allow it to be lengthened? What is the fabric, exactly? Oh, yes, do you know the season/collection in which this appeared? Thanks for your reply. Regards, M.M.

Sample Response

Hi M.M., thanks for your interest. The Versace dress measures sixteen inches from the shoulder to the waist, going straight down the front of the bodice. The hem is three inches deep. The fabric of the dress itself is 100 percent wool, but it is lined in 100 percent silk (so it isn't scratchy). As for the collection in which it appeared, I'm afraid I can't say precisely. However, my educated guess would be that it's from the mid-1990's, when this wonderful designer was still with us. Hope this helps! All the best, Dressed-up Diva

We answered the questions and mentioned another positive feature of the dress (that despite being made of wool, it wasn't scratchy).

While your auction is running, another businesslike thing

you must do is to check on the amount of hits your page is getting; this is the electronic version of doing a head count of the customers in your shop on a given weekend afternoon, for example. Only a percentage of them will buy something, true, but if they don't walk through your door in the first place, you are in trouble. The way to do this head count with an eBay auction is to look at the counter at the bottom of the auction page. If the item has been listed for three days, say, and only five people have even looked at it, you ought to consider changing the title to include more keywords or, at least, more popular keywords. This is easy to do: As long as there are no bids yet (and chances are, if only five people have looked at it, there aren't any), you can change most things about the auction page. Simply access the page and look for a link at the bottom of the first section that reads: "Seller: if this item has received no bids, you may revise it." Click on this, and you'll be taken back to the "Sell Your Item" form you originally filled out. Change the title (and even the category, if you'd like), using the guidelines discussed earlier.

Now, what if your counter is showing that lots of buyers are looking at your auction page, but there still aren't any bids? There are a number of possible explanations. Perhaps your item is being watched by some clever late bidders (read about "sniping" in Part One), in which case you'll be pleasantly surprised to see all sorts of activity as the end of the auction nears, sometimes during the final minute. Or your opening bid may be set too high, and it's scaring everyone away. (Hint: If you're hoping to get $200 for a used cashmere sweater during the summer months, you may be setting yourself up for a disappointment.) If you think this might be the case, you can wait for the auction to close and relist the item, which is simple because all you need do is click one button and—presto—you've started a new auction. Alternatively, you can click on that revise link mentioned above and lower your opening bid. Of course, don't set this at a lower price than you'd ever dream of accepting; just consider that a friendlier opening bid will attract more attention, spark some sales activity, and perhaps even incite a little competitive bidding (always good for driving the price upward).

You will develop a feel for all this as you sell more items. Pricing clothes and accessories for auction—as well as gauging the heights to which these prices will rise at closing—is part art and part science with a dash of serendipity. We've often kept a collective eye on an auction of a truly scary-looking dress, just for fun, and witnessed a bidding frenzy, resulting, inevitably, in a stratospheric closing price that must have made the lucky seller smile all evening. We've also seen some incredible garments go virtually unnoticed and deeply regretted not participating in their auctions. Particularly when you're talking about something that is a little unusual—an avant-garde bustier by an emerging designer, say, or a funky men's guayabera with tiny fleurs-de-lis embroidered down the front—you shouldn't be shocked and disappointed if it doesn't sell the first time around. Reevaluate your opening price, consider if there might be some new keyword you could add to the title to attract more buyers to your auction page, and try again. Serendipity often comes to the ball dressed as timing.

ALL GOOD THINGS

Having come to an end, your auction page will now state "Bidding is closed for this item." Perhaps that 1930's wedding gown received thirty-four bids, in which case a tiny flaring match, subtly indicating the measurable excitement level of the bidding, will have appeared next to it once there were thirty bids and remained for the duration of the auction. Then again, that very gown might have received no bids at all. Either way, this auction is over. Any attempt to bid on the dress now will result in the hapless would-be buyer receiving a curt little message that she missed the train, as it were.

Let's assume that this wedding gown auction closes successfully. Shortly thereafter, eBay will send a confirmation e-mail to both the high bidder as well as the seller, stating the final price and listing the eBay user names and e-mail addresses of the two individuals to whom the responsibility for this transaction now falls: you and BlushingBride. Generally, the seller contacts the buyer first, but this is just an observation of ours and certainly not a rule. So, you'll send an e-mail, saying something like this:

Hello, [since you don't know a name yet]

Congratulations on your winning bid for the lovely 1930's vintage wedding gown, eBay item 99999999. I am guessing by your user name that you are soon to be married. This dress is a unique and beautiful choice, and I'm so glad it will actually be worn and enjoyed. Would you be kind enough to respond to this e-mail within three days and let me know your address; this way, I can prepare the package for shipping. The total, including priority mail charges, is USD $427; if you'd like insurance on this (and I certainly recommend it), please add another $5. If this is to be shipped outside the United States, please disregard these amounts and simply advise me of your address so I may quote you international rates. I accept PayPal and money orders, which should be sent to the following address: 1-4

The Road, Somewhere, Somehow 12345. I look forward to hearing from you.

Kind regards,
Anita B.

Some sellers prefer to wait until they receive the end-of-auction confirmation e-mail from eBay before sending out their "e-invoice," but far more do so immediately after their auction closes, having checked the final price via their My eBay page (click on "Items I'm Selling") or the bookmark of the auction itself. Also, if you're going to have a number of things listed, it is helpful to compose a template of the above invoice, leaving out the actual name, item number, and final price of the garment; save this as a word-processing document called "Seller Invoice." You can copy and then paste this document into your e-mail box when you're ready to ask for your money. Simply type in the appropriate data—this dress, this amount of money, this specific comment—and you're pretty much ready to click Send, as opposed to having to type the same thing repeatedly for each of your items.

You've Got Mail! Your Buyer Has Responded

Hi Anita,

I am thrilled to have won this wedding gown. It's gorgeous, and I sure hope my sister likes it! I will send you a money order tomorrow morning. Here's my address: 123 And Step, Anytime, Anyplace 45670. Thanks again. I look forward to seeing the dress.

Sincerely,
BlushingBride

P.S. Do you have any dyed-to-match pumps, size 12? Let me know.

IT'S A WRAP!

The money order arrived today, and you're almost finished with your first transaction. All you need do now is wrap the gown and send it off. Most sellers use the United States Postal Service priority mail. One advantage is the abundance of free, self-sealing boxes. These come in a few different sizes: a couple of really small ones that are perfect for costume jewelry, scarves, and slender belts plus two larger ones suitable for shirts, slips, skirts, pants, jackets, suits, dresses, and gowns (although perhaps not the antebellum ones). If you need to ship a heavy, full-length coat, the post office will accept your own big coat–containing cardboard box and slap some festive red-and-blue priority tape on it.

Of course, you can also use United Parcel Service, Federal Express, or another delivery service. The important thing is that you use a reliable method that will deliver the item safely, preferably one that offers insurance should the buyer wish to pay for it.

Regardless of the shipping method you choose, you should always wrap the item in tissue paper. May we jump onto a giant jewelry box for a moment and state that stuffing a vintage garment into a box (or, worse, an envelope) and sending it on its wrinkle-accumulating way is nothing short of a heinous breach of etiquette on a seller's part? Consider how you would feel if you had just sent over $400 to a total stranger, and the vintage wedding gown arrived looking as though it had been dragged

1970's Diane Von Furstenburg wrap dress; 1960's white carved-plastic bangle. *Deborah Newell Tornello*

through the bushes backward. Needless to say, it is disappointing to open such a package. A seller who treats your purchase this way is saying to you, whether intentionally or not, that she cares only about receiving your money, not about your satisfaction with the purchase and certainly not about the garment itself.

It's this simple, Fashion Fanatics: Tissue paper is extremely inexpensive, it helps keep the clothing from wrinkling too much in transit, and it conveys the idea that you looked after this garment right to the end. For most garments, you simply lay a large sheet of tissue on a table, place the garment facedown on it, and add another sheet or two on top of that. Now, as you gently fold the whole thing into a rectangle, the paper will cushion the creases somewhat, which is a nice touch when someone has just paid you a week's salary for a silk skirt. Wrap this with one more sheet, tape it closed, and, voilà, you're ready to ship.

A small note is another pleasant way to tell your buyer you appreciate her business, and it costs virtually nothing. You can do a form-letter version with your word-processing program, as with all your other time-saving documents. A sample follows.

Thank you for your purchase from GhostofClothesPast. Enjoy! I appreciate your positive feedback. Be sure to bookmark my seller page and check back regularly for more fabulous vintage items.

Affix the note to your tissue-wrapped package, place this inside your addressed priority-mail box, and take it to the post office. Remember to ask for insurance, if your buyer has requested and paid for it. That's it!

You should ship things as soon as money-order payments arrive, after a personal check clears, or once electronic payments are confirmed, and notify your buyers that their purchases are en route. Aim for a good track record in this respect, as no one likes having to wait after the excitement of having won something. "Next business day" is a wonderful turnaround time to aim for, if you can manage it, but shipping within a few days of receiving payment is perfectly acceptable. If, for some reason, you cannot send the garment out promptly, e-mail your customer to apologize and explain when the item *will* be sent.

Sellers who ship abroad will take a few extra steps. For the majority of items being shipped to most countries, you'll need to fill in a customs declaration form. Be scrupulously honest on this document, and don't get into the habit of declaring everything a "gift," as this seemingly innocent lie will probably do nothing toward reducing your customer's duty charges, and, furthermore, it might get you into trouble. There is nothing wrong with stating that a package contains used personal clothing, however, as this is true.

Once you've banked the money and mailed the wedding gown, going back to our earlier example, you'll want to leave positive feedback for your buyer. The easiest way to do this is to log on to eBay as usual (hooked now, aren't you?) and go to your My eBay page. Once there, you'll see the feedback button in the upper right-hand side of the screen. Click on that, and scroll down to the option that lets you see all the transactions you've completed in the past ninety days, buying and selling alike, about which you may wish to leave feedback. The eBay people say it, and so will we: Be careful. Negative feedback is a potent weapon, sort of an electronic poison pen, and while you may be sorely tempted to complain about the fact that BlushingBride waited two weeks to mail the money order, at least it eventually arrived. We recommend reserving negative comments for those who commit serious infractions: buyers who, despite being sent four increasingly impatient e-mails, never send payment, or buyers who bounce checks and will neither repay you nor send back the garment. Once you've submitted the feedback, it can't be retracted.

At this point, you are no doubt wondering, other than leaving (or not leaving) negative feedback, what options *are* available to a seller if payment doesn't arrive? Well, you should start by sending the buyer a copy of your original "please send money" e-mail (the seller invoice), with the following note in front of it:

> Hi, I haven't heard from you or received payment as detailed below. Knowing that e-mails sometimes get misdirected or lost, I'm resending the original request. Would you be kind enough to respond at your earliest convenience and advise when payment will be made? Thanks so much for your attention to this.

If, after another week (or whatever period of time you feel is reasonable), there is still no response, you will need to do one or more of the following:

1. E-mail your nonpaying bidder one last time.
2. Request her phone number from eBay and call her.
3. Relist the item (if you report this bidder to eBay, they may waive the relisting fee) and do not leave feedback about the bidder.
4. Relist the item and leave negative feedback, perhaps something to the effect of "Ignored four e-mails; never sent payment. I don't recommend her." There's no need to vent or

resort to name-calling; just keep the comment specific to this sale.

Once you've got a few transactions under your jeweled Judith Leiber belt, you'll find that not only does the process of selecting, photographing, describing, and posting things get easier every time but also you develop a sort of rhythm, for lack of a better word, that fits your style and schedule. Some sellers like to post things in batches in order to have all their auctions more or less end at the same time. Others like to take the photographs, write the descriptions, and fill in the actual "Sell Your Item" forms on three different days, breaking up the significant time commitment into smaller, more manageable chunks. You will continue to learn as you go, and you will begin to meet some fascinating people in the course of events. Without goodwill, the enterprise of online selling would fall flat on its electronic face. Human beings give computers their purpose in this world, and human values—things like honesty, creativity, trust, responsibility, and respect—are what enable us to confidently conduct business with strangers via the magical electronic marketplace.

A FEW MORE MISCELLANEOUS SELLING SUGGESTIONS

1. If you select a seven-day auction (this is eBay's default selection), remember the date and time when you click the Submit button, as these will be directly reflected in the date and time of the closing, to the very second. Therefore, if you would like your auction to close at a time when we fashion fanatics are most likely to be sitting at our computers, able to enter last-minute bids (hint: when bidders are not at work,

commuting, or involved in child care, and it will usually be dark outside), you should start your auction at this time, too. If you live on the East Coast, consider your potential California customers and avoid early-morning auction closings. Your thoughtfulness will be rewarded.

2. Use your word processor's spell check, dictionary, and even a fashion reference book, especially when writing a title. Titles whose most important keywords—the name of the designer or the era and style of garment—are misspelled get far fewer hits, and their end prices reflect this. If your spelling is really dreadful in the description text, your buyer won't know what you mean and may decide she doesn't have the time and inclination to try to find out either.

3. Learn how to identify different fabrics, because if you are unfamiliar with them, it will be difficult to describe vintage clothes accurately. Recently produced items usually have fiber-content labels, but most older garments offer no such clues. All libraries have books on fashion, sewing, and upholstery, but the best source for fabric information is a fabric store. We suggest visiting one to experience the difference between silk shantung and cotton poplin firsthand. You may even want to bring some vintage items and ask for help identifying the fabric. An experienced salesperson could examine that old prom dress and perhaps help you find some matching hem tape.

4. In each group of auction listings, include one bestseller, since many buyers will click on your "Other Auctions" link to see what other goodies you're offering. This is a great way to draw attention to an obscure-but-wonderful garment that, had you listed it alone, would not have generated many hits through the keyword search. A bestseller is defined as a de-

signer or style that consistently sells well. Browse the current eBay listings for shoes, for example, and you'll notice that a few name brands always sell extraordinarily well. Try to have at least one such sure thing in every batch of auction listings you do.

5. Placing the garment's size in the title is helpful. Your buyer will know immediately if something will work for her. She will probably remain interested and content to wait for the pictures to appear.

6. Find a good dry cleaner, purchase a decent iron (and perhaps even a clothes steamer), and keep your eyes open for an interesting-looking mannequin or dressmaker's dummy.

REMITTANCE FOR THINGS PAST: WAYS TO PAY— AND GET PAID—FOR YOUR WARES

Please see page 30 for detailed pros and cons of each type of payment:

- money orders
- cashier's checks
- personal checks
- BidPay
- PayPal
- Billpoint
- cash
- credit cards (direct acceptance)
- escrow services

SETTING YOUR SIGHTS ON A SITE:
ADVANCED SELLING

*V*intage clothiers are a fairly consistent bunch. Ask the owner of a boutique how she got started in this business, and her answer will inevitably begin like this: "I always loved the fashions of the past and I've been collecting for years. . . ."

It's *personal.* What starts out as a flickering interest—ignited when progressive individual style coexists with limited means—eventually becomes a heated passion. This is when practical considerations become a factor for many people: When will they ever have an opportunity to wear all these fabulous things, and, more important, where on earth can they store them in the meantime? And with all the upgrading they've been doing lately, thanks, in large part, to the Internet, there now exists a veritable roomful of perfectly lovely garments that have been replaced by more recent obsessions.

Selling your wearable treasures online is a terrific way to recoup your investments—perhaps even make a tidy profit—and finance your current and ever-diversifying fashion interests.

It's also a wonderful way to start a small business.

The notion of owning a vintage boutique in a charming, historical neighborhood—think redbrick roads, wrought-iron streetlamps, and window boxes brimming with petunias—is undeniably romantic. The reality of this enterprise is anything but. First, you'll have to locate a suitable space and come up with key money (deposits, first and last month's rent, and so forth). Then you'll have to deal with all manner of issues: overhauling the lighting so customers can see your merchandise, battling with the landlord to upgrade the plumbing—you can't take a chance on having a pipe burst all over the designer department—and finding affordable liability insurance, for starters. And you haven't even sold gown one!

Alternatively, you may consider expanding your current online selling into your very own vintage website. This way, you'll be able to enjoy the benefits of owning your own business—controlling every aspect of it, from display to marketing to accounting, and deciding how and when you go to work—without the daunting setup costs involved in opening a bricks-and-mortar store.

The various web-design software programs available now make it almost ridiculously simple to do, even if you've never learned HTML, which stands for "hypertext markup language" and is the programming language of the World Wide Web. If you've already mastered listing your vintage clothes on auction sites like eBay, Yahoo!, or Amazon.com, you're familiar with the ins and outs of using a digital camera, loading photographs into your computer, and writing an item description—all of which are covered in the previous chapter.

Anyone contemplating starting a small business should begin by doing a little research. Midnet is a wonderful website where you can do just that; it offers specific tips on business ownership, record keeping, and tax issues, as well as links to numerous key government agencies (www.midnet.sc.edu/smbiz/smallbus.htm).

The American Express company has also produced a comprehensive guide to help get you started. Entitled "Creating an Effective Business Plan," it may be accessed at home3 .americanexpress.com/smallbusiness/tool/biz_plan/index.asp. Finally, for even more helpful information about starting a small business, including common mistakes to avoid, assessing your entrepreneurial skills (a self-administered test), and a section on applying for government grants, visit Starting a Small Business Guides (www.small-business.co.il).

VIRTUAL CAPITALISM, RETRO STYLE

Taking matters to the next logical level—starting a vintage website of your own and maintaining a small business—mainly involves using enhanced versions of skills you already have. And the nice thing about it is this: You can still keep your little (or not-so-little) eBay enterprise going. In fact, many sellers do just that, listing attention-grabbing items on the auction sites—taking advantage of their massive global audiences—and mentioning their own websites in the description. We should inform you that eBay has recently begun disallowing the insertion of direct links to a seller's own website into their auction pages.

The eBay Stores concept offers an alternative to auctions for sellers who want to take advantage of the site's formidable market reach. You can set up a type of online boutique that lists fixed-price ("Buy It Now") items and is housed under the eBay Stores roof, as it were. As you'd imagine, numerous rules and fees apply, but it's easy to get started and can cost as little as $9.95 per month to subscribe. A per-item insertion fee of $.05 (for a thirty-day listing) is also charged, and a final value fee will be assessed once the item sells. For items costing between $25 and $1,000, this is currently 5.25 percent of the first $25 plus 2.75 percent of the amount above that. Many sellers combine auction sales and eBay Stores listings. This is a smart approach, since items in your store will not be accessed by the auction department's search engines; however, your auction pages will display a banner that reads "Visit My eBay Store" and links the buyer directly to your store listings page, which will display both your store items *and* all your auction listings. For more information and up-to-date fees and guidelines, go to the eBay homepage and click on the eBay Stores icon, then click on "Open One Now."

How to know if one has enough inventory of the right sort of merchandise to even *consider* putting together a small business online? This is a question that only the potential vintage boutique owner can answer. But there are plenty of online examples from which to glean information and inspiration, and they're listed in Part Five. Visit as many of the boutiques as you can—even the ultrahigh-priced ones—and write down the features that impress you as well as the things that bother or annoy you. And be sure to read the "Heroes" section, in which we profile several excellent eBay sellers—some of whom have their own websites.

Designing the site itself can be an overwhelming task, or it can be a thoroughly enjoyable creative endeavor. This is where you are going to have to be brutally honest with yourself about your own abilities as a graphic artist, commercial writer, and, perhaps most important, computer software operator. If your budget allows it, by all means bring in the hired guns. A professional web-design service can work with you to create a unique and really eye-catching site. Not surprisingly, though, vintage clothing aficionados tend to be very visually oriented people, and often all that may be needed is a little guidance in the more technical aspect of web design. In this case, perhaps you might trade favors (or treasures) with a talented, computer-savvy friend and save yourself a significant portion of the customary start-up cost.

There are two popular web-design programs we can personally recommend. The first is Microsoft FrontPage, a user-friendly and relatively uncomplicated software package that employs WYSIWYG—or "what you see is what you get"—tool palettes; you needn't learn HTML, but, rather, you work with exactly what you see on the screen. FrontPage is designed for PC systems, and its most recent version requires, at the minimum, Windows 98 and 24 MB of available RAM, as well as a 133 MHz processor. (Pentium III is recommended.) To learn more about FrontPage, visit www.microsoft.com/frontpage. And if you feel up to attempting a more advanced approach, try Dreamweaver, a multifaceted web-design program with animation capabilities among its many features. Dreamweaver is available for both PC and Macintosh computers. The most recent PC version requires, at the minimum, Windows 95 with 64 MB of available RAM and a Pentium II processor. The Macintosh version requires OS 8.6 or 9x, a Power Macintosh processor (G3 or higher), and 64 MB of available RAM. For further information, go to: www.macromedia.com/software/dreamweaver.

And please note that these are only two web-design programs, ones about which we have firsthand knowledge. We strongly suggest you look into the numerous other software packages that are currently available, especially if one of them comes with the high recommendations of a brilliant tech-head friend.

Another important issue: What will you call your website? Sometimes it's easy to select a name, register that domain, and proceed with your launch. Oftentimes, however, you'll enter your fabulously clever website title into the domain registry only to be informed that someone else thought of it first. *Sigh.* These days, many individuals are creating websites, and domain names are in short supply. You want to select something that's easily identifiable as a vintage clothing website, but all the obvious choices—and many of the obscure ones, too—have already been taken, even the ones that incorporate the name of your cat or the main character in your favorite novel. There will soon be more suffixes available to supplement .com, .net, and .org, but until such time, try using numerals—perhaps drawing from your address—or the name of an item in which you specialize, for example, www.beadedsweater.com. The idea is to keep the name as simple and memorable as possible, while implying an association with vintage fashion.

Assuming you have designed your website, and you've loaded the first photos and descriptions into it and chosen a domain name, what now? A website must be hosted, which is an imprecise way of saying that your business now needs a street address somewhere in cyberspace. In order to be out there, you'll need to secure some bandwidth. This is usually accomplished via a web-hosting company, but many Internet service providers (ISPs) actually include a certain amount of web space for personal or business use in your overall package. If you're unclear about this, contact your ISP to determine exactly how much space is available and what steps you'll need to take when uploading (launching) your site.

The fees charged by web-hosting companies are wildly disparate, ranging from free, which invariably means you must allow advertising banners and pop-up applets to be plastered all over your site, to substantial. The costlier services provide round-the-clock technical support—which we appreciated tremendously—and often include such extras as FrontPage extensions (files that make it easy to use the aforementioned software). Also consider using a service such as Dynamic NetAnnounce, a web-optimizing company that will, for a fee, embed supplied keywords as code into your home page and then submit your site to every major search engine. This can be a boon for new vintage businesses, because someone who logs on to Google or AltaVista, say, and types in keywords like "vintage clothing" or "antique fashion," will be directed to a page on which *your* vintage business is neatly listed, complete with a link. To learn more about Dynamic NetAnnounce, check out their own site (www.dynamicnetannounce .com/aboutus.html).

As for the web-hosting services themselves—far too numerous to list here—you may research the different programs and price structures currently offered by asking your virtual entrepreneur colleagues for their recommendations. Alternatively, you can enter the words "web hosting" into your favorite search engine.

STAPLES (AND PINS AND NEEDLES)
FOR YOUR ONLINE VINTAGE BUSINESS

Hey, you're a professional now. It's time to tidy up that little guest room and start organizing yourself. We can't possibly know the extent of the inventory you plan to move online, nor can we guess how many start-up dollars you're willing or able to spend. Even so, we'll offer the following laundry list of things that are, in our opinion, useful and sometimes essential to have around, and we'll wish you all the success in the world. The way we see it, the more wonderful vintage websites there are, the better time we'll have indulging our favorite passion.

The Must-Haves

- A good digital camera that has as many pixels as you can afford (more pixels mean higher resolution, ergo clearer photos)
- A sturdy garment rack or two (wheeled ones come in handy)
- An attractive—or at least interesting-looking—mannequin
- A sewing kit, some clothespins, a tape measure, and an iron and ironing board
- A large white sheet or photographer's seamless backdrop paper and some duct tape
- A dictionary, a thesaurus, and a copy of *The Elements of Style,* by Strunk and White (for help with *writing,* as opposed to style of the sartorial kind)
- Packing supplies, such as boxes, tissue paper, and tape; office supply warehouse stores offer the best pricing for these items (and many carriers, including the post office, provide sturdy boxes free of charge)
- A desktop file holder for pending orders and a filing cabinet in which to store records of your completed sales
- A bulletin board to hold (at least) a few photos of your loved ones along with some inspiring fashion tear sheets

The Nice-to-Have Extras

- A custom-made rubber stamp with your company (or website) name and address

- Colorful computer paper for printing invoices and thank-you notes
- Panels of vintage fabric for creating interesting backgrounds
- Photographic lighting
- A library of books about fashion—focusing on the designers and eras represented in your inventory
- A vintage vase filled with your favorite flowers
- A CD player loaded with Mozart, Miles, Zappa, or Sinatra—your choice

SELLERS' RESOURCES

HANDLING TRANSACTIONS

For information about setting up a merchant account so that you can accept credit cards, visit the following sites: Visa (www.visacardusa.com); Cardservice International (www .cardservice.com); www.creditcardprocessor.com.

DRESS FORMS, DUMMIES, AND MANNEQUINS

For display mannequins, dummies, and torsos of every shape, color, and size, visit Store Fixtures (www.storedisplays.com).

Value Store Fixtures' website (www.valuefixtures.ab.ca) also sells a wide range of display mannequins—both new and used. Call for current availability and information on the preowned models.

Visit *Threads* magazine's website (www.taunton.com/threads/ pages/+00002.asp) and learn four inexpensive ways to make your own dress form.

APPRAISING YOUR VALUABLE VINTAGE ITEMS

Find an appraisal service in your area by visiting the site of the International Society of Appraisers (www.isa-appraisers.org).

Here are some appraisal companies that may be contacted online. For a flat fee (currently $9.95), WhatsItWorthToYou (www.whatsitworthtoyou.com) offers instant appraisals.

Various types of antiques appraisals are offered by the Motley's Group (www.motleysgroup.com/frm_appraisals.htm).

Sewtique (http://members.aol.com/sewtique/home.htm) specializes in appraisal of textiles, clothing, and costumes; they also offer fabric-restoration services.

New Yorkers can take advantage of the walk-in appraisal day at William Doyle Galleries (Tuesdays from 9:30 to 11:30 A.M.; alternatively, appointments can be scheduled by contacting them: 175 East 87 Street, New York, NY 10128, 212-427-4141, x260, info@doylenewyork.com). See their website at www .doylenewyork.com. Their couture and textile specialist is Jan Glier Reeder (jan@doylenewyork.com).

AUTHENTICATING COLLECTIBLES

Online Authentics (www.onlineauthentics.com) specializes in authenticating autographs, but you can also inquire about clothing. Sports-related garments have always caught the eye of collectors. The New York Rangers jersey worn by Wayne Gretzky in the 1999 great good-bye game was sold online at www .lelands.com. Leland's is the last word in sports auction houses, boasting the single most famous transaction in sports memorabilia history: the sale of Mickey Mantle's 1960 New York Yankees jersey for $111,100. While focusing on sports memorabilia (including cards), Leland's also conducts charity auctions, including one for the Jackie Robinson Foundation.

To order books with up-to-date pricing of vintage clothing, textiles, and jewelry, visit Collector Books (www.collectorbooks .commercepak.com). You can also order collectors' price guidebooks from large booksellers such as Amazon.com, Barnes & Noble (www.barnesandnoble.com), and Advanced Book Exchange (www.abebooks.com). Use the keyword "collecting" for your search.

CLOTHING AND TEXTILE RESTORATION AND CONSERVATION

After a Fashion: How to Reproduce, Restore, and Wear Vintage Styles by Frances Grimble: Read about and order this book via its Lavolta Press website (www.lavoltapress.com).

To find a fabric conservator call or write the American Institute for Conservation of Historic and Artistic Works, 1717 K St., N.W., Suite 200, Washington, DC 20006, 202-452-9545, for a list of textile conservators in your area.

A multitude of stain-removal tips may be found at Fabric Link (www.fabriclink.com/holidaystain.html), Barefoot Lass's Stain Removal Page (http://members.tripod.com/~Barefoot_ Lass/index-2.html), Do It Yourself (www.doityourself.com/ clean/stainremoval.htm), Textile Affairs (www.textileaffairs .com/stains.htm), and Silk Road (www.srfabrics.com/care/stain .htm).

DIGITAL CAMERAS: INFORMATION ABOUT THEM
AND PLACES TO BUY THEM

To compare prices for specific models, visit My Simon (www
.mysimon.com), Imaging Resource (www.imaging-resource
.com), Digital Camera Resource Page (www.dcresource.com),
Amazon.com (www.amazon.com), B & H Photo (www
.bhphotovideo.com), Kodak (www.kodak.com), Photoalley
(www.photoalley.com), Ritz Camera (www.ritzcamera.com),
and 800.com Electronics (www.800.com).

AUCTION TOOLS

Note: The following tools, software, and services are currently
available only for PC users, with the exception of Auctionhelper and Andale, which are offered in both PC and Macintosh versions.

All My Auctions downloadable software manages your listings from eBay and handles numerous tasks, including calculat-
ing listing fees and final value fees, invoicing, shipping records,
and more. It is capable of organizing "hundreds of simultane-
ous auctions"; the software costs $29.95, and a free time-
limited trial version is currently offered at www.rajeware.com/
auction/index.html (requires Windows 95/98/ME or above).

To learn about Internet Scrapbook, the free auction tool
built into Microsoft Internet Explorer—Mac version only—
visit Right On Mac! (www.rightonmac.com/articles/00/11/03
-scrapbook.html).

The AuctionWatch company (www.auctionwatch.com) offers various programs to manage, launch, and track all your auctions in one place with Auction Manager; bulk-launch auctions using Auction Manager Pro; and sell items directly from your AW Storefront. They also offer image hosting, page-design assistance, and much more. Fees for using this service are based on the number of items you sell. If you list fewer than ten auction items per day, the cost is as low as $12.95 per month with a $.05 fee per item added to that. Be sure to read "The Beginner's Guide to Online Auctions" (www.auctionwatch.com/awdaily/features/beginnersguide/index.html).

Auctionsubmit is free, downloadable auction software that is compatible with eBay, Amazon.com, and Yahoo! auctions. It offers page-design templates as well as numerous organizational, listing, and data-management functions. To learn more, visit their website (www.auctionsubmit.com).

For a fabulous selection of free, downloadable PC-only auction software tools, including sniping software, a "bidder-blocking" program, page-design assistance, a background-check tool, and the very popular Auction Pro 2000—which allows you to create full HTML ads for eBay, Yahoo!, or any online auction that accepts HTML ads—go to WebAttack (www.webattack.com/Freeware/misctools/fwauction.shtml).

Easy Auction (www.auctiontools.net/easyauction) is another comprehensive Windows auction software tool that provides an auction database, an auction tracker, an accounting tool, a correspondence manager, an auction and feedback submitter, a dual time zone clock, and more. It costs $39.99 and provides free updates.

Auctiva (www.auctiva.com) offers a free auction-management tool, Auctiva Basic, which includes the Showcase gallery for listings, automated listing tracking, and Auctiva support.

Additionally, the more comprehensive Auctiva Pro is available for a fee, starting at $10 per month; this option includes posting and management tools (ePoster and eBud), software that helps sellers create professional-looking listings, post them in bulk, track their progress, generate reports, and more.

AuctionHelper (www.auctionhelper.com) allows sellers to manage inventory, schedule and list items, relist unsold items, and e-mail and invoice winners; it offers numerous other helpful functions, especially for sellers who deal in large numbers of items. AuctionHelper also handles tasks once your auctions end, for example bulk e-mailing your winners and directing them to fill out their own invoices, and keeping track of who has paid. Various packages are available, but the minimum fee is $10 per month and $.15 per transaction.

AuctionSite Manager (www.web-bazaar.com/cgi/auction_site .html) offers sellers three levels of auction management software, ranging in price from $14.95 to $29.95: Basic, with auction listing display and browser-based manager, hosted under Strictly Listing, Inc.; Image Hosting, which includes all the basic services plus image upload and image hosting for your auctions; and Complete Site, which includes all the above as well as domain hosting and FTP access.

Shooting Star (http://foodogsoftware.com) is a PC-only auction management program that is workflow based. It not only manages data but also walks the seller through the processes of posting, selling, and invoicing and customer relations. The one-time fee for downloading it from Foo Dog Software is $49.95.

Andale (www.andale.com) is a widely used auction-management tool that offers numerous valuable programs, services, and templates to sellers using eBay, Yahoo!, and Amazon auctions. Different packages are available for personal, power, and corporate-level sellers, and pricing ranges from $10.50 per month to $169.95 per month.

EBay's Seller's Assistant Basic (bulk listings and tracking plus correspondence assistance) and Seller's Assistant Pro (a complete sales management package designed for high-volume sellers and small businesses), designed by Blackthorne Software, are two extremely popular PC-only auction management tools. The Basic version costs $4.99 per month, and the Pro version costs $15.99 per month. Visit http://pages.ebay.com/sellers_assistant/index.html to explore these two eBay-specific programs.

Finally, be sure to check out Alan's Internet Auction Resource page (www.alanelliott.com/auction). Online auction authority Alan Elliott provides sellers with a wealth of helpful information and links to useful sites, such as appraisal services, auction tools, and online payment establishments like PayPal and Billpoint.

With over twenty years of experience in digital art, Cynthia Beth Rubin is a wellspring of technical information on web design and uploading images. Visit her website (http://CBRubin.net/digital_skills) for tips and tutorials.

Interested in finding, joining, or creating a web ring? Contact www.webring.com.

Part Four

FITTING, FIXING, AND FLAUNTING

Making Your Purchases Wearable and Wonderful

FIT FOR HUMAN CONSTRUCTION:
MAJOR LEAGUE AND PRO DIVISIONS

$\mathscr{N}$ow that you've discovered the world of online vintage clothing shopping, it's all too easy to accumulate one-of-a-kind pieces; in fact, your closet is crammed with one *FABulous Fifties Unique Bombshell Dress!* piled on top of another. Take heart, Gentle Shopper: We will help you wade through and take arms against the sea of troubles in your wardrobe. We will deal with all the little difficulties—the repair jobs, the size discrepancies, the inevitable wear-and-tear issues faced by every collector of vintage clothing—and we'll see the light at the closet door.

The first order of business is to take a good look at all the misfits hanging around in your closet and decide which ones you're going to tackle yourself. Truthfully, now, you are the only one who can speak for the level of your sewing skills, and you alone can say how much time you're willing and able to devote to alterations. Our goal is to get your closet up and running: Whether this happens courtesy of your own hands or those of a paid professional is less important than the fact that it *does* happen, hopefully sooner as opposed to later. So, let's start by discussing those missions improbable, namely, the jobs that are best left to the professionals.

Alterations of constructed, tailored, and lined pieces should be handled by a tailor or seamstress. Sartorially speaking, there is nothing quite like wearing a jacket that fits perfectly—you feel confident, stylish, and sensational. If your jacket or coat is too wide in the shoulders or extremely loose in the waist, however, it will not generate this attitude; more likely, you will feel somewhat sloppy and ill situated. A professional can reduce a shoulder up to an inch on either side by removing and replacing the sleeve—don't try this at home—and he can also open the lining and nip in the waist along the side seams, the back seam, and—if they exist—the darts. Heavy winter coats with linings should also be shortened by a tailor. Oftentimes, with pants and skirts, reducing the waist beyond an inch or so requires complete removal of the waistband, a task that's definitely best left to a professional. It may also be possible to deal with excess fabric by adding pleats or gathers; bear in mind that the garment's silhouette will now be rather different. Ask for any remnants resulting from your alterations, as the fabric scraps can be useful for patching or test washing in the future.

Enlarging tailored garments is somewhat trickier. You might have to hunt down a piece of matching fabric to add to a waistband (fabric store remnant bins are great sources for this), or you could decide to refashion a pleated skirt or trousers into something slightly less pleated but more roomy and comfortable. If you're putting together a maternity wardrobe, finding a good seamstress is one of the nicest things you can do for yourself—in addition to eating well and getting plenty of rest, of course. Matching sash ties can be inserted into side seams so you can custom-fit a dress that is—for the moment, anyway—overwhelmingly voluminous, and stretchy panels can be added to men's trousers.

Note the exquisite construction and detailing of this vintage Christian Dior wool blouse. *Linda Lindroth*

Evening gowns, wedding gowns, and all expensive clothing made of light-colored or delicate fabrics should really be altered by those who know what they are doing, and even these professionals will tell you that removing stitches from silks like peau de soie is risky business—little stitch holes will inevitably remain. Avoid buying silk garments that will need letting out—indeed, this is a great time to point out a basic rule of thumb for alterations: It is generally much easier to make large things smaller and achieve acceptable results than to make small things larger.

Resolve to click the Back button whenever you find yourself tempted by a skirt with a twenty-two-inch waist or a pair of pants with hips that might work if you were to shun all manner of carbohydrates between now and Christmas. Besides, every top stylist says the same thing about separates: Trousers and skirts—especially pleated ones—that are just *slightly* too big will hang more attractively on the body and make you look slimmer.

Let the Pros Handle It

- Adjustments to tailored, lined, or constructed garments
- Detailed, multiple-seam alterations
- Alterations of expensive, delicate, or light-colored fabrics that show stitches, for example, wedding gowns and formal wear
- Replacing linings of jackets, coats, and most dresses
- Reweaving holes in expensive knitwear (professionals skilled in this art always command high fees, so be sure the garment is worth restoring)
- Taking up or letting down the hems and cuffs of *lined* garments
- Most letting-out (enlargement) projects
- Reducing the bodice of a lined dress
- Shortening jeans

HELP WANTED: FINDING A PROFESSIONAL SEAMSTRESS OR TAILOR

If you have never experienced having a garment professionally altered so it fits you perfectly, you are in for a treat. Perhaps your vintage 1960's Oleg Cassini "Jackie O suit"—or, if you're more of an Armani guy, your new trench coat—needs a little custom body work to be truly wearable. But you're just beginning to acquire the sort of clothes that warrant this special attention, and you're unsure where to find a seamstress or tailor who can meet your needs.

As we mention in the section on menswear, word-of-mouth advertising is, by far, the best kind of recommendation for a dry cleaner; you should take the same approach when hiring a seamstress or tailor. Ask a well-dressed friend about the person to whom she takes her fine vintage gowns when they need to be fitted to her small frame. Perhaps there is a colleague in your office whose suits are always impeccably made—indeed, even his shirt collars appear custom-sewn; he may point you in the right direction. And fine boutiques and menswear shops are always staffed with people who know where to send a customer should his purchases need alterations; sometimes the store will have an on-site tailor who also does outside work. Boutiques that cater to brides and prom-goers will always be able to recommend at least a few good seamstresses if you ask politely: "I just inherited this lovely formal gown from the 1950's, but it's a little big for me. I was wondering if you might recommend a seamstress who is accustomed to working with beautiful, high-end clothes like the ones in this shop?" Also, try visiting a fine-quality fabric store—one that carries real silk and wool, as opposed to cheap synthetics—and asking the store owner for the name of a talented tailor. It is highly likely that she will not only be able to recommend someone but also have her business card handy. Finally, check out the Professional Association of Custom Clothiers website (www.paccprofessionals.org/referrals.htm) for a list of seamstresses and tailors in your state.

Once you've chosen a seamstress or tailor, you'll need to decide which piece to hand over first. Of course, it's entirely up to you, but we advise against schlepping the entire alterations pile from your house to his workshop, even if budget constraints aren't an issue. Select one trial piece to take to your newfound pro, perhaps a jacket or coat that needs to be custom-fitted to your torso. The trial garment should not be an irreplaceable heirloom. Save those for later, when you're standing in front of a closet that's practically overflowing with the fruits of your seamstress's labor, and you're convinced she is actually a fairy godmother with a seam ripper instead of a wand.

Since most tailors and seamstresses are terribly busy, try to be as prepared as possible when you take your garments to one. When you call to make your appointment, ask if you'll need to purchase your own thread or notions, or whether those will be provided. Briefly describe the work you'd like performed and ask if it's possible to get an idea of the cost involved. It's also helpful to write down the alterations you'd like done, even if you've mentioned these to your seamstress over the phone; this way, you can both refer to your list while you're being fitted. Remember to wear appropriate clothes or undergarments and bring along the shoes you will be wearing with the outfit, as they will help determine not only hem length but also the fit of a jacket or dress bodice. Your natural posture does vary according to what is on your feet.

Finally, once the fitting is over, you should be given a receipt for your garment and a fairly accurate estimate of the charges—if not a straightforward invoice—along with the date on which you can expect to collect your outfit. If the work being done is extensive, for example, fitting a wedding gown or altering the shoulders, waist, and sleeve length of a jacket, it is quite possible that two or more fittings may be required, and you'll schedule those now. Otherwise, once your garment is ready for you, try to collect it as soon as possible and be ready to try it on for a final going-over.

One last thing: In many metropolitan areas, it's customary to tip the person who just made you look like a million bucks, bearing in mind that if the work is exemplary, you will most likely become a repeat customer. It is courteous to tip 15 to 20 percent of the alterations charge, based on the difficulty of the work. Professionals always take good care of those who value their handiwork and tangibly express their gratitude, and they are more likely, in the future, to accommodate special requests if they're coming from appreciative clients.

FIT FOR HUMAN CONSTRUCTION: MINOR LEAGUE DIVISION

$\mathcal{A}$re there fitting problems and alterations that you can address on your own? Yes, absolutely. How many of these tasks you're comfortable tackling, however, depends on a number of factors: your experience, the time frame in which you'd like to have the alterations finished, your willingness to learn, and your patience. You can easily access all sorts of sewing-related instructions, from threading a needle to mending and simple tailoring, on the Mississippi State University's Extension Service website, "4-H Clothing Project Reference Manual" (www.msucares.com/pubs/pub1302.htm). Also check out *Threads* magazine's collection of fit-related links (www.taunton.com/threads/pages/th_feat_fitting.asp).

Following are some simple alterations that can be handled by anyone with basic sewing skills; remember that time is a cost factor, too, so if your schedule is characterized by eighteen-hour workdays and you can afford to delegate, don't hesitate to hand simple repairs and button replacements over to your seamstress along with the more complicated projects, unless, of course, you find sewing relaxing and enjoyable. Most important, know your measurements: If you've been buying fashion online, chances are you've already bought and used a tape measure, but if you're unfamiliar with your own personal stats, there's no time like the present. Write them on a card and keep them near your sewing supplies.

HEMS

Ever present is the possibility that you will need to shorten the skirt or pants (or shirt sleeves) of something you purchased online. Hemming a skirt is simple enough; you can easily do it yourself. First remove the stitches of the previous hem. Stand in front of a full-length mirror and place a few strategic straight pins on the shortened hemline where you think it should be. Put the garment on a table or bed and place the pins around the hem as evenly as you can, perpendicular to the fold. Try the garment on and check again in the mirror, turning slowly, and make any adjustments. When you are satisfied, gently press the new hemline with an iron. Remove the pins and determine how deep you want the hem to be, including the part you will turn under for your stitches. Cut off the excess fabric, turn the raw edge under, and gently press the whole thing with your iron. Repin or baste the hem and, using either blind stitches or slip stitches, finish the hem.

Sleeves can also be shortened this way, provided the shirt or jacket is unlined: unpick, pin to desired length, trim excess fabric if necessary, finish edge, and hemstitch. With heavy fabrics like denim, you can turn under the existing hem and sew it in place—using a thicker hand needle.

Hemming leather may be challenging, but it is not impossible to accomplish. Use chalk to mark the hemline—avoid using pins on leather or leatherlike materials. Paper clips are best for holding the hem in place. If you feel comfortable topstitching on your sewing machine, switch to a wedge-shaped needle made for leather and use a fairly long stitch (six to eight stitches per inch). You can also use rubber cement or a self-stick hem tape. Turn the hem up and press it in place with your fingers (or use a plastic mallet). If the hem is curved you may need to ease it by cutting small triangles in the fullest areas, squeezing the cut edges together.

If, on the other hand, you wish to let down a hem to lengthen a garment, examine the current hem. Pull it in opposing directions with the thumb and forefinger of each hand so the fold flattens out. Is the hem crease faded? Is the hem itself a different, less-faded color? In either case, rethink your hem-lengthening plans: Perhaps you can live with the shorter length if the alternatives appear worse. If you're committed to lengthening the garment no matter what, you might try your hand at dotting the faded crease with a permanent marker in a matching color (available at craft stores); if you use the fine tip and apply a dotted line of closely matching color to the crease, you may significantly disguise it.

Depending on the garment, you could also sew ribbon, lace, or other trimming over the crease.

If you decide to proceed, you'll find that letting down a hem—whether it's on a skirt, dress, sleeve, or trouser—is relatively simple to do. Unpick the original hem, and press the garment as well as possible so the crease disappears. You may wish to spritz the crease with a little water and press using a hot iron—on the wrong side of the fabric, of course—or use a dampened press cloth. Try on the garment and pin the hem at the desired length. If the original hem was less than generous, you will have even less with which to work now; in fact, you may need to use bias hem facing tape or stretch lace seam binding in order to create a hem in the first place (you'll still need at least a half inch of fabric to turn under). Once you've taken care of the raw edge, either by turning it under or sewing on the tape or lace, simply hemstitch as normal. To set the new hem and help remove any trace of the old crease, wash the garment and iron it while it's still slightly damp, concentrating your efforts—naturally—on the hem area.

Taking in the waist or bodice of a dress or unlined jacket is another fairly simple alteration you can do with the help of a friend. The best way to do this is to turn the item inside out and try it on over your usual undergarments. In order to perform a symmetrical alteration and have your garment hang properly, you must do the same thing to each side. If the zipper is in the center back, you may take in both side seams. Have your friend place the pins in a line that's parallel to your body, on both sides, so the fit is close but not tight. Take off the garment. Baste the new seams with contrasting thread, remove the pins, and try the garment on again, right side out this time. Finally, sew the seams with your machine. Trim the excess fabric if necessary and finish the new seam edges with pinking shears, seam binding, or hand overcasting.

If you're considering altering a dress from the 1950's or earlier, there is a good chance the zipper will be located in the left-hand side seam, and it's always preferable to leave a perfectly good zipper in its original location if possible. In this case, work with the center back seam, if one exists. If not, perhaps there are vertical darts at the waist, making a symmetrical reduction possible; this is how Chinese cheongsams are constructed. Grasp both the front darts with your hands, gathering some extra fabric, to see how the garment hangs with a more fitted waist, and remember there are probably back darts that can be exploited, too. If you wish to take those in, we'd once again recommend enlisting the help of a friend. Have her pin the darts—now deeper—on each side, smoothing out the surrounding fabric so the garment truly fits without being tight. Don't worry if they aren't completely even, as you will adjust the pins when you take the garment off. Try it on again, with the pins adjusted for symmetry. Remove the garment and baste the darts with contrasting thread. Try it on with the pins removed, right side out. If you're happy with the new, sleek look, sew the darts with a machine, and press darts toward their original direction—usually, they face the middle of the dress or jacket when looking at the wrong side of the garment.

BUTTONS AND BUTTONHOLES

If the garment you bought is missing a prominently placed decorative button, it is unlikely you will find a match. Replacing all the buttons also gives you an opportunity to adjust the fit of your garment.

A jacket or blouse that seems a little full can be adjusted by moving the buttons. There are a few guidelines to remember. While women's garments always have the buttons on the left side of the garment and men's on the right, the neck button at the back is always on the left-hand side. Moving the buttons means realigning the button placement line that corresponds to the buttonholes on the opposite side. Selecting the key buttonhole positions for your new placement means you will need to adjust for the neck, waist, and fullest part of the bust. Additional buttons are placed between these on the new button placement line across from their buttonholes. You can mark that line with dressmaker's chalk or basting stitches. Sometimes you may find that a button has been placed on a vintage garment to cover up a hole. You will need to take this into consideration when placing the other buttons. We sometimes use safety pins to stand in for the buttons to check the placement before resewing the buttons.

Suppose you do not like the original buttons on a garment and you select new ones that are smaller: Buttonholes can be altered by adding a few stitches to each in order to reduce the opening.

Repairing buttonholes that have come unraveled involves more complicated needlework; if you've never attempted this before but would like to give it a try, consult a good sewing manual that has diagrams and clear instructions. We like *The Vogue Sewing Book* and *Reader's Digest Complete Guide to Sewing*.

Taking in the waist of a skirt or pair of trousers can be as simple as moving a button or as complicated as removing the waistband. If the garment is only slightly too big, moving the button will probably suffice to create a better fit. Of course, you might be working with snaps, hooks and eyes, or a hook and bar instead of buttons, but the task is something you can do yourself. First, remove the button by carefully snipping the stitches; a small seam-ripper tool works well for buttons that have been tightly affixed. Tug gently on the button to remove it, and brush away any remaining threads. Now try on the garment, close the zipper, and hold the waistband together with your thumb and forefinger, making sure it's positioned for a comfortable fit. Slide your marking pencil through the outer edge of the buttonhole and make a small dot on the waistband beneath where you'll resew the button. If the waistband has a hook and bar or snaps, unpick and reposition the bar (or bottom snap), after first trying on the garment and marking the new spot, as before.

BELTS

Belts can be made smaller by adding holes with a leather punch, although you'll need to visit a good shoe-repair shop if you want to trim length and reposition the buckle. Many worn areas on belts can be repaired quite easily with shoe polish (make sure you rub it into the leather well enough that it doesn't leave streaks on your favorite John Bartlett white T-shirt). You can also use shoe dye or one of a wide range of permanent Pantone marker pens sold in art supply stores. If the belt has been constructed of two pieces of leather glued back to back and the pieces are separating, use contact cement, rubber cement, or Elmer's or Sobo glue to reattach them.

If you need to add extra holes, you can do so with a punch, a metal tool with a sharp circular tip that, when struck with a hammer, makes a neat hole. Remember to check where the designer's name has been branded in order not to lose it in the alteration.

ALTERNATIVE ALTERATIONS

Besides sewing, there are many fabulous, creative ways to address fitting problems. At the top of the list is a good, uplifting padded bra; credit this miracle of engineering with the rescue of many an ill-fitting evening dress. Often a pair of control-top panty hose is all you need to achieve a smooth line under a knit dress. If you can handle a little temporary discomfort, waist cinchers and corsets can reduce you, as opposed to your gown, and will act as insurance against splitting your seams. Jackets with slightly too wide shoulders look better if a thin shoulder pad is tacked inside; use the natural-shaped ones that are made from layers of cotton batting rather than the thick foam wedges so characteristic of 1980's clothes. A dress bodice whose waistline falls just beneath your rib cage and above your waist feels and looks peculiar. A very wide belt, worn at your natural waist, can cover the gathers of the skirt and the waistline and create the illusion of a correctly proportioned bodice. And, finally, try wrapping and tying your oversized garments. Shirts can be knotted in front, Elly May Clampett style; if there is enough fabric, you can unfasten the bottom buttons, cross one shirttail over the other, and tie them in a tiny knot at the small of your back, à la Audrey. You can even play with an oversized silk dropped-waist dress in a similar fashion—gathering and overlapping the fabric to create a sarong effect that flatters your figure and using an antique brooch to hold everything in place.

Shoes that are slightly large can be fitted with half insoles or insoles, which are available in drug stores as well as shoe-repair shops. Now they're not just wearable, they're extremely comfortable. Oversized hats can be fitted to the head using this ingenious trick: Grasp a two-foot piece of wide horsehair braid—the fine nylon bias-mesh stuff, available in fabric stores, that's often used to make the hems of wedding dresses and ball gowns stand out—and fold it in half lengthwise, making a springy roll. Sew the edges together, and then sew this "sausage" around the inside of the hat, attaching it to the inner band. Voilà—a custom-fitted hat that stays on your head without uncomfortable pins.

When it comes to certain wardrobe items, however, you really must know when to fold 'em. A good shoemaker can sometimes stretch a pair of shoes a little, but there is nothing one can do about shoes that are a full size too small. We've tried that spray-on liquid that is supposed to stretch leather and can confidently advise you to save your money—it doesn't work. The same thing applies to tiny hats and belts: Collect them if you love them but don't expect to be able to alter them and wear them.

OUT, DAMNED SPOT! THE ART AND SCIENCE OF STAIN REMOVAL

*L*et's deal with those stained garments next, focusing on the vintage finds you've been meaning to spot-reat, soak overnight, or take to the cleaners. For goodness sake, don't spend a fortune dry-cleaning anything you aren't sure you're going to wear once it *has* been refreshed. However, we trust you'll carefully review the following recommendations for cleaning things and proceed accordingly. Some fabrics really do require the attention of a professional, especially if you intend to wear the garment in its original form, as opposed to a "deconstructed" version.

CHEMICAL WARFARE: TAKE IT TO THE CLEANERS

Dry-clean-only items with stains should be handled by professionals. This seems obvious, but many a well-meaning person has ignored the care label and attempted spot removal. Tell the cleaners what fell on your garment—if you have any idea—and point out the fiber content if you can; faded labels can often be hard to read, but photocopying them, using the darkest setting, may allow you to determine if something is silk or rayon. Almost all lined garments should be dry-cleaned.

Dry-clean any stain of unknown origin, since really old stains seldom respond to gentle home methods (more on aggressive at-home stain-removal methods later).

Dry-clean any beaded, sequined, or elaborately embroidered garment, and ask the cleaners to use a mesh bag. Certain establishments have more experience with fine, ornate clothing; ask around for recommendations.

Dry-clean velvet, taffeta, and leather. Leather requires a special cleaning process; if a cleaner handles it improperly, your once-soft leather skirt could wind up feeling stiff and extremely unpleasant.

Dry-clean anything you fear will shrink. Tell the cleaner about your apprehension and ask that they take the necessary precautions to avoid shrinking and damaging your garment.

Consult a fabric conservator if your garment is a costly hand-painted or hand-dyed treasure. For a list of such professionals in your area, call or write to the American Institute for Conservation of Historic and Artistic Works, 1717 K Street, N.W., Suite 200, Washington, DC 20006, 202-452-9545.

STAINS AND MESS ON THE PERMANENT PRESS . . . WHADDYA DO?

A 1970's television commercial finished the above line: "Well, if you can't . . . use . . . regular Clorox, use Clorox Two." And thus the world was introduced to the marvels of nonchlorine bleach. Today, we have more brands of spot removers, stain lifters, and fabric brighteners than ever before, yet some of the best methods for tackling stains are the old-fashioned, time-tested ones. Carbona's Stain Devils line features ten different formulas for lifting all manner of stains, from coffee to blood. All are dermatologically tested and environmentally friendly. Visit their site (www.carbona.com) for information or to order products.

For colored prints, especially cotton ones, we love Biz powder. This product is not recommended for wool and silk, since the proteins that constitute these fibers may be damaged. The recipe for getting rid of those weird little brown age stains is quite simple. Throw two scoops of Biz in a five-gallon bucket and fill it with the hottest water possible. Stir this white, chemical soup with a large stick or spoon, and add the stained item, pushing it beneath the suds until all the air is removed. Allow it to soak overnight—the longer it soaks, the better the results—and rinse it repeatedly. Now wash it with a delicate soap like Ivory Snow liquid (fabric softener is optional), and hang to dry. Not only will most if not all of the stains be gone, but the colors and white background will be brighter, too.

For white washables, try the Biz soak first; Clorox should be used only as a last resort. Chlorine bleach gradually eats away at fabrics and should be used only if nothing else seems to help the garment. After the Biz soak and gentle wash, try this trick, which is often used in the Caribbean: Drape the wet white garment over a clean shrub or hedge so that it is perpendicular to the sun's rays and allow it to be solar bleached. This method is great for restoring a white oxford shirt to its original brilliance. If you must use chlorine bleach, start with a diluted solution in your washing machine's gentle cycle, as soaking things in bleach for days will really break down the fibers.

Disappearing Acts

Age Spots
Try the Biz soak described on page 223.

Blood
Soak the garment in cold water and wash; if this doesn't lift all the stain, try the Biz soak, which is virtually guaranteed to remove blood.

Coffee and Tea
Rinse the garment as much as possible before washing it. If any signs of the stain remain, try the Biz soak.

Grease
If the stain is fresh, blot up as much of the stain as possible with a paper towel or other absorbent material, then use a stain-removal product like Shout or Spray 'n Wash (we like the solid versions best) before washing. If it's an old stain, the Biz soak might help.

Ink
A tried-and-true solution for removing ballpoint ink is aerosol hairspray. Use a plain, inexpensive one, like Aqua Net, as opposed to a hairspray that contains conditioners or oils. Spray the mark until it's saturated, rub gently, and rinse with cold water. Then wash normally.

Makeup
Baby wipes are terrific for impromptu cleanups of your boyfriend's collar, and they can gently remove foundation and lip-

stick from your face, too (unscented ones are best). Solid or gel stain-removal products like Shout and Spray 'n Wash are also effective (on clothes!).

Perspiration

This one is tricky, since underarm stains are themselves vintage items, and, unfortunately, some of them refuse to budge—much to our chagrin. Start with the most gentle method—sponging the stain with a fifty-fifty vinegar-and-water solution, and then try an overnight soak in the much-beloved Biz.

Rust

Several rust removers are available, and we've had success using Whink; however, some rust stains are permanent. Be sure to wear gloves and follow the instructions on the bottle, since it is possible to burn yourself and ruin your garment with this caustic fluid if you aren't careful. A gentler treatment involves sprinkling the stain with salt, then pouring a little lemon juice on top of that; allow the garment to soak this in for a few minutes before rinsing and laundering.

Wine

For red wine stains, try a hair-of-the-Russian-dog approach: Pour a little vodka into a saucer and press the stained part into it until it's submerged. Leave this overnight, then rinse and hand wash normally. For white wine or Champagne stains, sponge the stain with a fifty-fifty vinegar-and-water solution, then wash.

ON YOUR MARKS (AND SCUFFS AND DINGS): ACCESSORIES

Sometimes the shortest distance between scuffed and wearable is a line drawn with a permanent marker. The Kiwi company, well-known for its range of shoe polishes and leather cleaners, makes a scratch-covering product that comes in black and brown and works beautifully on purses as well as shoes. When applying either marker ink or scratch cover, build up the pigment slowly and avoid overapplying the dark color or it will appear obvious. Many leather goods can be cleaned with saddle soap, but please bear in mind that some lighter leathers may be permanently darkened afterward. Finally, there is a product called Sneaker White that's great to have around for refreshing athletic shoes, many of which can first be washed in the machine. Don't forget to replace the laces with new ones.

If, after your best rescue efforts, your shoes still seem blemished, your belt looks spotty, or your purse appears to have been tossed around a runway by angry baggage handlers, there are still a few things you can try. Satin shoes, for example, can be decorated with rhinestones, beads, buttons, and small flowers—all good ways to camouflage spots and stains. High-end belts and handbags can be repaired and restored, for a fee, by their namesake boutiques; many fine department stores also offer these services. And patent leather and vinyl pieces can sometimes be brought back from the brink with a little denatured alcohol, applied with a cotton ball. If the purse seems really sticky, however, it is probably irredeemable.

OPERATION RESTORATION: FIXING AND REPAIRING DAMAGE

$\mathcal{V}$intage clothes are fashions from another era, worn by another generation. In the old days, people were not that different: They barbecued and played outdoors, drank and smoked and danced until dawn, and generally made happy messes of themselves, as evidenced by the sorry condition of some vintage garments. Bravo to them! But what are we to do with all these damaged goods? Here are some ideas that might work, depending on the nature and extent of the injury.

MISSING OR FRAYED RIBBON AND LACE

You can often replace ribbon and lace and refresh a piece of vintage lingerie. Good craft stores and fabric shops carry a wide range of lace and ribbon in various widths and colors. If the original ribbon was silk you might want to order the real thing, since most fabric store ribbons and trims are made of synthetic fibers. A great source for real silk ribbon—offered in two widths and numerous colors—is the online shop Quiltware (www.quiltware

.com/silk.asp). For a wide range of lace, including some that can be dyed to match, be sure to visit Laceland (www.laceland .com).

HOLES

Small holes can be patched with tiny pieces of fabric snipped from the seam allowance. Pin this to the underside of the garment and, working on the right side now, turn the raw edges inward—using the tip of a very fine needle—to sew the patch in place. Alternatively, if a hole is near a seam or hem, the garment can be taken in (or up) slightly, absorbing the hole into the seam or hem allowance. And, of course, you could always cover the hole with beads, sequins, buttons, or ribbon—or wear a beautiful, strategically placed brooch or scarf.

If you wish to darn a small hole, use an embroidery hoop to pull the fabric taut. Use a very fine needle and a matching thread (for patterned fabric, choose thread to match the lightest color), knot the end of the thread, and, starting from the wrong side, draw the needle through, close to the hole. Make a few parallel stitches, then go back over them with another set, perpendicular to the first, weaving over and under as you go. Don't create too much bulk, or the darn will be very noticeable.

For torn lace, it's possible to loosely connect the pieces of separated fabric using a single thread. If the tear is located in a high-stress area like a seam, you might also want to reinforce the garment on the underside, using a piece of flesh-colored illusion netting. This is a stretchy, sheer mesh fabric that's often used in costumes (like those worn by figure skaters) and is available in larger fabric stores.

FADING

"Black is black, I want my baby back. Gray is gray since she went away-ay-ay . . ." Humming these lyrics, we head to the washing machine with a couple of bottles of liquid black dye and a few pairs of vintage black jeans in need of renewal. This is a pretty simple activity unless those jeans are already skintight and the hot water required might shrink them further.

A bit more difficult is matching the color of something, for example, that is lighter than periwinkle and darker than sky blue. Bring the garment with you to the dye display in your fabric or craft store or local supermarket and consider how you will like the item in this new, albeit brighter, variation. Remember that the best dyeing results are obtained using the stove-top method, however, so have plenty of old rags around for immediate cleanup, especially if you're dyeing something dark in a light-colored kitchen; alternatively, you might use an outdoor hot plate for your dye project and spare yourself the mess and stress of cleaning a dye-splattered stove. Black, navy, or burgundy dye, used in double-strength concentration, will refresh a faded linen outfit. Most synthetic threads used for topstitching will not take dye: A contrasting finish will result instead. Some craft stores offer cold-water batik dyes that may be preferable for use on wools or silks. All hand-dyed garments—especially dark ones—should be washed separately henceforth.

BROKEN BAUBLES

The very qualities that draw us to vintage costume jewelry, namely its sparkle and delicacy, are often the primary reasons for its ruin.

If you collect vintage costume jewelry, it's a good idea to invest in a small repair kit that contains tweezers, tiny screwdrivers, pliers, and wires. A couple of different types of adhesives will be useful, too. Keep an eye out for damaged costume jewelry when you're rummaging through the thrift-store bins, as old, broken pieces are terrific sources for stones and spare parts. Your trusty craft store undoubtedly stocks rhinestones. Finally, while some of our friends will attack a grimy rhinestone bracelet with a toothbrush and jewelry cleaner, we prefer to avoid overusing water, as it can loosen the stones, and, in the case of some municipalities whose water is chemically treated, it can even damage the finish of the metal parts. Instead, we suggest spot-treating your vintage costume baubles with Q-tips dipped in jewelry-cleaning solution.

LAST DANCE, LAST CHANCE . . . FOR LOVE

You love that vintage dress with the black-and-white graphics, but the stubborn perspiration stains on the bodice have caused you to cast it aside in disgust. And what about the fabulous cut-velvet Issey Miyake coat you snapped up from a consignment boutique, the one with the torn sleeves and shredded lining? You may well be thinking that you should give these things away.

Or perhaps you could "re-purpose" the garments. We invite you to think outside the blanket box and imagine a new life for these once-glorious pieces. When all else fails—when the garment is a write-off but you can't bear to part with it—why not draw on the innate creativity possessed by all vintage clothing aficionados? We're not advising that you waste your time if the item in question isn't absolutely dear to you. By all means, give it away and move on. Otherwise, consider the following inspired suggestions.

A dress with a ruined bodice can become a skirt. Use fabric harvested from a deep hem to make the waistband, or purchase a solid-color neutral fabric for facing a clean waist (one with no band). A good sewing manual like *The Vogue Sewing Book* offers illustrated instructions for working with waistbands; alternatively, your dressmaker can do this.

Anything made of sumptuous fabric can be converted into a luxurious pillow sham, shawl, or table runner.

Broken costume jewelry can be used for spare parts. Alternatively, intact pieces (for example, a section of a rhinestone necklace) can be sewn onto a vintage purse, conveniently covering one of those wine stains. If there are two matching pieces, you've got a pair of sparkly shoe clips in the making: Simply glue them to backings purchased from a fabric store. And be sure to save all interesting loose beads and faux pearls in a big jar. Your daughter or niece will love making herself a fabulous necklace.

Jeans that are stained or torn at or below the knees can be turned into cutoffs—nothing too original there. But consider, for a moment, denim's similarity to canvas: Fabric paints are easy to work with and readily available at craft stores and fabric shops. The Belgian designer Martin Margiela offered jeans with black leather knees a few seasons ago. What a perfect use for the leather skirt that no longer fits you. Perhaps you can create a pair of fantasy jeans with your inspired paintbrush and a few well-placed brooches, safety pins, or rhinestones. Certain Italian designers recently did just that, and their creations sold for thousands of dollars. Just don't throw your masterpiece in the washing machine. Hand washing in cold water—and then, only when needed—is the way to go.

Clearly, a little imagination goes a long way. And if you resolve to attempt just one manageable "rescue effort" every week or so—whether that means replacing a button, taking a jacket to the tailor, sun-bleaching a dingy white shirt, or embroidering a tiny heart on a silk nightgown and covering a flaw in the process—you will soon have an entirely new wardrobe of clothes, accessories, and *choices* at the ready.

Part Five

WHERE, OH WHERE WILL

MY LITTLE MOUSE GO?

An A to Z of Online Vintage Boutiques

SITE DIRECTORY

$\mathcal{T}$he following list of websites represents a broad cross section of online vintage and preworn clothing boutiques. Whether you're a newcomer to the world of vintage clothing—someone who's just looking for a unique prom dress or some interesting costume jewelry—or a serious collector or costume designer armed with lots of experience and an enviable budget, chances are you'll find all sorts of gems among these sites. And if you'd like to sell a garment directly to an online boutique, you'll encounter several, if not many, interested parties; be sure to contact a site with a description of your garment, and the owners will ask for photos if they're interested.

While it would be impossible to list every single vintage site on the World Wide Web, we have put together a comprehensive list that will inspire you and, we hope, provide you with a starting point for your own treasure hunt. At the time of this writing, all the sites reviewed herein were fully operational; unfortunately, you may find that a few of them have since closed their cyberdoors, and for this inconvenience we apologize in advance.

We visited each online boutique using our own home computers—Linda's is a PowerMac G4, Deborah's is a Compaq PC laptop—which have 56K modems and connect to the World Wide Web via ordinary dial-up Internet service providers. Those readers who subscribe to high-speed Internet services such as DSL can expect faster page loading, especially where images are involved; on the whole, however, we found that the majority of sites offered a wonderful shopping experience for any wired fashionphile, whether or not she was satellite-assisted.

When reviewing the vintage websites, we rated them both with dollar signs and little shoe icons. The dollar-sign rating gives you an idea of how much you'll be spending, as follows:

$ Inexpensive. Most items in their inventory cost less than $100.

$$ Moderately expensive. Most items cost between $100 and $500.

$$$ Expensive. Most items cost over $500.

After visiting each website and exploring the different sections therein, we rated them based on the following criteria: the overall selection and quality of the merchandise; the attractiveness and user-friendliness of the site; the inclusion of clear, appealing photographs and helpful, detailed item descriptions; and the difficult-to-define qualities, such as the enjoyment level one experiences when shopping at the site. The stiletto shoes were awarded as follows:

👠 Poor. Walk on by this lackluster site.

👠👠 Fair. A step in the right direction; there's room for improvement.

👠👠👠 Good. Hitting their stride and worth a visit.

✈ ✈ ✈ ✈ Very good. Run—don't walk—to this site.

✈ ✈ ✈ ✈ ✈ Excellent. Really on their toes. They're dancing out in front.

Smart shoppers always familiarize themselves with a store's return guidelines before committing to a purchase. If you're considering buying something from one of the many online vintage and preworn clothing boutiques, be sure to read its return policy carefully before placing an order and contact the owners if you have any questions.

Happy hunting!

Aardvark Jeans
www.aardvarkjeans.com

$ ✈ ✈ ✈

As the name implies, this site is for jeans, the conditions of which are graded from 1 to 4. Levi's 501's as well as other pants can be ordered by condition and size (men's sizes only). Jean jackets are also available. Ordering is easy through a PayPal button, which brings up a partially completed "send money" form. They buy jeans and post a picker's list. Be sure to have your reading glasses ready, as this site has small photos and teeny type. Mailing address: 500 West Spring Street, Fayetteville, AR 72701 (800-336-4694).

Aloha Vintage
www.alohavintage.com

$ ✈ ✈ ✈

This is a fun-filled site that offers numerous affordable Hawaiian shirts, cheongsams, and sundresses in small, well-organized departments like vintage, Aloha wear, and furnishings. We especially liked the eclectic group of small beaded purses and the $15 hand-painted cotton dresses that were displayed when we visited. The photos are fairly basic—and there is one per item, in most cases—but they can be enlarged for better viewing by clicking on them. The descriptions are adequate, and interested buyers can always e-mail the site for further details about an item offered for sale. Checks (with a wait), money orders, and PayPal are all accepted. Refunds and exchanges are not permitted, so be certain of your purchase. The address and phone number are not currently mentioned on the site, and neither is the availability of international shipping—e-mail the owner for this information.

Angelica's Attic

www.angelicasattic.com

$ 🪡🪡🪡

Deni Sinnott's site was recently redesigned using new software and hot colors and backgrounds. We searched the dress category by long, cocktail, and prom, and then we browsed through separates, loungewear, and accessories. Her men's clothing category (items are listed with nicknames!) included Hawaiian shirts ("Aloha!") and 1970's club shirts ("Disco Dude"). In women's wear a sleeveless black cocktail dress ("Black Diamonds!") with a rhinestone-studded neckline was listed as sold (relatively inexpensively at $40). The FAQ page covered credit card info (Visa and MasterCard) as well as shipping via UPS and the USPS, sizing, security, privacy, and international orders.

Antique & Vintage Dress Gallery

www.antiquedress.com

$$–$$$ 🪡🪡🪡🪡🪡

If money is no object but there is only enough time to visit one vintage site, consider checking out this medium-large online boutique that truly offers something to thrill vintage wearers of every stripe (and floral). The deceptively plain-looking home page lists the many eras represented by the clothes—and what divine clothes they are. We especially loved the "1930's–Today/ Designer" category, which went on for pages, offering clear photographs and detailed descriptions of everything currently for sale: a vintage Halston gown with iridescent sequins, a slinky bias-cut velvet 1930's dress, a crisp taffeta Ceil Chapman 1950's frock, and an ethereal pink and green chiffon Adolfo gown that we'd have seriously considered ordering if the waistline had been a tiny bit more accommodating than twenty-three inches. Returns are accepted—be sure to notify the owner within two days—but only for items costing at least $150; in other words, be sure to ask lots of questions before buying a less expensive piece, since the sale will be considered final. Visa, MasterCard, and Discover are all accepted, as are PayPal, money orders, and personal checks (with a wait). International shipping is available. Mailing address: Antique & Vintage Dress Gallery/Deborah Burke, P.O. Box 600353, Newtonville, MA 02460-0003 (781-891-9659; please limit calls to business hours: 9 A.M. to 7 P.M. Eastern standard time). No physical store is mentioned.

Biddington's Auction Galleries
www.biddingtons.com
$$-$$$ ✗ ✗

Biddington's offers online auctions of upmarket art, antiques, and fine items. They have a category for antique and vintage clothing as well as contemporary designer resale. These can be accessed from their home page. Despite a heavy, unimaginative site design and small inventory, the site often features excellent interviews, for example, one with choreographer Matthew Nash about collecting vintage clothing (see www.biddingtons.com/content/expertnash.html), making this site worth an occasional online visit. Mailing address: 425 East 50 Street, Number 5, New York, NY 10022 (212-838-3572).

Butterfly Vintage Clothing
www.butterflyvintage.com

$ 🦋 🦋 🦋

Cheerful butterflies invite the vintage shopper to browse the departments of this site, which include dresses, skirts, costume jewelry, coats, and more. The descriptions for the medium-sized inventory of 1930's to 1970's merchandise tend to be spare. The photos are excellent. E-mailed questions are welcome, and the site is easy to navigate. International shipping is available. Master-Card, Visa, American Express, money orders, cashier's checks, and PayPal and BidPay are accepted. All sales are final (no returns). No physical store is mentioned. Mailing address: P.O. Box 16738, San Diego, CA 92176. No phone number is mentioned.

Buy-Gone Days
www.buy-gonedays.com

$$ 🦋 🦋 🦋 🦋

Buy-Gone Days specializes in gently worn couture and designer clothing from the 1920's to the 1970's. Fabulous fabric backgrounds grace pages of exquisite examples of vintage clothing. You can click on the designers link and scroll through Chanel, Courrèges, Jean Muir, Zandra Rhodes, Pauline Trigère, and Betsey Johnson. A hard-to-resist Norell red gown from the 1970's was lined in silk and had eighteen covered buttons down the front; the long sleeves ended at zippered wrists. In excellent condition, this hot holiday beauty was $160. A Missoni black wool two-piece dress with a capelet, from the late 1960's, was $250. But the highlight of our visit was seeing an early-1980's gold lizard-textured-leather minidress lined in gold silk. Spectacular at $850.

Items are offered in impeccable condition and are dry-cleaned and carefully packaged. Orders are placed by telephone. Payment methods honored include credit cards through Billpoint and Bid-Pay, certified checks, and money orders. Returns are not accepted. International buyers are welcome. Mailing address: 655 Oregon Trail, Pine Bush, NY 12566 (845-744-6422).

Carla's Vintage Wedding Gowns
www.members.aol.com/gown4you/home.html
$-$$ ✂ ✂ ✂

Carla's Vintage Wedding Gowns is a specialty site dedicated to vintage and preworn wedding gowns from all eras. Order by e-mail and she will ship to you via UPS. Visa, MasterCard, and personal checks or money orders are accepted. Returns are subject to a 20 percent restocking charge. Her "one last thing . . ." caveat may be the perfect credo for vintage shoppers: "Don't buy vintage as a way to keep the budget in limits, buy it because you love it and can't live without it."

Carol Lane Antiques
www.laneantiques.com
$$-$$$ ✂ ✂ ✂ ✂ ✂

Carol Lane sells rare and important estate jewelry and beautiful Modernist, Arts and Crafts, Art Nouveau, and handmade jewelry and objects in silver and gold. Browse or use her search engine to locate your favorite items. The website has a versatile design that allows for several different views of each piece of jewelry from both her eBay listed auctions and this site. It's easy to make inquiries (she responds quickly to e-mails), and there's a secure order form. Credit cards, personal checks, money orders, and cashier's checks are acceptable forms of payment. This well-known and highly reputable dealer is located in Riverdale, New York. Mailing address: P.O. Box 434, Riverdale, NY 10471 (718-548-5750).

The Cats Pajamas
www.catspajamas.com
$-$$ 🐈 🐈 🐈 🐈 🐈

It's hard not to love a site with such a playful splash page, and visitors will find all sorts of treasures. The searchable inventory is huge, but everything is well organized into departments such as kids' decor, men's, lingerie, weddings, plus sizes, and bargains. Pictures and descriptions are excellent. Their wonderful collection of white cotton Victorian petticoats shouldn't be missed. Returns are accepted if you e-mail them within twenty-four hours of receipt. Goods must be received within three days of receipt; buyer pays a 10 percent restocking fee. They'll ship "anywhere on the planet," and they accept Visa, MasterCard, Discover, American Express, personal checks from repeat customers, money orders, and PayPal. No physical store is mentioned. Mailing address: 335 Maynard Street, Williamsport, PA 17701 (866-CATSPJS, 866-228-7757; fax: 570-601-1734).

Chelsea Girl Vintage Clothing
www.chelsea-girl.com
$$ 🐈 🐈 🐈 🐈 🐈

We thoroughly enjoyed visiting this whimsical, well-organized site. The graphics on the "Let's Go Shopping" page—well-dressed "girls"—are clicked in order to visit departments like day dresses, evening dresses, suits, and separates. Scattered throughout the beautiful, carefully edited inventory are quotes from Oscar Wilde, Diana Vreeland, and Woody Allen. The clothes themselves include such iconic treasures as an ultrafeminine 1950's Suzy Perette frock, a custom-made 1960's cocktail dress, a fabulous tweed nipped-waist 1940's suit, a 1930's floral bias-cut dress, and a 1920's silk kimono coat. Chelsea Girl accepts Visa, MasterCard, American Express, money orders, and checks (with a wait). International shipping is available, and returns are accepted with two days' notice. Owner Elisa Casas also operates a popular, well-regarded vintage boutique—The 1909 Company—in New York's SoHo district; it's located at 63 Thompson Street, New York, New York. Mailing address: Chelsea Girl, c/o The 1909 Company, 63 Thompson Street, New York, NY 10012 (212-343-1658).

Clothes Heaven
www.clothesheaven.com
$$-$$$ 🛍️🛍️🛍️

This is the online version of Larayne Brannon's Pasadena, California, shop. The shop and site feature recent vintage designer clothes in gently worn condition. Text is clear and complete, describing moderate- to high-priced designer clothing from the closets of the rich and famous. Store location is 110-112 East Union Street, Pasadena, CA 91103 (626-440-0929).

Curbside Couture
www.curbside-couture.com
$ 🛍️🛍️🛍️

Pink roses decorate the splash page of this site, where vintage shoppers will find a small- to medium-sized collection of clothing that mainly hails from relatively recent decades (1960's through 1980's). The photos and descriptions of the clothes are good, but the inventory itself seemed a little bland. No mention of international shipping is made, so e-mail them if you live outside the United States. The owners of this online shop are located in Albuquerque, New Mexico, but no physical store or business address is mentioned. Phone: 505-275-2601 and 888-255-7731 (New Mexico only); fax: 505-275-1155.

Dandelion Vintage Clothing
www.dandelion-vintage.com

$ 👡👡👡

The inventory is diverse and affordable, the photos are good, and the items are carefully described, making the site worth a look. You'll find Victorian pieces along with 1930's through 1970's clothes, lingerie, and a selection of petite and plus-sized items. Checks (with a wait), money orders, and credit cards are accepted (the latter via PayPal). International shipping available. No addresses or phone numbers are mentioned.

Davenport & Co.
www.davenportandco.com

$$ 👡👡👡👡

Davenport & Co. has offered fine vintage clothing online since 1997. This site features about thirty categories in which to browse. Victorian clothing, 1940's hats and accessories, 1960's/1970's polyester, men's vintage clothing, vintage movie magazines, size 12 and up, and wedding gowns all contain terrific items in a range of prices. We liked a 1960's Lilli Ann green wool calf-length coat with three-quarter sleeves, lined in green silk crepe with a wide white-mink collar. Linda was intrigued enough to click on the thumbnail photo; the site then showed pictures of the front and back view and a close-up of the mink collar. Lots of other items did not have labels, and there was no search engine. This fast-loading, well-stocked site is regularly updated, and there were links to other vintage clothing and jewelry sites. International orders are accepted, and it is easy to order either by clicking on the money order or check link or their credit card order form that accepts Visa, MasterCard, American Express, Diners Club, and JBC. Shipping is via U.S. priority mail, and requests for a refund must be made within three days of receipt. Returns are subject to a 10 percent restocking fee. They accept layaways for items over $75 with a 25 percent deposit. Mailing address: Dee Davenport Howe, 146 Bowdein Street, Springfield, MA 01109.

Decadestwo
www.decadestwo.com
$$–$$$ 🦋🦋🦋

This promising site was created by the owners of the legendary Los Angeles vintage boutique Decades—the original flagship store for high-end designer and couture vintage clothes—and its newer store downstairs, Decades Two, which specializes in consigned "contemporary couture," or items of recent vintage. Although in its early stages at the time of this writing, Decadestwo offered a small but intriguing sample of things to (hopefully) come: Richard Tyler gowns, Alaïa suits, and all manner of exquisite high-end designer goodies. We look forward to seeing the inventory expand, as this site will undoubtedly become a must-see for those shoppers who are prepared to splurge for something really special. International shipping is available; returns are accepted within forty-eight hours only. Accepted payment methods are Visa, MasterCard, American Express, or check-card. Mailing address: 8214 Melrose Avenue, Los Angeles, CA 90035 (323-655-1960; fax: 323-655-1450).

Designer Exposure
www.designerexposure.com
$$–$$$

Frequent visits to Maria Williams's excellent website over the last couple of years have provided us with hours of shopping pleasure. There are many ways to browse the inventory: by designer, sale items, new arrivals, and gift suggestions as well as recent additions of auctions and classified departments. Though this website is based in Auckland, New Zealand, items can be shipped from New York, Los Angeles, and Sydney. On a recent visit this extremely user-friendly site listed 214 of our favorite designers from A to Z. One might not find pieces by designers all of the time, particularly after one of Maria's big sales: Once you register you will be invited to these. Heads up! You'll have to hurry. The popular items sell out quickly as this is a well-trafficked store, registering 1.2 million hits a month. You'll enjoy seeing multiple views of the clothing though the descriptions are minimal. One click sends selections to your dressing room for a week or more, though they are still available for others to buy. A click on "Buy Now" will calculate your shipping charges (usually by UPS), and you can change your mind just as easily with the "Delete Item" button. Credit cards are accepted. Returns are accepted for credit within seven days. Williams rates her clothes' condition from new to very good. She doesn't stock vintage clothing as such but offers a wealth of fabulous recent preworn designer clothing. Shipping can be expensive, especially if the item is being sent from Sydney or Auckland. However, the clothing arrives quickly. Packaging is decidedly no-frills. Both

Maria and the webmaster, who is eager to help you work out
technical problems, answer e-mails promptly. We've shopped
this site long enough to have noticed improvements, particularly
in page-loading speed. This site is at the top of our Book-
marks/Favorites list. Mailing address: 14 Gillies Avenue, Newmarket, Auckland, New Zealand (011-64-5245954).

dresshopnyc
www.dresshopnyc.com
$$ ✗ ✗ ✗ ✗

You're greeted by a vintage black-and-white photo of a woman
with a bird on her head. Then you can rummage the virtual racks
of this site and find all sorts of iconic treasures, from a Bonnie
Cashin trench coat to a Lilly Pulitzer golf skirt to a fabulous Lilli
Ann skirt suit from the 1940's. Most of the smallish inventory
hails from the 1920's through the 1960's, and, while some prices
seem a little steep, there is a section of goodies that are offered for
less than $65. The photos are clear and the descriptions are de-
tailed and helpful; alas, a number of items were marked "sold."
Visa, MasterCard, Discover, and American Express are all ac-
cepted (as well as money orders). Returns are subject to a 15 per-
cent restocking fee. No physical store or business address is
mentioned. Phone: 212-260-5474.

1860–1960
www.1860-1960.com
$$ ✗ ✗ ✗ ✗

This is an elegant, spare site that focuses on the Victorian era,
despite the dates implied by its name. A costume designer for
Merchant-Ivory films would have a field day here, as there are
some truly exquisite antique dresses and skirts in their inventory.

Sizes tend to be small—an unfortunate characteristic of turn-of-the-century clothing—but the quality and historical value of the garments make this site worth a look. Shoes, dresses, hats, and accessories can be bought using Visa, MasterCard, and PayPal. Returns are accepted within three days of receipt. They maintain three shops within antique markets in Southern California: Santa Monica Antique Market, 1607 Lincoln Boulevard, Santa Monica, CA 90404 (310-314-4899); Gift Garden Antiques and Collectibles, 15266 Antioch Street, Pacific Palisades, CA 90272 (310-459-4114); and Cranberry House Antique Center, 12318 Ventura Boulevard, Studio City, CA 91604 (818-506-8945).

Emma Good's Fine Antiques
www.emmagood.com
$$ ⤳⤳

This Internet-based antique shop has an outstanding but small inventory of antique clothing from 1840 to 1900, hats and bonnets and other accessories, and quilts and coverlets. They participate in antique shows, "predominantly in northwest Indiana." Inquiries may be sent via e-mail. They accept checks, money orders, and cashier's checks. Returns are accepted. A 1998 or 1999 vintage clothing calendar is free with a purchase: Although it's out of date, it's great for research.

Enoki
www.enokiworld.com
$$ ⤳⤳⤳⤳⤳

Expect to spend a few hours at this inventive and impressive online vintage clothing and department store. This site keeps its massive audience constantly amused and informed. You'll start at a photo and enter a site filled with places to go. Stylish and upbeat, Enoki lists the frequently updated departments by date and subject. On one visit we found outerwear by North Beach Leather, John Anthony, Bonnie Cashin, Pauline Trigère, and Mario Valentino. The vintage Azzedine Alaïa boutique is a must for his fans. Included are links to info, lifestyle, accessories, clothing, *Space* (their magazine of style news), and contact information. Some listings include pertinent background information on the designer. Clicking on the "fist full of dollars" logo takes you immediately to their order form.

They grade the clothing from flawless to poor, though Enoki does not sell garments in fair or poor condition. Enokiworld is happy to provide additional measurements (they describe their sizing and measuring methods) beyond what is given. You'll find their customer testimonials in "Buzz." Shipping is via UPS, and Missouri residents will be charged sales tax. Enoki accepts Visa, MasterCard, and American Express. Returns are accepted within ten days of their shipping date with a 20 percent restocking fee, and you must e-mail them immediately with your intentions. Shipping charges are not refundable. Be sure to check out Enokiworld's other departments, including furnishings, magazines, books, music, and toys and games.

Enokiworld is one of the most stylish vintage sites we visited. Located in St. Louis, Missouri (314-725-0735).

Eureka, I Found It!

www.eureka-i-found-it.com

$ ✈ ✈

Scan the long list of categories on this antique site and you'll see vintage clothing, vintage hats, and jewelry. In the clothing area, we found a men's Hawaiian shirt and a batik sport jacket. The most interesting items were the hats: A Schiaparelli tall hat made from swirls of ivory netting resembled a marshmallow and was in excellent, clean condition for $65. The inventory is small, but the site is worth a look. Checks or money orders as well as Visa and MasterCard through PayPal are accepted.

Evalueville
www.evalueville.com
$–$$ ✂ ✂ ✂ ✂

Also known on eBay by the seller name evalueville, this huge volume seller, located in Hattiesburg, Mississippi, offers men's and women's designer clearance clothing and shoes and accessories from major department stores like Bloomingdale's. Thousands of items are up for auction on any given day. We bought a John Galliano cutting-edge jacket, with its original $1,485 price tag still attached, for $104.50 and a pair of $310 Yoshiki Hishinuma pants for $17.50. Items are new with tags and graded for the degree of their shopworn condition. This secure website e-mails you a link for credit card checkout. They ship via USPS, offering a reduced rate for multiple purchases on the same day. This is a very professional operation, but communication is difficult, front and back pictures of garments are small, and minimal narrative description is provided. When our garments arrived, they had been squeezed together into an envelope and needed pressing. Still, the price is right! There are no phone numbers or e-mail address posted on this site.

Fashion Design on Sale
www.fashiondesignonsale.com
$$ ✂ ✂

The authors found this site before we found each other! Fashion Design on Sale offers very recent (last season) designer fashions from cutting-edge contemporaries like Martin Margiela, Junya Watanabe, Veronique Branquinho, Prada, Gaultier, Ghost, and Yohji Yamamoto. The site has certainly grown more sophisticated over the last couple of years, but there are annoying factors: For example, some pictures are too small to view and others are too large to load quickly. Fashion Design on Sale offers only the briefest of descriptions and doesn't provide a garment's measurements. E-mailed questions are answered but not always in a helpful way. Items that are no longer available are tagged with flashing "sold" signs, and occasionally there is distracting music playing. Obviously this website is still evolving. Also known on eBay as fashiondesignonsale@yahoo.com. Credit cards are accepted and multiple sizes of some styles are often available.

Fashiondig Mall
www.fashiondig.com

This site is well designed for browsing and buying. It's not possible to search the individual Fashiondig sites for specific items. However, there is a profile of each seller on the right-hand side of his or her home page in a panel called "Fashiondig asks."

All That Glitters
www.fashiondig.com/allthatglitters/

$ ✂ ✂

We loved the graffiti-printed capri pants, perfect for that rare individual with thirty-two-inch hips. There are lots of rock and roll T-shirts here along with an offer to turn our wardrobes into rock and roll regalia. Credit card payments are accepted through Billpoint or PayPal, as are checks and money orders. Returns are accepted within five days.

Divine Finds
www.fashiondig.com/divinefinds/

$ ⚘⚘⚘

This Buffalo seller has great style and an outstanding collection of vintage handbags. You might find a spectacular 1950's cocktail dress accented with metallic colored ribbon, taffeta filler, and an outer layer of nylon net, or a mother-of-pearl compact in excellent condition. An order form pops up when you click the Order button. Checks, money orders, and credit cards are accepted through PayPal. Returns are accepted within seven days, subject to a 15 percent restocking charge.

Ellen Christine Eclectic
www.fashiondig.com/ellenchristine/

$$ ⚘⚘⚘

This site includes a hat history and examples of Ellen Christine's own handmade hats, which she designs using antique textiles and trims, and the site also features some very elegant vintage dresses, coats, and accessories from the nineteenth and twentieth centuries.

She accepts payment by MasterCard, Visa, American Express, Discover, postal and bank money orders, and personal checks (which require clearance before goods are shipped). No returns or refunds are allowed, so ask questions before ordering. Wholesale inquiries are welcome. Ellen Christine has two store locations:

Ellen Christine Millinery, 255 West 18 Street, New York, NY 10011 (212-242-2457), and Ellen Christine Millinery . . . by the sea, 668 Washington Street, Cape May, NJ 08204 (609-884-3888).

Frontino & Vaz Vintage
www.fashiondig.com/frontino-vaz/
$$ ✗ ✗ ✗ ✗

This is a superb spot to browse and shop for costume jewelry from the past century. Supersharp photographs of jewelry set with stones abound. New York sellers Georgene Frontino and Lucille Vaz sell their jewelry at antique shows on the East Coast. Names to look for here are Coro, Haskell, Eisenberg, Dior, Boucher, Trifari, and others. They accept MasterCard, Visa, and Diners Club as well as checks and money orders. Returns are accepted within seven days. Condition reports on request.

Mid Century Chic
www.fashiondig.com/midcenturychic/index.htm
$-$$ ✗ ✗ ✗ ✗

Heavily weighted with 1960's items, this is the place to visit for cool magazine clutches, Peter Max scarves, and the odd Pucci piece. The items appear in no particular order, but the inventory is fairly small, so it won't take long to scroll through its entirety. Be certain of your purchases, as there are no returns (with very limited exceptions), and pay for them with credit cards through PayPal or with money orders. International shipping is available. No physical store, phone, or business address is mentioned. Fax: 212-213-5225.

Nostalgic
www.fashiondig.com/nostalgic/index.htm
$$ ✗ ✗ ✗ ✗

For wonderful high-end vintage jackets and coats, you can't beat Nostalgic, another member of the Fashiondig virtual mall.

You'll find fabulous faux fur, real leather bomber and biker jackets by Schott, and one-of-a-kind outerwear pieces that will see you through many chilly seasons in serious style. This company is located in Port Reading, New Jersey, although it does not maintain a physical store. Returns must be made within seven days. MasterCard, Visa, American Express, and money orders are all accepted; international shipping is not mentioned (call or e-mail this company for more information if you live outside the United States). Phone: 732-636-4333; fax: 732-636-4280.

Orlando Vintage
www.fashiondig.com/orlandovintage/index.htm
$$ ✗ ✗ ✗ ✗

Here is another member of the Fashiondig group, and it's a great boutique indeed. You'll find all sorts of treasures "from flappers to Afros and everything in between." You might discover a rare Cuban souvenir bracelet, an alligator clutch, a Dior chain belt, and a vintage Oscar de la Renta gown, all during the same visit. Although the merchandise is listed in no particular order—making it a little tricky to search for specific items—the goods are interesting enough that sorting through them is a pleasure. At the time of this writing, there was a superb selection of vintage Lilly Pulitzer pieces available. Who knows what goodies will turn up next? Returns are accepted within seven days; no mention of international shipping is made, so e-mail or call first. Pay for your finds with Visa, MasterCard, American Express, Discover, money orders, or personal checks (with a wait). There is a physical store—near Orlando—at 2117 West Fairbanks Avenue, Winter Park, FL 32789; this is also the business address. Phone: 407-599-7225.

5 and Dime Vintage
www.510vintage.com

$-$$ ✄ ✄ ✄

This Denver store has operated online since 1998. Since 1993 their retail outlet has offered vintage jeans in both worn and new old stock from the 1970's. Bell-bottoms style 684 (big bells!) were priced at $75. Many of the dresses we browsed had no labels, though the Hawaiian shirts did, and there were lots of vintage T-shirts. They also buy vintage items, and you can check their want list. Payment is accepted by money order, check, MasterCard, Visa, or Discover. Returns are accepted on a case-by-case basis. Retail store address is 606 East 13 Avenue, Denver, CO 80203 (303-818-8107).

Funk & Junk
www.funkandjunk.com

$$ ✄ ✄

If you apply the brakes when you spy a tag sale with lots of funk and junk to sift through, then this is the website for you. Funk & Junk claims to have tens of thousands of items, though it appeared that only some of them were posted. If you are looking for something in particular, use their search engine. There were 422 items listed in their vintage clothing category, though we were never quite sure what we would find or if it was still available. We found a *Mork & Mindy* Na-No Na-No T-shirt for $40. There are many ways to search this site, and the descriptions were quite adequate. They will accept items for consignment. Credit cards (Visa, MasterCard, and American Express), checks, and money orders are accepted. UPS shipping. A request for a refund must be sent within twenty-four hours of receipt of the item and is subject to review.

Gansevoort Gallery
www.gansevoortgallery.com
$$$ ☆ ☆ ☆ ☆

Located in the meat-packing district of New York City, this gallery is owned by Mark McDonald, formerly of the legendary Fifty/50 Gallery. It is the place to go for museum-quality mid-century jewelry by American and Scandinavian designers. There is always a particularly wonderful selection of work by Art Smith and occasionally a piece by Alexander Calder. Mailing address: 72 Gansevoort Street, New York, NY 10014 (212-633-0555).

Glorious Vintage: Vintage Treasures from the '40s to the '70s
www.gloriousvintage.com
$ ☆ ☆ ☆

A stylish black-and-white page invites buyers directly into the many departments of this interesting vintage clothing site. The medium-sized inventory is divided into 1950's little black dresses, 1960's high fashion, prom dresses, blouses, gloves, and lingerie, though most impressive is the collection of men's smoking jackets. The majority of the clothes are reasonably priced, well described, and nicely photographed. Returns (for exchange) are accepted with three days' notification. Pay for your selections with BidPay, money orders, or certified checks only. This site is based in Montreal, Canada, though no physical store is mentioned; the owner requests that buyers e-mail her for the address and phone number. International shipping is available.

Gotham City Online
www.shopgco.com
$-$$ ☆ ☆ ☆ ☆ ☆

This is a very special feel-good site that is not only well stocked and easy to use but also the premier charitable clothing retailer in the New York City area. Highly visible as an eBay power seller (using seller names etreasures and missvintage), the website and retail warehouse outlet offer men's, women's, and children's clothing. In addition to gently used and vintage clothing, Gotham City Online offers new-with-tags designer clothing and retailer overstocks and returned merchandise. Search by designer names, types of garments, and sizes, as well as men's, women's, girl's, and baby categories. Christian Dior, Bob Mackie, Yves Saint Laurent, Prada, Banana Republic, and Kenzo were available when we visited. Click on thumbnail photos that lead to two more excellent views of each garment. Questions are answered within the day, and your satisfaction is guaranteed. Free shipping for orders over $75. Credit card payment via PayPal. Retail outlet at: 800 31 Street, Union City, NJ 07087 (212-625-8208).

Groovy Juice
www.groovyjuice.com

$ ♪ ♪ ♪

Lanajean Vecchione started selling vintage clothing in Providence, Rhode Island, in the 1970's and has since relocated to San Mateo, California. She sells 1960's and 1970's men's and women's clothing, dress patterns, and vintage denim; she also has a category called "Fun Stuff." She accepts checks, money orders, or cash; and you can order via e-mail. There are links to her online auctions through eBay or BidPay. Ms. Vecchione is the author of *Fashion Flashbacks 1960–1979*.

Hemlock Vintage Clothing
www.hemlockvintage.com

$ ✍ ✍

Categories on the home page of this online store include accessories, shoes, women's and men's clothing, updates and new additions, gallery, fashion in history articles, and links. Though it was
easily navigated by period, from 1800 to the 1970's, and by garment type, such as sweaters, lingerie, and coats—and the photographs were good—there were many more items listed as "on
hold" than there were offered for sale. More items appear in the
1940's through the 1950's category than do in the 1960's and
1970's groupings. Hemlock's sales policy informs us that their
measurements are taken flat (making it easy to compare measurement to those of garments we own), that they guarantee the authenticity of their items, and that they encourage questions. Pay
by credit card, money order, or personal check. Their phone number is furnished on request, and there is no return on sale items.
Other returns require prior notification and will be charged a 5 to
10 percent restocking fee. Shipping is not reimbursable, and their
return policy stipulates that you must not have worn the garment.
Hemlock Vintage Clothing is located in Minneapolis.

Hip Resale
www.hipresale.com

$$ ✍ ✍ ✍

This is a "portal" website that allows online shoppers to visit a
number of participating vintage and resale sites. Bookmark
this site if you love handbags, as the majority of the goods of-
fered by its member sites were designer purses: gently used
ones and discounted new ones. At the time of this writing,
there was a limited amount of clothing on one site and a link

to the Nordstrom online sale site. Most sellers offer international shipping.

Ho-Hose Vintage & Classic Nylon Stockings
www.ho-hose.co.uk

$ ⚔ ⚔ ⚔

We love sites with counters. This one that specializes in vintage and classic nylon stockings had racked up 336,650 visitors on the day we logged on. You can click on Ho-Hose's Top 50 or visit a web ring of similar items. Many brands are listed, and they accept credit cards through PayPal. We particularly enjoyed the glossary of hosiery terms. Shipping to the United States is by international recorded delivery, airmail insured.

Identity.com
www.external-identity.com

$$-$$$ ⚔ ⚔ ⚔ ⚔

If you are fan of the Belgian designer Martin Margiela, you will love this stylish and trendy website. Starting at a Rorschach blob of cobalt blue on a white ground, you'll select from men's or women's preworn or new garments and browse through designers from a who's who of the European avant-garde: Comme des Garçons, Costume National, Ann Demeulemeester, and Helmut Lang. The site is easily navigated and has super photographs. You will enjoy the clean organization of this website. Garments are graded 5 (mint) to 1, though nothing under 2 appears on this site. A gorgeous pair of Costume National pointy-toe men's loafers, size 9½ (but fitting like a 10), was $450. The owner of the site prefers that you fax your credit card number, as the site does not have a secure server, or you can send the number in three separate e-mails. MasterCard, Visa, personal checks, and money orders are all accepted. No return policy was given. Identity.com also lists items on eBay. Inquiries were promptly answered. Shipping is free anywhere in the world, however this policy does not extend to their eBay auctions. Mailing address: P.O. Box 6168, North Dunedin, Dunedin, New Zealand.

Iguana Vintage Clothing
www.iguanaclothing.com
$$ ⚘ ⚘ ⚘

An agreeable iguana that's all dressed up in a blue bow tie and sweater vest welcomes you to this well-illustrated website that presents an online selection from their retail store (pictured on the home page). Styles from the 1940's through the 1980's, men's and women's clothing, accessories, shoes, wigs, and eyeglasses are featured as well as new items made for the store. You may want to double-check on the availability of anything you see here before ordering. Discover, Visa, MasterCard, and American Express are accepted. All sales are final: no returns, refunds, or exchanges. Mailing address: 1422 Ventura Boulevard, Sherman Oaks, CA 91403 (818-907-6716).

Isadora's Antique and Vintage Clothing
www.isadoras.com
$$$ ⚘ ⚘ ⚘ ⚘ ⚘

This is the beautiful online version of the vintage and antique clothing store of the same name in Seattle. Isadora's sells attractive men's and women's antique clothing, accessories, and collectible estate jewelry; they also offer bridal gowns and evening wear. Excellent photos and descriptions are provided by Paisley Rae Buescher, the manager of online sales. She can be reached by e-mail for your special requests.

A pair of turn-of-the-century black silk and satin lace-up boots for an extremely narrow size 7 were in excellent condition and gorgeous; the price was a little steep for us, though, at $525.

Checks, money orders, Visa, MasterCard, and American Express are accepted. Returns are accepted after notification by e-mail less shipping and handling charges. Estate jewelry comes with appraisals. Mailing address: 1915 First Avenue, Seattle, WA 98101 (316-343-1484).

It's in the Past Vintage Clothing & Accessories
www.itsinthepast.com

$ ♞ ♞ ♞ ♞ ♞

There is a cartoonish whimsy to this site that offers a tremendous, searchable inventory of vintage clothes listed by categories, including "30's–70s," men's, ties, sewing/decor, and even boy's and girl's. The impressive selection of vintage handbags is not to be missed. They accept Visa, MasterCard, and American Express, and they ship internationally. Returns are accepted within five days of receipt, less shipping and a 10 percent restocking fee. Mailing address: 3706 Windyhollow Way, Mason, OH 45040 (513-339-0354).

Justsaywhen
www.justsaywhen.com

$$ ♞ ♞ ♞ ♞ ♞

The home page says it all: recent updates, designer names, and a "$150 and under" section. "Glam News" is a chance to win prizes like a vintage Pucci scarf. This is a great site for the harried shopper: You can click on "New Stuff" and see what's up or rush right into the "Contempo Closet." The "$150 and under" section offered a 1970's Geoffrey Beene, a 1960's Louis Féraud, a 1960's

Adele Simpson, and a fabulous Bill Blass one-shoulder, floor-length beaded gown with magenta sequins from the 1970's. Sizes and measurements are included in the thorough descriptions. A secure order form allows you to pay with Visa, MasterCard, and Discover. This site will ship internationally (a currency converter is available). Refunds within ten days, less credit card fees.

Milan, the site's owner and proprietor, offers her own personal closet for viewing. Don't forget to check out her favorite links. She has been selling vintage clothing for twenty-one years and is a frequent participant in the New York vintage clothing shows. (You can call Milan at 917-568-3784.)

Karen Augusta Antique Lace & Fashion
www.antique-fashion.com
$$$ ❧ ❧ ❧ ❧ ❧

(See the "Heroes" section of this book.) If your passion for vintage clothing includes museum-quality eighteenth- and nineteenth-century frocks and coats, you are in for hours of viewing pleasure at this website. Karen Augusta is one of the premier dealers in antique vintage clothing. Her collection is located on the third floor of the 1863 Gage House in southern Vermont. Museum curators, designers, stylists, and serious collectors can visit by appointment. In addition, Karen Augusta participates in the New York Vintage Fashion and Antique Textile Show.

The website can be searched by category (ladies' costume, ladies' undress, et cetera) and by era. The antique items are exquisite and expensive, including a women's hooded cloak circa 1780–1800 for $1,650. Superb descriptions that include country of origin are provided, as well as materials: "Pale gray silk satin, ivory china silk lining, silk ribbons. Gray silk used on the hood has a pinkish tone." Provenance for this is listed as "Ann Bolton Booth originally from Chestertown, MD, and later from Philadelphia, PA." In addition, a small paper label pinned to the cloak is dated 1791.

Linda gasped while viewing an 1878 Emile Pingat wedding gown from Paris for $5,800. Clothing on this website is photographed exceptionally well.

Karen requests that you call, fax, or e-mail to reserve an item. Visa and MasterCard are accepted for orders over $100. Money orders and bank or personal checks are accepted. Returns are by agreement: notification within twenty-four hours and shipped in the original packing within three days of receipt. Refund will be less shipping and handling charges. Each garment was artfully presented in this outstanding online store. Very unusual items included roller skates from the 1880's, a four-piece matador costume from the late nineteenth century, and a women's bicycle dress from the early 1900's. Karen also buys museum-quality items and includes a want list with her requirements. Highly selective, easily navigated, beautifully presented: an outstanding vintage site. Karen Augusta answered our inquiries quickly. Mailing address: 33 Gage Street, North Westminster, VT 05101 (802-463-3333).

Karma Vintage Clothing
www.karmaboutique.com
$ 🖊🖊🖊
A psychedelic pink-and-blue splash page welcomes the vintage shopper to a site well organized into departments and sizes (for example, women's small). There are plenty of affordable dresses and skirts in this collection; the wonderfully funky men's shirts

shouldn't be missed, either. No physical store or business address is mentioned; no phone number is given. Returns are accepted if notification occurs within three days. No further information about placing orders could be found on the site; it is suggested that interested buyers e-mail them.

Kickshaw Vintage & Antique Clothing
www.kickshawproductions.com
$-$$ ⚘ ⚘ ⚘

This Toronto-based group has been working as fashion historians and curators since 1978. They evaluate and appraise collections for museums and insurance companies as well as sell vintage clothing dating from the nineteenth century to the recent designer collections of Ann Demeulemeester. They are the curators of three traveling exhibitions that are described on their very straightforward and easy-to-use website. Search by era or categories. Prices are in U.S. dollars. Click on a thumbnail and more detailed photographs will appear. A purple velvet toque circa 1913 from John Wannamaker in excellent condition was $250. A black-chiffon-over-black-crepe evening dress from the late 1960's, in excellent condition, was $45. When we visited, sixty-two items—including shoes and vintage fashion photographs—were available from these sellers, known on eBay as kickshawproductions. Order by e-mail. There are no returns and no refunds. Shipping is via express insured (seven-day delivery from Canada to the United States) and was about $11.50 for our purchase. Pay by money order, cashier's check, or credit card through Billpoint. Mailing address: Jonathan Walford & Kenn Norman, 3 Church Hill, P.O. Box 1388, Fonthill, Ontario, Canada L0S 1E0 (905-892-9103).

Kismet Couture

www.kismetcouture.com

$ 🐾 🐾 🐾

Fashionable shoppers who favor the styles of the last two decades will enjoy this site, as they offer both men's and women's clothing—from the recent past—at reasonable prices. The site is very well organized and easy to navigate, and although the photos were very slow to load, they were clear and sharp. The detailed descriptions include measurements; read them carefully, as no returns are accepted. Visa, MasterCard, Discover, and American Express may be used to pay for your purchases. International shipping is available. No physical store is mentioned. Mailing address: 1390 Ocean Drive, Miami Beach, FL 33139 (305-534-2600).

Kitty Girl Vintage

www.kittygirlvintage.com

$$ 🐾 🐾 🐾 🐾

A photo of the red-haired model from the 1950's Suzy Parker welcomes you to this elegant site. We went to the Bamboo Room first where we found featured Hawaiian dresses, including an example by one of Deborah's favorite designers, Shaheen. Swimwear, play clothes, and vintage Hawaiian sarong dresses abound. There was a great assortment of Bakelite jewelry, including a pair of Scottie dog barrettes. This website has its own search engine, or you can browse pages on clothing from the 1910's–1930's, 1940's–1960's, lingerie, shoes, and Kitty's links and customer feedback. Credit cards (MasterCard, Visa, and American Express) are accepted on their secure site, as are checks and money orders. Shipping is via priority mail. Refunds are given on returns received within ten days in unworn and un-damaged condition, less their shipping charges. Phone: 415-386-6774.

La Boutique Resale
www.laboutiqueresale.com
$$–$$$ 𝒜 𝒜 𝒜

Here is a small but selective online resale boutique with a corresponding physical store in New York City. Typical offerings include suits by Chanel, Alaïa, and Trigère, as well as a smattering of accessories. While the no-frills site does not have the selection you'd expect of a Madison Avenue designer resale shop, bear in mind that the physical boutique itself undoubtedly has many treasures for those who are able to visit Manhattan; perhaps greater numbers of goodies will wind up on the website as online orders come in. Accepted methods of payment are MasterCard, Visa, Diners Club, and PayPal. There is no mention of international shipping, so call or e-mail the store if you live outside the United States. Store address (and mailing address): 1045 Madison Avenue, New York, NY 10021 (212-517-8099).

Language
www.language-nyc.com
$$–$$$ 𝒜 𝒜 𝒜 𝒜

Language is a New York City–based "department" store that sells a little bit of everything in its 2,500 square-foot space in the Nolita section of downtown Manhattan. From home furnishings to beauty products, Language sports a trendy mix of fashion, art, and lifestyle items. New clothing by designers like Miguel Androver and Chloé appear alongside vintage items like a $4,000 Hermès Kelly bag and a spectacular black beaded 1920's flapper full-length gown. We enjoyed browsing their back issues of *Visionaire*. Think of this as a full-service store. Credit cards are accepted; shipping is via UPS and priority mail. Returns are not accepted. Store is located at 238 Mulberry Street, New York, NY 10012 (888-474-5566).

Laura's Designer Resale Boutique
www.getchic.com

$$ ✈ ✈ ✈ ✈

This is a well-stocked online outlet for a store that presents "designer clothing from the closets of Hollywood celebrities." This fast-loading site offers a wide range of items, such as a child's size 10 David Charles black velvet jacket with gold bow and an Alaïa black leather belt. Order through a secure server (no credit cards were accepted for international orders). All sales at Laura's are final, and you can e-mail her with your special requests. The store address is 12426 Ventura Boulevard, Studio City, CA 91604 (818-752-2835).

Little Treasures Vintage
www.littletreasures.net

$ ✈ ✈ ✈

Gardenias decorate the home page of this site, some of whose clothes are sold at Antiques & More, 327 Pine Avenue, Long Beach, CA 90802 (562-437-3040). The site proclaims that clothing from this store graced the front and back covers of *Shabby Chic*. Jewelry and hats, as well as vintage compacts and perfume and powder sets, are included in their inventory. Visa and MasterCard are accepted through PayPal; also accepted are American Express, money orders, and personal checks. Your items are held in reserve until payment is received and then the item is marked sold.

Shipping is via U.S. mail. The site offers a layaway plan with a 30 percent down payment required. A return notice is requested within twenty-four hours, and the refund does not include shipping charges. No returns on sale or layaway items.

The Mod Haus
http://modhaus.com
$ ✗ ✗ ✗

A flower-power-meets-burlap-themed splash page welcomes the vintage shopper, who is invited to browse a very small—albeit interesting—inventory of clothes, as well as jewelry, art, and other nonfashion items. The funky wearables that were in stock at the time of this writing included a Lanvin coat, a Givenchy Qiana shirt, and a nice range of "art jewelry." Most pieces are from the 1950's through the 1970's. International shipping is not mentioned, but the order form includes a box for your country, implying its availability. Visa, MasterCard, American Express, and online checks and money orders are all accepted. No physical store or business address is mentioned. Phone: 617-464-4485.

Modvictoria.com: Fabulous Modernist Jewelry
www.modvictoria.com
$–$$ ✗ ✗ ✗

Victoria Tillotson is a jewelry dealer and designer who teaches jewelry design at the School of Visual Arts in New York. Her site features silver Modernist jewelry from American studio designers as well as work by Scandinavian and Israeli designers. Payment is by credit card through PayPal. Money orders and checks are also accepted. Shipping and insurance are $5. Mailing address: Box 1619, Radio City Station, New York, NY 10101.

Mopcloset
www.mopcloset.com

$ ⚞⚞⚞⚞

The clever layout of this site calls to mind the atomic-age-patterned tableware of the 1950's. The inventory is medium-large, and they offer lots of vintage basics for the beginning collector: swing dresses, shift dresses, and ugly-cute golf pants with some of the loudest patterns imaginable. Amid the whimsically named clothes—dresses entitled "Bake Sale Betty," "Retro Teacher," and "Fair Lillith," for example—are a number of serious bargains, such as a pair of vintage, low-slung Levi's ("Crack Problem"). The site takes Visa, MasterCard, and American Express, as well as personal checks with a waiting period. They accept returns up to fifteen days after purchase. No physical store is mentioned. Mailing address: 8503 Antler Drive, St. Louis, MO 63117 (314-863-1254).

M. Schon
www.mschon.com

$$ ⚞⚞⚞⚞⚞

This site features Modernist handmade jewelry from the 1950's. It's beautifully designed with clear photos and descriptions of important and unique jewelry. You'll find Danish (Georg Jensen), Mexican (Taxco), and American Modernists from New York City. There is a secure order form for Visa, MasterCard, and American Express. Checks must clear before shipping, and money orders are also an acceptable form of payment. This seller—who was featured in *Elle* magazine—offers a seventy-two-hour return policy.

Nancy's Nifty Nook

www.nancysniftynook.com

$ ✄ ✄ ✄ ✄ ✄

The roses-and-lace background suggests a delicate, fragile sort of site, but Nancy's is a force with which to reckon. Departments abound, from hats, accessories, "50's–60's," and lingerie, to bridal, sewing, and sale sections; there's even a helpful section on care and cleaning. The easily navigated site offers a search function to help you narrow things down while browsing its large inventory of treasures. Photos of the clothes themselves are clear and are accompanied by detailed descriptions. They ship internationally and accept Visa, MasterCard, and Discover. Returns are only accepted if they "misrepresented an item." No physical store address is given. Phone: 877-663-5977.

Neen's Vintage

www.neens.com

$–$$ ✄ ✄ ✄ ✄ ✄

Although this site seems a little cluttered and tricky to navigate smoothly, summon your patience, as the sheer volume of clothes, accessories, and shoes—mostly from the 1940's through the 1970's—makes Neen's worth a visit. The length of the formal gowns' listing rivals the height of the volcanoes that appear in the backgrounds of some of the Hawaiian vacation photos. And, yes, you'll find a wonderful section of Hawaiiana, for men as well as women, showcasing the exotic prints of the recent as well as distant past. Pay for your tropical treasures with Visa, MasterCard, or personal check (with a wait), and be sure to notify them within three days if you need to return something. International shipping is available. No physical store is mentioned, but they participate in several vintage clothing shows (consult the website for recent dates). Mailing address: P.O. Box 230178, Tigard, OR 97281 (888-343-0383).

Nelda's Vintage Clothing
www.neldasvintageclothing.com

$ ♘ ♘ ♘ ♘

This site has a decidedly feminine appeal, with its pink background and "hip chick" graphics, but the well-organized, medium-large inventory includes clothes and accessories for men, too. The designs from the 1940's to 1970's are Nelda's strong suit, so to speak, and you'll find everything subdivided into eras, making it simple to focus on your favorite look; the men's jacket section is a must-see. Everything is well photographed and described in detail. Choose carefully, since returns are only accepted for store credit and will incur a 15 percent restocking fee. International shipping is available. Pay with Visa, MasterCard, American Express, money orders, and PayPal. Business address: 1621 North Main Street, Suite 3, San Antonio, TX 78212 (210-271-7111).

No New Stuff!
www.nonewstuff.com

$$ ♘ ♘ ♘ ♘

Retro clothing and accessories are sold on this website for the fifteen-year-old vintage clothing store Jezebel, in Fort Lauderdale, Florida. There is a funky, pastel splash page with great typography and fun categories like "Groovy Garb," "Fabrics & Notions," "All Gussied Up," and "This Just In." Thirty-six items were listed in their "All Gussied Up" section, including a pink-and-purple Pucci robe from Formfit-Rogers, and a 1950's glitter-in-plastic bracelet and earrings set.

Their Laundry room includes lots of recommendations including, "Don't store your linens starched (a bug's gourmet treat!)." A product called "Sharon's Solution," a gentle wash for linens and lace, sells here at $12.99. Payment methods accepted include Visa, MasterCard, American Express, and money orders. You order is placed on hold until you call in your credit card number or mail your payment. No return policy was stated. Store address: 1980 East Sunrise Boulevard, Fort Lauderdale, FL 33304 (954-761-7881).

The Outskirts Vintage Garb
www.theoutskirts.com
$ 🪡

Offering a selection of vintage clothes and accessories from "pre-40's to 70's," this site has a small inventory that is described in a truly minimalist way; a buyer who's interested in any particular item should definitely e-mail the site for more information. The photographs are small and grainy, and many of them did not load, despite repeated visits to the site. Returns are accepted within ten days if buyer notifies them no more than twenty-four hours after receiving the item. Visa, MasterCard, Discover, checks (with a wait), money orders, and PayPal are all accepted. A "Base Store" is mentioned, the address of which appears to be The Outskirts Vintage Clothing, Farmington Falls, ME. No phone number is mentioned.

Piece Unique
www.pieceunique.com
$$$ 🪡 🪡 🪡 🪡 🪡

This intriguing consignment site bills itself as a "Recent and Vintage Haute Couture Online Catalog." You can expect to find flawless garments by Chanel, Gucci, Gianni Versace, and Armani, to name only a few of the well-known designer labels on virtual display. You can also expect some breathtaking prices: When we visited, Piece Unique was offering—in the "Recent Garments" department—a bandage dress by the French designer Hervé Léger for $1,450, a fox-fur-trimmed Hermès parka for $1,690, and a paillette-covered suit by Fendi for $1,980. Of course, as style mavens are well aware, these stunning clothes would be even pricier in retail boutiques. Other departments include "Recent Accessories," "Vintage Garments" (a great source for 1980's Chanel), and "Vintage Accessories." This online boutique is based in Los Angeles, California; no address is mentioned. Accepted payment methods include Visa, MasterCard, and money orders; foreign buyers must pay with an international money order in U.S. dollars. To place an order or inquire about selling high-end designer and couture pieces, contact Piece Unique directly, either via e-mail or telephone: 310-444-0452.

POSH Vintage
www.poshvintage.com
$$ ❧❧❧

The inventory is still on the small side at this promising new site, but fans of chic 1960's and 1970's clothes will enjoy browsing the slinky knit dresses and made-for-dancing jumpsuits. Departments include dresses, handbags, coats and jackets, shoes, and—our favorite—a combo platter that offers all manner of interesting vintage pieces, for example, a genuine 1940's Jantzen ruched "starlet swimsuit," a fabulous floral 1960's cocktail gown, and a flawless vintage silk dressing gown fit for a modern-day diva. POSH accepts Visa, MasterCard, PayPal, money orders, and personal checks (with a wait). Returns must be made within three days of receipt and are subject to a 20 percent restocking fee. International shipping is not mentioned, although there is a space provided for "country" on the purchasing form; e-mail them to confirm. No phone number, business address, or physical store is mentioned; however, we presume this is a Florida site, since residents of that state are advised of the additional sales tax they will incur.

Red Rose Vintage Clothing
www.rrnspace.com

$-$$ ✗ ✗ ✗ ✗

This is a cool retro site that uses a TV set from the 1950's in its home page design. Established in 1979, Red Rose Vintage Clothing has a retail store in Indianapolis.

Men's clothing is well represented, and the prices are good. We found a Catalina snowflake cotton shirt for $25 and a 1940's double-breasted black topcoat for $75. Store policies are clearly stated, including shipping (via UPS). Website buttons are labeled decades, men's department, bargain basement, sale items, links, et cetera. There's plenty of good humor at this site, with references to a cat named Ralph, who is the store manager. Their FAQs even posture a bit on the quality of the Chicago Cubs baseball team! Clicking on the thumbnail photos reveals large clear photos. To order you must e-mail your request along with the item number or call them. Since this website is an annex of their retail operation, this is the best way to secure your purchase. Store and mailing address: 834 East 64 Street, Indianapolis, IN 46220 (317-257-5016).

Reminiscing Vintage Fashions
www.reminiscing.com

$$ ✒✒✒

This site specializes in women's clothing from the turn of the twentieth century to the 1940's. We encountered a large group of 1940's ball gowns. Photos are very good on this site. There are multiple views in extremely sharp focus along with detailed descriptions. Order via e-mail. Credit card payment can be made through Billpoint; checks and money orders are also accepted. Shipping is via priority mail. No refunds or returns. Mailing address: P.O. Box 1822, Pompano Beach, FL 33061 (954-941-0665).

Repertoire and Company
www.repertoireandco.com

$$ ✒✒✒✒

Set aside a little time when you visit this gorgeous site, because, if you're like us, you'll enjoy browsing the lovely photos of rich-colored gowns and textiles. Dresses from the early 1900's, mid-century suits, and 1970's evening wear are showcased in two galleries; also offered are accessories like signed costume jewelry, embroidered handbags, and beaded scarves and capelets. The owner—declaring herself "a collector with no more room"—describes each piece in detail. Designer labels abound. There is no information about international shipping, so e-mail the site first if you're outside the United States. The only possible downside is that credit cards are not accepted; instead, you'll need a money order, cash, or a personal check (with a wait period) if you want to add that amethyst velvet flapper dress to your own gallery. No physical store is mentioned. Mailing address: Dianne L. Magnusson, P.O. Box 833, Georgetown, CT 06829 (203-227-0415).

RetroActive
www.designervintage.com
$$ ⚘⚘⚘

The owner of this emerging—and very promising—vintage site maintains a strong presence on eBay, under the seller name Dexterdoggie. The vintage shopper will find plenty of enticing goodies here, including a small boatload of designer vintage clothes, an awe-inspiring collection of Hermès scarves, and a large array of vintage cashmere sweaters (the latter of which is accompanied by a piercing little screed regarding the geopolitics of this luxury fiber). Be aware that RetroActive's unique pieces sell quickly, so it's a good idea to call the owners before you get your heart set on a special scarf or a rare gown.

Also included on the site are useful sections about care and cleaning as well as tips for determining whether a garment is real couture or merely an off-the-rack piece. International shipping is not mentioned; e-mail them your inquiry. Visa, MasterCard, American Express, Discover, and money orders are accepted; returns require a $5 restocking fee. Mailing address: 58 River Street, Milford, CT 06460 (800-588-6050).

Retrodress
www.retrodress.com
$ ⚘⚘⚘

Here is a simply designed website using pink, black, and white that is easily navigated though modest in size. Retrodress is stocked with 1950's to 1980's women's suits, dresses, separates, coats, and shoes. Brief narratives describe their condition. Photos were a bit small but very sharp and clear. Oscar de la Renta, Lilli Ann, Burberry, and Vicky Tiel are represented here. A shopping cart system is used; credit cards are accepted (Visa, MasterCard, and American Express), as are personal checks and money orders. Shipping is via priority mail at a $5 flat rate. Returns within five days are subject to a 15 percent restocking fee. Mailing address: P.O. Box 312, Lakeside, CA 92040 (619-443-4933).

Revival Vintage
www.revivalvintage.com

$ 🛩🛩🛩

This is the online selection offered by a vintage store of the same name in Westwood, New Jersey. Clicking on the categories—which include Victorian to the 1930's, accessories, 1940's to 1950's, men's clothing, jewelry, and 1960's to 1970's—produces a grid-type chart with descriptions of items. Condition ratings range from near mint to fair: "These items," they state, "are available at discounted rates. But for the creative, they are still interesting pieces." Order by sending an e-mail to their order department. MasterCard, Visa, American Express, and Discover are accepted as well as money orders and personal checks. A full refund, less shipping charges, is available with notification postmarked within two to three days of receipt of garment. There is also an eBay link to this site. Mailing address: Kathy and David, Revival Vintage, 186 Center Avenue, Westwood, NJ 07675 (201-722-9005).

Romance Remembered by Cresa: Vintage Textiles of Yesterday
www.rrbycresa.com

$ 🛩🛩

This site offers a nice selection of old lace hankies and hats within its dark, misty pages. And prices are so reasonable, a buyer might feel as if she'd entered a time warp. Not too much is offered in the way of clothing; there is a limited amount of home textiles (like tablecloths and doilies) available. These feminine finds may be purchased using Visa, MasterCard, and electronic checks; contact them for information on international shipping. Returns are accepted with two days' notification. Based in Texas, although no physical store or business address is given. Phone: 877-449-3683.

Rusty Zipper Vintage Clothing and King Poodle
www.rustyzipper.com, www.kingpoodle.com
$-$$ ✂ ✂ ✂ ✂

These online boutiques are linked, and both websites are extremely easy to navigate. Jen and Rob Chadwick offer over five thousand unique items of men's and women's 1940's to 1980's vintage clothing, accessories, ties, sewing patterns, and fabrics. A size chart is provided. You can easily search by decade, accessory type, dress style, jacket, fabric, size, and price. A keyword search for a 1950's bowling shirt in a women's size medium turned up two vintage shirts and five reproductions. Established in 1996, Rusty Zipper posts some of their magazine and newspaper reviews. The King Poodle site is their discount vintage site where everything is priced below $10. You can easily go back and forth between the two sites and search and order from both. The owners used to have a vintage clothing store but now do all of their selling via the web. Sign up for their mailing list and enjoy. This site is easy to use, and the prices are great. Order using Master-Card, Visa, and American Express. The site provides no hassle returns and delivery in one week or less for $6 in the United States. International shipping is available. We think this boutique pairing is one of the best on the web.

Sazz Vintage Clothing
www.sazzvintage.com

$$ ✗ ✗ ✗

Sazz Vintage is a relatively new website based in Philadelphia. It offers many categories for the rockabilly fan: Western shirts, swing dresses, 1970's disco shirts, accessories, coats, jackets, and even some kids' clothing. You can search for all available items, like 1950's cowgirl skirts with buckles and fringe, by list or descriptions. This is quite helpful if you're looking for something specific. Payment is accepted through PayPal or money order, and $5.50 covers the shipping. International shipping is offered, and the seller will hold an item for three days. Returns accepted within seven days, and refunds do not include shipping charges.

Sleek 'n Chic Vintage Lingerie
www.sleeknchic.co.uk

$$ ✗ ✗ ✗

While the website is located in the United Kingdom, all prices are in U.S. dollars. Click on rare items and see luxurious delights like 1950's vintage silk stockings (not panty hose and not nylon!) for $79.99 and a vintage black Strapless Delight slip with a wired bodice and side zippers in new, unworn condition for $175.49. This site also has retro eyewear, though there are no guarantees that the glasses can be fitted with contemporary lens material. They accept credit card orders through PayPal along with checks and money orders. U.K. orders have a different shipping address, and customs may apply for them. This site is linked to Frilz and Lace (www.frilzandlace.com), a site for contemporary and new undergarments. Mailing address: P.O. Box 4106, Clifton Park, NY 12065 (518-371-4722).

AZillion SPARKLZ
www.sparkleplenty.com
$-$$ ✈ ✈ ✈ ✈ ✈

This site is true to its name and will literally dazzle the vintage jewelry collector. Do you adore Bakelite or covet Schiaparelli? Are most of your mad-money pennies reserved for funky little jeweled pins, or, on the other hand, do you seek the ultimate Miriam Haskell necklace? It's all here. The orderliness of the site is impressive, considering the sheer volume of baubles offered. Be sure to check out the mesh evening bags and 14-karat gold vintage charms, too. International shipping is available; returns are generally handled on an individual basis, so choose carefully. Payment is accepted via MasterCard, Visa, Discover, money orders, or personal checks (with a wait). No physical store is mentioned; mailing address: Janet Lawwill, P.O. Box 1029, Kemah, TX 77565 (520-907-2839).

Talisman & Token
www.talismanandtoken.com
$$ ✈ ✈ ✈

This site is a full-service stop if you are interested in vintage and "nearly new" jewelry from Scandinavian, British, and other European designers. In addition to their online catalog, they offer consultancy to stylists, costume designers, and the general public regarding searches, repairs, commissions, and historical expertise. They also maintain a database of working and student jewelers.

Tangerine Boutique Vintage and Couture Wearables
www.tangerineboutique.com
$-$$ ✈ ✈ ✈ ✈ ✈

This is a unique site, from its pen-and-ink drawing splash page to its excellent descriptions of the merchandise, divided into categories like "Le Salon" (designer), day dresses, formal wear, and even "Statuesque—for the Womanly Figure." The big, bright photographs take a while to load, but the medium-large inventory of 1950's to 1980's goods is definitely worth browsing, as it offers something for everyone. Reasonably priced, funky pieces abound, as do pricier items. They accept Visa, MasterCard, American Express, checks (with a wait), and money orders. Returns on nonsale items only, and you must notify them within three days and pay a $5 restocking fee. No physical store, business address, or phone number is mentioned.

Then Plus Now 2 Vintage Purses and Accessories

www.thenplusnow2.com

$-$$ ✈✈✈

Looking for the perfect bag? This vintage purse site offers a large assortment of handbags with new items added weekly. Along with the vintage purses, there are accessories, a category called "a little newer" (items from the 1970's and later), a "TLC" section for things that need a bit of repair, and a wedding page. You can search by era or click on the photos on their home page. There was no search engine to look for a Hermès Kelly bag, but browsing provided some gems—a mod trapezoidal purse in red and white, for example. Additional views of the purse were supplied. Edie and Jess recommend telephoning or using e-mail to check availability, or you can use their order form. Your credit card is accepted through PayPal, along with personal checks and money orders. Shipping is via priority mail. Their return policy promised a full refund minus shipping charges and a 15 percent restocking fee if returned within three days of receipt in the same condition as received. Mailing address: 15036 North Main Street, Buchanan, MI 49107 (616-695-2462; 877-276-6292).

Tias

www.tias.com

This is a large mall site boasting 1,300 categories and 330,000 items. It's similar to eBay Stores or Fashiondig in that members can list items for sale online. These might include a 1950's classic fitted dress with buttons, 1933 vintage collegiate sports sweaters, and Hawaiian shirts. Credit cards, money orders, and personal checks are accepted. From the Tias home page you can use a search engine to select vintage clothing.

Tias is an excellent site offering a community of vintage clothing sellers at a variety of prices.

Decades

www.tias.com/stores/decades

$　✂ ✂ ✂ ✂ ✂

Part of the large Tias virtual mall, this online shop has an enormous inventory of vintage clothes and accessories. The site itself has a no-frills look, leaving room for the numerous categories and subcategories; there are well-organized sections devoted to the late 1800's through early 1900's, "Aloha Wear," 1920's flapper dresses, mid-century suits and frocks, men's haberdashery, lingerie, and jewelry. You'll find all sorts of treasures here: colorful Bakelite bracelets, well-priced cocktail dresses, charming Hawaiian shirts, and even vintage sterling silver and copper jewelry. International shipping is not mentioned; call or e-mail if you live outside the United States. Accepted methods of payment include Visa and MasterCard through PayPal as well as money orders and personal checks (with a wait). Returns are accepted with three days' notification. No physical store is mentioned; mailing address: The Villa at Captiva Bay, 4960 Red Bank Road, Galena, OH 43021. No phone number is given.

A Midnight Sparkle
www.tias.com/stores/midnightsparkle/

$-$$ ✈ ✈ ✈ ✈ ✈

This animated, eye-catching site offers a large, searchable inventory that's well organized into departments, including 1930's–1950's items, 1960's–1970's pieces, men's suits, smoking jackets, sweaters, blouses, coats, wedding gowns, and lingerie. The vast costume jewelry selection is nothing short of amazing, as it includes not only signed pieces but also collectible Bakelite bracelets and sterling silver baubles. The photographs and detailed descriptions are superb. They accept Visa, MasterCard, Discover, checks (with a wait), and money orders, and allow returns with three days' notice; they don't charge a restocking fee. International shipping is available. No physical store is mentioned. Mailing address: 114 Timberlane Drive, Haysville, KS 67060. No phone number is mentioned.

One Black Swan
www.tias.com/stores/obs/

$ ✈ ✈ ✈ ✈

This site offers costume jewelry from the 1940's to the 1960's, including Mexican, Native American, designer costume, and Bakelite. Payment is via credit card through PayPal; they also accept checks and money orders. Free shipping is provided on orders over $125. The site also lists items on eBay.

Trashy Diva
www.trashy-diva.net

$$ ✈ ✈ ✈ ✈

What a sexy, eye-catching site. You click on "shop the site" and begin browsing the virtual racks, where you'll find a beautifully organized and displayed inventory of corsets, jewelry, lingerie, and vintage jewelry from the 1920's through the 1940's. We loved the vintage-inspired Victorian jacket—perfect for wearing over a skimpy top or bustier. Returns—of nonsale items only— are accepted within ten days, tags attached; a 20 percent re-stocking fee will be charged. International shipping is available. Pay with Visa, MasterCard, or American Express. Physical store and mailing address: 829 Chartres Street, New Orleans, LA 70116 (888-818-DIVA; 504-581-4555).

Unique Vintage
www.unique-vintage.com

$ 🦋 🦋 🦋 🦋 🦋

The splash page is impressive: clear, colorful, and well laid out. This site would seem to have it all: terrific merchandise (including many collectible American labels like Lilly Pulitzer and Pauline Trigère), affordable prices, an easy-to-use shopping-cart system, and clear photos and descriptions. Unique Vintage also stocks signed cos-tume jewelry. No mention is made of international shipping; call or e-mail first. Pay for your purchases with Visa, MasterCard, American Express, money orders, or personal checks (with a wait). No physical store or phone number is mentioned. Mailing address: P.O. Box 10814, Burbank, CA 91510 (818-219-9306).

A Victorian Elegance
www.avictorianelegance.com

$$ 🦋 🦋 🦋 🦋 🦋

Reminiscent of a very cluttered attic filled with treasures, this site boasts a large inventory, very detailed descriptions, and plentiful photographs. The name implies turn-of-the-century merchandise, but there are many offerings from the 1930's to 1980's also. Other departments include coats, men's, children's, sewing and textiles, and even books (on vintage clothing, of course, and conveniently linked to Amazon.com). They accept Visa, MasterCard, Discover, Novus, and American Express. They allow returns if the buyer notifies them of a problem within two days of receipt. No physical store is mentioned. Mailing address: P.O. Box 2091, Plant City, FL 33564 (800-660-3640; 813-719-8013).

Vintage Baubles
www.vintagebaubles.com

$ ✂ ✂ ✂

The departments of this large website include designer vintage, accessories, costume as well as fine jewelry, and wedding items. Whether you're looking for something from the 1940's, a more-recent 1980's outfit, or a treasure from one of the decades in between, you'll find plenty of well-priced choices here. Many items include more than one photograph, and everything is described in detail, even flaws. MasterCard, Visa, checks (with a wait), and money orders are accepted. At press time, free shipping was being offered for U.S. customers. International shipping is available. Returns are accepted with twenty-four hours' notice (buyer pays a 15 percent restocking fee). No physical store is mentioned. Mailing address: Pamela Browne–Vintage Baubles, 2825 Sawyer Bend Road, Franklin, TN 37069 (615-377-6482).

Vintage Blues
www.vintageblues.com

$ ✂ ✂ ✂ ✂

A blue splash page welcomes the shopper, who can click on a black-and-white photo to enter the site, where she may request that the page be translated into French, German, Italian, Portuguese, or Spanish. Whew! This site has a small- to medium-sized inventory. Those in search of collectible denim and military clothing will be very pleased, as there are many such items offered, and prices are very reasonable. The ladies' section offers 1950's circle skirts in a range of witty patterns, as well as extremely affordable basic day dresses. International shipping is available—to all countries except where prohibited by law. Returns are accepted within ten days, for store credit or exchange only; a 15 percent restocking fee will be charged. Payment methods accepted are Visa, Master-Card, and PayPal. Store and mailing address: 2212 East 12 Street, Suite 208, Davenport, IA 52803 (563-323-2552).

Vintagebuzz
www.vintagebuzz.com

$ ✗ ✗ ✗

You'll be greeted by four vinyl records labeled red room, atomic gifts, "guys," and "dolls," and although this his-and-hers online inventory is rather modest, it's worth a look if you're hunting for unusual jackets or cheap, cheerful costume jewelry. There is also a range of household goods and knickknacks for sale. Vintage-buzz accepts Visa, MasterCard, money orders, and checks (with a wait). International shipping is available. Returns are accepted within five days of purchase and two days' notification. For more vintage goodies, visit the physical store at 5229 Lanker-shim Boulevard, North Hollywood, CA 91601 (this is also the mailing address) (818-769-8900).

Vintage Couture
www.vintagecouture.com

$$–$$$ ✗ ✗ ✗ ✗

This site is a "consignment-classified" hybrid, meaning the vintage garments listed therein will be either consigned pieces or classified listings. With the first type of listing, you'll be dealing directly with the site; with the classified listings, you'll buy the item from the individual (and if you have any questions, that's whom you'll contact). That said, the medium-large inventory of high-end fashion is impressive, and it's easy to navigate the departments, which include recent clothing, recent accessories, vintage clothing, and vintage accessories. Designer pieces from Chanel, Gucci, Pucci, and Dior abound, and prices are accordingly steep. Should you wish to sell your own designer goods with Vintage Couture, e-mail them for their most updated policies and charges. They are located in Canada and accept MasterCard, Visa, money orders, and cashier's checks, provided your selection is a consignment item. International shipping is available, and returns are permitted with immediate notice and require payment of a 20 percent restocking fee. For payment, shipment, and return policies that pertain to classified listings, you must consult the individual sellers.

Vintage Fiber Works
www.vintagefiberworks.com
$ ✗ ✗ ✗

Although they offer a small collection of vintage clothing, including wearable pieces from the 1920's through the 1960's, and a modest array of costume jewelry, this colorful site really shines in the fabric department. Hard-to-find vintage barkcloth, in several whimsical mid-century patterns, is available here, as are some interesting ribbon and floral trims for clothing and hats. At the time of this writing, only one wedding gown was on virtual display in the bridal department. They accept all credit cards, checks (with a wait), money orders, and cashier's checks. International shipping is available; these items must be purchased with credit cards. The retail store's address is 1200 Main Street, Lynchburg, VA 24504 (804-845-3601; 877-754-6978).

Vintage Martini
www.vintagemartini.com

$$ ⚘⚘⚘⚘

The name is tempting enough, but Vintage Martini's gorgeous inventory will have you feeling quite stirred, if not shaken; certainly you'll be light-headed enough to picture yourself wearing some of the movie-star dresses offered for sale. When we visited, we were treated to—among other things—several beautiful photographs of the most amazing one-of-a-kind 1960's Bill Blass evening dress: It was almost completely covered, from shoulder to floor, with pearl-centered cream-organza flowers. Of course, there are lots of choices for the slightly more down-to-earth girl, too, whether she's looking for a sharp 1940's suit or a pair of witty and colorful capri pants. Departments include ladies' (and this is further divided into Edwardian, Victorian, 1940's, 1950's, and so forth) as well as men's, accessories, and patterns. Returns are accepted with twenty-four hours' notice; a 20 percent restocking fee will apply to multiple-item returns. Money orders, checks (with a wait), and MasterCard and Visa (through PayPal) are accepted. No physical store, telephone, or address is mentioned on this site, nor is international shipping discussed; please click on Vintage Martini's contact link to e-mail them for this information.

Vintageous
www.vintageous.com

$$ ⚘⚘⚘⚘⚘

Here is another site that offers wonderful antique dresses and suits for the budget-minded fashionphile and serious collector alike. The medium-large inventory covers all the bases: Looking for a unique 1950's skirt? Vintageous had several wonderful examples, including one with embroidered dancers. And if name-brand evening gowns are what you're after, you'll love clicking through the pages of floaty chiffon skirts, fitted bodices, and exquisite beadwork that make up the formal wear department. There are also sections dedicated to outerwear, accessories, and vintage patterns and some wonderful links—for example, a retro hairdo site—that vintage fans will enjoy. Returns are accepted with a two-day notification. Pay for your treasures with checks (with a wait), money orders, or MasterCard and Visa through PayPal. International shipping is available. No physical store or telephone number is mentioned; contact: Naomi Goldstein c/o Vintageous, P.O. Box 11111, Norfolk, VA 23517.

Vintage Silhouettes
www.vintagesilhouettes.com
$$–$$$ ✄ ✄ ✄

This is the online store for an eleven-year-old, five-thousand-square-foot vintage clothing store owned by Janene and Art Fawcett. In addition to vintage clothing and accessories from 1830 to 1965 they have a special interest in men's vintage clothes described as "New Old Stock." A late 1930's–early 1940's mocha double-breasted men's suit in a burnt orange windowpane pattern was offered in a size 36 regular. Pants with a thirty-six-inch waist were never worn or cuffed, and the suit's price was listed at $300. Ladies' dress patterns were sold for around $6 each. A 1952 red silk Dior cocktail dress that, alas, had been seriously altered, was priced at $1,000. A 1970 Rudi Gernreich long-sleeved dress was priced a bit lower at $350. A Pucci silk jersey dress from Saks was priced at $925 along with a disclaimer that they sold faster than they could be listed. There are gems to be found here, but the site could use serious redesign. They accept credit and debit cards and offer an 800 telephone number. They also accept checks, though they hold the item till it clears. Returns are accepted within three days (except for sale items), and they use a "reserved" designation on the item until the transaction has ended satisfactorily. Their news flashes were posted months earlier and needed to be removed or updated. They have an excellent list of links. Store and mailing address: 190 Parker Avenue, Rodeo, CA 94572 (510-245-2443; 800-636-1410).

Vintage Textile
www.vintagetextile.com
$$–$$$

This attractive, well-organized site offers the vintage aficionado a wonderful inventory of fine vintage clothing through which to browse. The designer section will take your breath away, especially if you're in the market for a one-of-a-kind Galanos dress or an envy-inspiring Hattie Carnegie gown from the 1950's. Be warned: Magnificence doesn't come cheap! The photos are large and abundant; there are several different angles shown. International shipping is available. Visa, MasterCard, money orders, PayPal, and personal checks (with a wait) are all accepted. Returns are accepted with twenty-four hours' notice, and returned items costing over $300 will incur a 10 percent restocking fee. Mailing address: Linda Ames, 18 Lee Street, #10, Keene, NH 03431 (603-352-6338).

Vintage Trends
www.vintagetrends.com
$$

This seriously stylish and easy-to-navigate website claims to have the world's largest inventory of vintage, military, recycled, and designer clothing and accessories. This major online vintage retailer (founded by Kevin Torf, an e-commerce entrepreneur) is the creation of Reaction Labs, a venture design firm.

Categories include clothing for men, women, and kids, and items for the home. Search swimwear by thumbnails in an easy-to-see grid—there were seventy-four swimsuits on the day we visited. One click will take you to an in-depth description while another will give you a larger view.

A Rudi Gernreich scarf from the 1970's was $100. A Bonnie Cashin rust-colored suede jacket with fabulous brass closures (but a crease in the collar) was $140. A search for Claire Mc-Cardell turned up a black wool dress from Townley in our size (with a tear in the back yoke) for $120. A Jean Muir cashmere sweater from the 1980's was $100.

Their customer service link answers all of your online shopping questions from sizing and condition to their return policy. (They accept returns within twelve hours of delivery.) Credit cards are accepted through a secure site, and they ship internationally. They even have an intellectual property statement that might make particularly interesting reading if you are thinking of creating your own vintage website. Vintage Trends is located in Southern California.

Vintage Voola
www.vintagevoola.com
$ ✂ ✂ ✂ ✂

The cool green boomerang-patterned home page offers men's and women's clothing and accessories as well as children's items and recordings (LPs, 78s, tapes, and CDs). Their 1930's to 1970's inventory is divided into categories and includes a link to eBay. A

1960's black velvet minidress was presented with good photographs, measurements, and a narrative description and priced at $22. Jewelry items were expensive, for the most part, and included a large selection of rhinestone pieces and big clear photos. Their menswear selection included Hawaiian, Western style, and dress shirts, and a short-sleeved vertically striped graphic shirt from the 1970's. The order form allows for payment by money order, personal check, and credit cards through PayPal. Returns—unworn with tags attached—are accepted with notification within two days. Wigs and records are not returnable unless defective.

Vintage Voola is owned by Al and Cheryl Farlow. They started selling at flea markets and antique malls before opening a vintage clothing store in downtown Seattle in 1992. In addition to the website, they sell on eBay. If you connect by link to their eBay auctions you will be able to read their feedback. Store and mailing address: 705 East Pike Street, Seattle, WA 98122.

A Vintage Wedding
www.vintagewedding.com

$$ 🪡 🪡 🪡 🪡 🪡

A bride-to-be who loves vintage clothing will be completely thrilled by A Vintage Wedding. She will start at the pretty ivory invitation page and proceed into what can only be described as a wedding wonderland. Myriad gowns (from the Victorian era through the 1980's), shoes, purses, gloves, and of course, bridal veils are nicely photographed and extensively described. There is even a section dedicated to vintage groom's clothes. Since most bridal wear is made of light-colored fabrics, be sure to make specific inquiries about marks or stains on any item you're considering, although this site does accept returns with two days' notification. Accepted payment methods include MasterCard, Visa, Discover, money orders, and personal checks (with a wait). No physical store is mentioned. Mailing address: A Victorian Elegance, P.O. Box 2091, Plant City, FL 33564 (813-719-8013; 800-660-3640).

VintageWonderland.com
www.vintagewonderland.com

$ ⚞⚟ ⚞⚟ ⚞⚟

A curvy pinup girl adorns the splash page. There are links to the men's and women's sections and to the seller's eBay auctions. The website's small inventory includes a nice range of affordable mid-century dresses, several coats from various eras, Hawaiian wear, and menswear. Credit cards are accepted via PayPal; personal checks (with a wait), money orders, and Billpoint are also honored. International shipping is available. At the time of this writing, no information on returns or store policies could be located; the address and phone number were also missing.

The Way We Wore
www.thewaywewore.net

$ ⚞⚟ ⚞⚟

A bright turquoise-and-pink welcome screen invites shoppers to visit the martini room, the love room, and the disco room (which house pre-1950's and 1950's, 1960's, and 1970's goods, respectively). The medium-sized inventory is well organized, but the minimalist descriptions lack detail (though you are welcome to e-mail the site's owners for further information). In addition to clothing, you'll find sunglasses, wigs, Western wear, and Hawaiiana. They'll accept returns for exchange only. No information was provided regarding the methods of payment accepted or whether international shipping is available. Store address: 2602 Waugh Drive, Houston, TX 77006 (713-526-8910).

Whiskey Sour Vintage

www.whiskeysourvintage.com/new_home_frame.htm

$ ✗ ✗ ✗

A sexy splash page lets the vintage shopper click on a pinup girl's curves to enter the site. There, a somewhat small inventory of mainly twentieth-century clothes is offered; categories include women's, men's, and accessories. Items are described in careful detail. The large, lovely photographs take a while to load, however. Many items in the inventory showed a little Sold tag next to them, which could frustrate a shopper. This site only accepts credit cards via PayPal and personal checks with a waiting period, and they don't offer any information on their return policy. No physical store, business address, or phone number is mentioned.

Woodland Farms Antiques

www.woodlandfarmsantiques.com

$-$$ ✗ ✗ ✗ ✗

The name might not shout "vintage clothing," but Woodland Farms Antiques is definitely worth a visit if you'd like to start acquiring some designer vintage pieces without completely emptying out your piggy bank. Also on cyber display are textiles, quilts, sewing patterns, cookbooks, and fabrics, but it was the dresses and suits—from the Edwardian era through the 1970's—that captured our interest. On one visit we saw a gorgeous royal blue silk Ceil Chapman dress, a beaded Adele Simpson gown, a Lilli Ann coat with a dramatic furry hood, a

fabulous nipped-waist tweed wool suit from the 1940's, and a se-
quin-encrusted knit sheath from the 1960's. The departments
include ladies, gentlemen, hats, shoes, purses, and lingerie, to
name a few. The owners are quick to respond to a potential customer's e-mailed questions and do accept returns if they're notified within twenty-four hours. Checks, money orders, and
MasterCard and Visa (through PayPal) are accepted. No details
about international shipping, physical address, or phone number are given—e-mail the owners for further information about
any or all of these.

Yu Japanese Designer Clothing

www.yu-nyc.com

$$ ⚘⚘⚘

When we shopped in Yu's store in lower Manhattan we left with
our purchases wrapped and encased in Yu's beautiful handmade
cloth shopping bags. Her online identification site offered a
small inventory, including several Issey Miyake rarities. Inquire
about price and availability by phone. Store address: 151 Lud-
low Street, New York, NY 10002 (212-979-9370).

Zvintage

www.zvintage.com

$$ ⚘⚘⚘⚘

We love their online store motto: "Bad taste is better than no
taste at all!" This is a very professional site that sells vintage pieces
that have been either never worn or only gently used. This boutique also provides a history of clothing, from the Egyptians
through Louis XIV, to the accessories of the 1940's, 1950's, and
1960's. A search of evening dresses in their current specials
turned up a leopard print slip dress from the 1970's by Stephen

Burrows on sale for $15! A quick click could add the item to your shopping cart; another click on 1950's dresses produced thumbnail photos of all their items. Searches can also be done from the 1920's to the 1980's. Register to use this site and they will also e-mail you if something special comes in. They welcome inquiries from other dealers. This is an extensive, fast-loading, and easily navigated site. Melissa Griffin offers appraisals. Mailing address: 872 Copeland Road, Columbus, OH 43212 (614-291-8692; 866-ZVINTAGE).

HEROES

There are online vintage clothing sellers, and then there are our favorites: those stylish and enterprising individuals whose love of fashion is genuine, whose professionalism is obvious, and whose merchandise is consistently appealing and intriguing. We asked them to share their thoughts—about vintage clothes and online selling, both on eBay and, in two cases, through their websites—and their responses were wonderfully articulate and enlightening. (Our heroes are listed here in alphabetical order; several appear in the Site Directory as well.)

Karen Augusta
www.antique-fashion.com
If eighteenth-, nineteenth-, and very early-twentieth-century vintage clothing is your thing, you will want to visit Karen Augusta's website or arrange a special visit to see her collection in Vermont.

Karen Augusta, 33 Gage Street, North Westminster, VT 05101 (802-463-3333)

"For thirty years I have studied, appraised, purchased, and sold antique costume, fashion accessories, fine laces, linens, and textiles. My childhood in New England fostered an artistic sensibility and love of beautiful clothing. My father is a portrait artist, my mother a fashion illustrator. Studying the designer garments my mother worked with and the clothing I saw in museum portraits gave me a deep appreciation of the connection between fashion and history.

"I started antique clothing collecting while a college student in the 1960's. In the mid-1970's, I opened an antique shop in western New Jersey and began exhibiting at antique shows throughout the Northeast. I maintain a web catalog of historic clothing and accessories.

"My studio and business are located in the spacious third floor ballroom of the historic 1863 Gage House, my home in southern Vermont. Often pieces from my inventory are featured in national and international publications, including *Country Living, Mademoiselle,* French *Vogue,* and *Victoria* magazines.

"Museum curators, movie and theater costumers, fashion designers, stylists, and serious collectors are among my clientele. For many years I have offered an appraisal/consultation service for individuals, museums, historical societies, institutions, and auctioneers."

Designer Exposure
www.designerexposure.com

For most of the two years that Maria Williams's site has been online, we have been fans. We have purchased items and enjoyed the variety of clothing offered as well as her great sales.

Maria Williams, 14 Gillies Avenue, Newmarket, Auckland, New Zealand (011-64-5245954)

"I have sold or collected vintage clothing for seventeen years. I specialize in hip designer clothing that is less than two years old but not particularly vintage, in labels like Chanel, Dior, Prada, Gucci, and Chloé. We have a large selection of clothing: Bags, shoes, and clothing items are all 'one offs' so we do not have more than one of anything. We get 1.2 million hits a month, and our customers come from all over the world. We have our own online auction and classified sections that bring buyers together.

"We offer a secure site for taking credit cards, and we answer e-mails within twenty-four hours at the outside. We are online at least twelve hours a day. If you are not satisfied with your purchase it must be returned within seven days of receipt for store credit.

"WEBENZ, New Zealand (Jacqui Jones and Chris Hope) designed our website.

"We offer good customer service and extremely easy navigation in a fast-loading, readable site. We have over one thousand items online at any one time, and our inventory is updated daily."

Gotham City Online

www.shopgco.com

800 31 St, Union City, NJ 07087 (212-625-8208)

"Gotham City Online is the premier charitable retailer in New York City. We have been online selling vintage men's and women's clothing and accessories for two years. Working with a variety of nonprofit organizations like Partnership for the Homeless, Dress for Success, and Housing Works, Gotham City Online offers their administrative services including pickups, coordination of clothing drives, barter arrangements for furniture and books as well as fund-raising. We sell a variety of quality new, used, and vintage clothing and books and housewares to an international clientele. Almost all of our merchandise originally comes from the amazing stores and boutiques of New York.

"The secret to our success is our focus on quality and our utilization of digital technology. We have developed a robust digital production facility that enables us to accurately manage large volumes of unique items. We do our own system development on our website, which gets 150,000 visitors per week. Most important to us is the site's appearance, color, and readability. Our site is easy to navigate and well stocked. Less important to us is animation, sound, or anything that borders on annoyance.

"The efficiency and sophistication of our systems are enabling us to help revolutionize the way bulk clothing is resold. In turn, proceeds from the goods we sell enable us to raise tens of thousands of dollars a year for these nonprofit organizations.

"Our merchandise is sold online via auctions, directly through this online store, and through our new metro New York fashion warehouse. Our website allows users to search through thousands of items by *size, brand,* and *style.* This integration allows shoppers to find exactly what they're looking for from the thousands of items we have for sale.

"We accept all forms of payment and respond to all questions within six hours.

"We are one of the few that have integrated our eBay activity within our online store. EBay has acknowledged our accomplishments by honoring us with the power seller title that is assigned to large sellers that maintain *customer satisfaction of at least 98 percent.* There is a direct link to our eBay auctions from our website or by the seller name etreasures or missvintage."

Kenokid

www.ebaystores.com/kenokid

Linda: "My first purchase from Kenokid was something of a comedy of errors. The Issey Miyake sewing pattern I had just won was sent by mistake to another buyer in Maryland, and that buyer's pattern was sent to me. Site owner Anne Pobst was away when I e-mailed her about the problem. Anne's husband quickly replied and assured me that Anne would resolve matters on her return. She did just that, and with such disarming congeniality I was hooked. I sent my pattern to the buyer in Maryland and she sent me mine. We each received free shipping for three subsequent purchases. I am well over that free-shipping incentive and have filled my closet with Romeo Gigli, Dior, Dries van Noten, Issey Miyake, and Matsuda from her eBay auctions. I always look forward to asking questions about the garments so I can catch up on her news. Packages from her 'store' in British Columbia usually arrive within seven days and they are always exactly as described or better."

Anne Pobst, Coquitlam, BC, Canada (no store location, Internet sales only) (604-524-3901)

"I have been online since 1998 and collecting and selling vintage clothing since 1990. I specialize in Japanese designers such as Issey Miyake, Yohji Yamamoto, Kansai Yamamoto, Kabuki, Junko Shimada, and Matsuda; vintage pieces of Dior, Kenzo; Chanel jewelry, clothing, and handbags; Moule Rayon Clothing (Canadian designer); Emilio Pucci (when I can find it); Dries van Noten; Custo; and Jane Doe. I almost always have something available by Chanel, Moule, and Miyake.

"My customers come from all over the world. So far I have done business with clients in thirty-six countries. Most of my business is with customers in the United States, and only a small percentage of my business is with customers here in Canada. I can accept Billpoint payments for electronic checks or credit cards. This is a secure website and does not have to be linked to an eBay sale. I use it for private sales as well. I accept personal checks and can accept domestic forms of U.S. money orders (the green ones) even though I am in Canada. European and Asian customers often like to pay by BidPay as it is convenient for them and cheaper than purchasing a money order at their countries' banks.

"I am online daily and can usually answer a question the same day.

"Regarding returns: If I have failed to find an important fault in an item I sell or have misdescribed it in some way, I will refund your money, including the shipping costs you paid and those for shipping back to me. If you find I described the item okay but you discover that you just don't like it after all or it doesn't fit as you hoped, I will accept its return in the same condition and will refund your purchase price, but you are responsible for the shipping costs each way. If it is an auctioned item, I may ask you to hold it while I resell it and then mail it to the next buyer, as that saves me hassles with Canadian customs. If insurance was not available on the item (as is the case with small-packet mail from Canada), and it is lost in the mail, I will refund your payment including shipping.

"For me, eBay provides an easy marketplace. If I had my own website I would have to figure out how to draw people to it. Then I would have to worry about the logistics of setting it up to be a secure shopping environment. For a small monthly fee, eBay does all that for me. The online store is a bit primitive (no shopping carts), but it is easy and convenient and people can find my store easily when they look at any of my auctions.

"I think an auction site should have clear descriptions, clear photos, and a respectful attitude toward its customers. Customers cannot try on the clothes, so it is important to make it as clear as possible whether this item is something they want and can use and enjoy. I used to use counters on my items as it helped me determine not only which labels were most desirable but also which categories to post in. Now I only use counters on items I haven't sold before to help me see if perhaps it is not visible enough because I have placed it in the wrong category. (I'm referring to auction counters, not website counters.)

"Many customers still write to me and ask me to translate sizes from one country to another: 'Is that a U.S. size 8?' 'What is that in Italian sizing?' I always encourage online customers to ignore the size and use a measuring tape to determine the best fit. I suggest they measure their own best-fitting clothes and use those measurements as a basis for comparison.

"Doing business successfully online takes learning on both the seller's and the buyer's part. Even though I do not have a website I respond to ones that have a clean appearance and are easy to see.

"In my former profession (usability testing of web-based technology for business and learning) we used to call animation and sound on websites 'dancing macaroni.' In general, animation and sound are distracting and annoying. They may be cute at first but can detract from your message and worse—if they take too long to load, they can drive your business away. An interesting fact I learned about development of websites is that women do not respond positively to 'dancing macaroni.' Some of this has to do with our biology. Generally, women have better peripheral vision than men do, and movement in the corner of the eye can elicit a 'threat response.' Because of this, animations that move across the screen and have nothing to do with the object of the site (i.e., the items for sale) can actually drive women customers out of your website, often for reasons they can only articulate as 'It is too busy' or 'It made me feel uncomfortable.' Color and readability are critical: no red and blue contrast; larger fonts with serifs (e.g., Times Roman is more readable than Arial). And, last, if you can't get anywhere in three steps, the site is overly complex."

Kookiepuss
www.stores.ebay.com/store=2765514
Vintage clothing fans who admire the feminine styles of the 1950's are always snapping up Diane Makasian's dresses and skirts. Indeed, if you enter the phrase "50's dress" in the eBay keyword box on any given day, you will undoubtedly find numerous offerings from Fresno, California's "Kookiepuss." The colorful, well-priced, fine-quality garments reflect her philosophies about vintage clothes and fashion in general.

"The main thing that attracts me to vintage clothing is the classic and timeless style that it possesses. What makes an item 'vintage'—as opposed to just something that was worn during a different decade—is a garment's ability to actually represent, or even define, an era. You can look at it and feel drawn into another moment in time.

"I have owned a vintage clothing store for eight years, and I was selling pieces for four years prior to that. And having actually collected vintage for fourteen years, I can look at new clothing by top designers and see the influence of vintage designs in the styles or fabrics. Almost all modern-day fashion appears to be influenced by one vintage look or another. A customer of mine actually buys pieces in order to reproduce their fabrics for clothing lines sold in very mainstream stores.

"The 1950's styles interest me most, probably because there was such a nice variety of styles produced during this era: whimsical, sophisticated, or vampy, for example. The clothes were made with great attention to detail, and the fabrics often featured unusual prints and color combinations.

"I have a very broad customer base that includes young, trendy women as well as sophisticated collectors. As for pricing the clothes themselves, I believe that consumers should decide the value of an item, since it is only worth what someone is willing to pay for it. Previous selling experience is also a factor, of course.

"At this time, I sell on eBay and I have a retail store, Retrorag. I have not tried any of the other auction sites. I use an auction tool called Auction Poster, and I list new items regularly—I'm online about eight hours a day. So, anyone who e-mails me a question can expect a very prompt reply. I do sometimes use the reserve auction option, but I have not used the other eBay features with any regularity. I am currently trying out the new "eBay Stores" feature, but I don't think enough buyers know about it or understand what it is. I do think that eBay needs to refine their feedback procedures, perhaps by involving themselves more and offering only eBay-selected comments about certain situations instead of permitting a free-for-all. The bid retraction process also needs to be monitored more closely.

"I am working on my own vintage clothing website, www.retrorag.com, which I am pleased to say will be up and running by the time you read this."

MoreBigFun

www.stores.ebay.com/store=22333846

Jessica Morse started out as one of our favorite eBay sellers, morebigfun, and has since upgraded to the eBay Store category. Her enthusiasm and love for vintage clothing and accessories are evident in her lively item descriptions and her 100 percent score as a Reliable Merchant. Almost like the Better Business Bureau, the Reliable Merchant designation comes from a network of select auction merchants who have shown outstanding reliability in past auction transactions.

Jessica Morse (323-227-1613)

"I have been an eBay seller for a year, but I've collected vintage clothing forever. I remember buying a bunny-fur coat at a yard sale when I was eight or nine years old. I started selling vintage clothing by accident. I was trying to supplement my meager waitressing income while going to art school on a scholarship. I used to wear my 'finds,' and my friends always asked me where I got them and whether or not I would sell them. It just escalated from there.

"I don't have a specialty. If I had to choose, though, I'd say vintage men's clothing. No, women's. No, jewelry. I love it all. Oh! Vintage Western wear and denim! My favorite.

"The single item that I have the most stock of at any given time used to be Levi's 501's. I still have a lot of those, but today I have a lot of 1960's dresses, vintage shoes, and *tons* of vintage jewelry.

"I accept almost all forms of payment, but I prefer PayPal. It's safe, quick, and a great way for me to keep track of payments. I'm online all day. From the time I get up (usually around 7 A.M.) until I go to bed (usually midnight) I check e-mail constantly. I try to answer questions immediately.

"I haven't gotten around to setting up my own website. My friends have told me for years that eBay would be the perfect place for me, and it is. Before the year is out I will have my own 'web store' on eBay. I have tried a few other online auction sites and have been very disappointed by them. EBay has the most traffic. I average about 180 visitors per week.

"I think the most important things for an auction site are: appearance, navigational ease, and most of all, the STUFF! If you have great stuff, everything else just helps. It's the goods that people really want to see."

RubySohoNY
www.chelsea-girl.com

Elisa Casas is the owner of The 1909 Company, located in New York's SoHo district, as well as the terrific online vintage boutique Chelsea Girl. Like many vintage aficionados, she was in the beginning drawn to the fashions of the past because they were affordable. "As a college student in Greenwich Village, I enjoyed the lower cost of vintage clothing. Pretty quickly, however, the history behind vintage fashions began to fascinate me. Now, having collected it for fifteen years, I feel that wearing vintage is all about having individual style, as opposed to following trends or conforming to the masses, and that's what attracts me to it. I cringe when I see celebrities dressed head to toe in designer clothing. People who wear vintage seem to possess an innate sense of design: They're definitely not put together by a stylist. Sorry, Gwyneth . . . you might always be voted Best Dressed, but who wouldn't be, with Calvin Klein outfitting her?"

Elisa Casas, 63 Thompson Street, New York, NY 10012 (212-343-1658)

"My New York store opened in 1994, and I was one of the

first 'vintage clothing pioneers' on eBay—I've been buying and selling with them for over four years. My website went live in January 2001. Designer pieces, as a rule, sell better on eBay than no-name garments do; I think this is because people can easily search for them. As a buyer, however, I like to search out items that fewer people are seeking. Bargains can still be had.

"You get to know the market pretty well after being in the business for so long. And because I'm also a collector, I intuitively know what someone will pay for an item, and I price it accordingly. My typical customer is in her thirties or forties and buys vintage to wear, not to collect.

"EBay is not my primary venue for selling. I find my own website is a lot more convenient to manage and less expensive. Additionally, I have better control over how to market my merchandise on my website. That said, eBay does have such a broad audience, and for selling certain items, it's unbeatable. Other auction sites, at this time, simply don't have the same quality and range of merchandise as eBay, nor can they offer sellers anywhere near the same size audience.

"I usually spend up to five hours per day online—it is extremely time-consuming! I reply to questions very promptly. I don't use any of the auction tools or selling programs, preferring the personal approach. I find that for nondesigner items, I just don't get the prices on eBay that I get in my NYC shop. But if I'm selling a Gucci bag, for example, I know that people interested in Gucci will find it with a search.

"EBay definitely does not meet all my needs: I don't like the herd mentality. Whereas my website is very individualistic: I can be in complete control of mailing lists, marketing, and presentation.

"As a buyer, I would advise any beginning seller to make sure that her pictures are clear: You could get double the price for your item just by using good, detailed photographs. Describe the item well. And don't sell flawed items. I find that if there's a flaw mentioned and described, it is usually *much* worse when I receive the item. So, I skip any flawed items as a rule.

"The Internet has completely changed the vintage market. As a buyer, the amount of merchandise that I have available to me is overwhelming, and the overall quality of my store merchandise has improved greatly. As a seller, I now have a vast audience to whom I can market my product: 150 customers might visit my shop on any given day, but 2,500 people look at my website. On the other hand, since the arrival of online vintage boutiques and eBay, I have noticed a downhill trend in the selection and overall condition of vintage clothing for sale at flea markets and shows, and I rarely come across the fine-quality items at these venues; however, on eBay, I do find them."

2ndhandprose

If you come across an eBay auction page that's written in such sparkling and playful language it practically jumps off the screen, chances are you've discovered one of Terri Wagener's listings. The lovely photographs of the garments are usually taken on the plant-filled porch of her Hollywood, California, bungalow, and whether she's describing a floral party frock or a 1940's suit from a Hollywood estate sale, there is always an interesting, complicated story involved. Terri's motives, however, are refreshingly simple: "I sell to get beautiful things to women with no access to them, to share stories, to get clothes to the right home, to meet people with interests similar to mine."

Having collected it all her life, Terri feels the main attraction of vintage clothing "is its style: It allows one to dress in a unique way without being trendy, tacky, or garish. I am interested in the individual history of the clothing—even the mends and stains—as well as where it has been and who wore it—in short, the romance of it all." She continues: "I was going to Goodwill as soon as I got my driver's license, to my middle-class parents' tremendous chagrin, and I've been selling online since March 2000.

"I find I am most interested in pretty, feminine attire, especially dresses, both casual and dressy, that were obviously someone's favorites. Hollywood glamour. Special-occasion dresses —garments designed and worn to make a specific impression on a certain person or group at a given point in time. Things that carried high hopes.

"As for setting pricing, within any one category, I start things at the same point. Dresses are $9.99. Skirts and blouses are $8.50. Special occasion dresses (tea length) are $14.99, and long gowns are $18.99. I may go lower but very rarely higher. The money isn't why I do it.

"My typical customer is in her thirties and is a stylish woman with her own disposable income. She's proud of her femininity, interested in history, and possessed of a sense of humor. She is quite savvy—a very nice person.

"My favorite experiences are when customers win something they love, something for which they have plans, and they write to me afterward to describe how the evening went. Or to tell me how they squealed when they opened the package or how their husband's eyes spun around. I like the continuation of the clothing's story—in someone else's life. I have many of these fun experiences, too numerous to mention.

"On the other hand, there are those people one encounters

online—just as one would in real life—who are unhappy in their lives and angry at the world. They have persecution complexes or some whacked-out ideas about other people as a whole. These strange beings, when the post office is slow, write e-mails in all capital letters, peppered with exclamation marks, canceling their credibility immediately, as far as I am concerned. Perhaps they'll level outrageous insults or make personal remarks: There will be all this amazing venting on my monitor. I recall one woman in particular who returned three things because they weren't wrapped in tissue paper—which I usually do use, as I explained to her, but this group of dresses had extremely full crinolines. Then there was another woman who reported me to eBay after I sent her a refund, per her request (read: demand), only to learn she had changed her mind and wanted the item again. These troubled individuals only account for about 1 percent of my customers, so they really are a very small group—but they take up my time. And this is time I could spend with my other excellent and delightful customers, which seems highly unfair.

"On average, I spend about two to three hours a day online; this could easily be less, if I didn't surf eBay for fun, too. I spend about ten to fifteen hours a week taking care of my selling concerns; I normally reply to a potential buyer's question within a few hours—always within the day. I don't use any of the auction tools, as I prefer the personal touch. Of all the different eBay features, I have only ever used the Featured Auction listing—just a few times, at that—in order to call attention to something I think everyone would enjoy seeing, something that was a beautiful representation of a designer or era.

"As for the relatively new eBay Stores concept, I don't get it. EBay seems to want to create spin-off businesses, when the original concept was fine as it stood. Like other large websites that constantly attempt to change direction, they will eventually compromise their pristine identity as *the* place for the world's online auctions. Not such bright marketing, I believe.

"I may very well have a website someday—but I would hope to incorporate auctions, too. I don't wish to be the one to set the price. I think an item should go to the person who wants it the most (much like the Golden Ticket went to Charlie in *Willy Wonka & the Chocolate Factory*). I know auctions don't guarantee that at all, but theoretically, at least, everyone has the same chance to dream about owning the item."

Part Six

RESOURCES DIRECTORY

All Dressed Up and Everywhere to Go:

Site-seeing for the Fashionphile

DESIGNER AND GENERAL
FASHION INFORMATION SITES

Alexander McQueen

www.alexandermcqueen.com

Alexander McQueen's designs are famous for their drama and originality; the manner in which this website showcases his exquisite creations can only be described as a masterpiece of dark theater.

Alfred Shaheen Hawaii

www.alfredshaheen.com

Alfred Shaheen of Hawaii designed beautiful fabrics—as well as dresses and casual wear—during the mid-twentieth century, and vintage versions of his creations are always sought after by collectors. His daughter Camille recently created a website to promote new Shaheen garments made from designs of the past; these feature traditional motifs of Hawaii, Tahiti, Asia, and Egypt. Vintage Shaheen dresses and shirts may be purchased online, too.

Barneys New York

www.barneys.com

Every fashionphile worth her salt—make that imported, rosemary-infused aromatherapy bath salt—loves Barneys New York, and now she can visit the store's official website; what's more, Barneys promises that online shopping will be available *very* soon.

Betsey Johnson

www.betseyjohnson.com

You'll have a ball when you visit Betsey Johnson's whimsical Flash-based site.

Beverley Birks Couture Collection

www.camrax.com/pages/birks0.htm

If you'd like to see some of the most astoundingly beautiful couture dresses ever created, visit this online gallery of twentieth-century French, Italian, American, and British designs.

Björk

www.bjork.com

Remember the swan dress that Björk wore to the 2001 Academy Awards ceremony? You'll see this and more on the Icelandic singer's website—a digital mix of fun, fashion, and photography.

Chanel

www.chanel.com/fb/index.cfm

Chanel fans will adore the company's elegant and well-designed site.

Colette

www.colette.fr/colette_flash.htm

Visit the amazing Parisian boutique Colette—where you can view and purchase fashion, music, and even food—without setting foot on the Concorde. This Flash-based site is a masterpiece of web design.

Dolce & Gabbana

www.dolcegabbana.it/eng/main.asp

Check out the latest from Dolce & Gabbana (this address will take you to the English version).

Donna Karan

www.donnakaran.com and www.dkny.com

Donna Karan's website links to eluxury.com for online shopping. DKNY is this designer's secondary line.

Fashion Planet

www.fashion-planet.com

This site features fashion stories, travel information, and daily news along with a wonderful page entitled "Windows on New York" that offers links to numerous museums, upscale designers' boutiques, and places of interest in the Big Apple.

Fashion Windows

www.fashionwindows.com/default.asp

Billed as "the Internet's database on fashion, visual merchandising and mannequins," this site features articles, up-to-the-minute fashion news stories, gossip, photography, and more.

Label France

www.france.diplomatie.fr/label_france/index.gb.html

For in-depth articles about numerous French haute couture designers, including Chanel, Saint Laurent, Dior, Lacroix, and more, visit this great website produced and maintained by the French Foreign Ministry. (The address provided will take you to the English version.)

Gianfranco Ferre

www.gianfrancoferre.com

Count on Gianfranco Ferre's creations to exemplify quiet taste and luxury; learn more about his signature style by visiting the designer's website.

Gianni Versace

www.gianniversace.com

The entertaining Versace site is packed with color, music, and animation; you'd expect nothing less from the design house famous for its "rock and royalty" sensibilities.

Giorgio Armani

www.giorgioarmani.com

View Giorgio Armani's numerous fashion collections and products when you visit this elegantly designed website.

Givenchy

www.givenchy.com

The site is quite beautiful: The haute couture photos should not be missed, and the history section—always appreciated by vintage aficionados—makes us wish more designers offered this sort of background information online.

Helmut Lang
www.helmutlang.com

View the most recent examples of Helmut Lang's edgy designs at this web address.

Hermès
www.hermes.com

At the time of this writing, the Hermès website was still under construction; however, the beautiful splash page—classic Hermès orange with animated galloping horses—suggests that this online boutique will quickly become a favorite, so we're listing it here and looking forward to shopping online for their must-have scarves and accessories.

Issey Miyake
www.pleatsplease.com

Issey Miyake's site is a multihued fantasy: In other words, a must-see for fans of avant-garde design, both in clothing and web pages.

Jean Paul Gaultier
www.jeanpaulgaultier.com

Long regarded as fashion's bad boy, Gaultier has a consistently inventive take on haute couture that is a balanced blend of the eccentric and the exquisite.

Kenzo
www.kenzo.com

Since the 1970's, Japanese-born Kenzo Takada has worked and lived in Paris. His colorful clothing draws from the Eastern and Western influences of traditional folk costumes. Using one of the most adventurous color palettes on the web, this website employs complex animated typography and music to introduce us to kOzen—"an old idea we had forgotten."

Lumière
www.lumiere.com
This online fashion magazine offers a wealth of articles about upscale designers, photographers, and style in general.

Oscar de la Renta
www.oscardelarenta.com/flash.html
Oscar de la Renta's site reproduces the fashion show experience for style surfers: In addition to seeing the latest designs shown on the catwalk, you'll also be able to hear unique soundtracks from the collections.

Plastic
www.plastic.com/index.pl?section=altculture&topic=Fashion
A fresh take on all culture issues is offered by the Altculture division of Plastic, a well-written online 'zine. Browse the style-related articles that often appear.

Ralph Lauren
www.polo.com
Check out Ralph Lauren's vision of quintessential all-American style at his official site.

Schiaparelli
www.schiaparelli.com
Schiaparelli fans will be pleased to learn that signature scarves, T-shirts, and handbags are being produced anew and may be

ordered through the company's website, which also has sections on Surrealism and books about the designer.

Sonia Rykiel
www.soniarykiel.com

Sonia Rykiel's designs are quintessentially French—elegant and sophisticated. The site is true to her style.

Style
www.style.com

Billed as "the online home of *Vogue* and *W*," this site offers a wealth of articles, up-to-the-minute fashion news, and links that allow shoppers to purchase clothes from the pages of the Condé Nast magazines.

Thierry Mugler
www.thierrymugler.com

French designer Thierry Mugler's website is an exercise in conceptual art: Roll your mouse over the stars in the sky and the faces of his fans and friends appear. Click on them, and you'll be able read their glowing testimonials.

Yves Saint Laurent
www.ysl-hautecouture.com

This is the official English-language version of Yves Saint Laurent's website; a retrospective of the retired designer's brilliant designs is on display in the collections section.

Zandra Rhodes
www.zandrarhodes.com

Colorful British designer Zandra Rhodes is as well known for her extraordinary textiles as for her dresses and products for the home. Visit this site and learn about the wonderful Fashion and Textile Museum in London—designed by architect Ricardo Legorreta—that Ms. Rhodes is backing; it is pure homage to the color-drenched architectural traditions of Mexico. There are also links to stores that carry the designer's furs and home products, along with the promise that dresses and gowns will appear on the site soon.

MUSEUMS

$\mathscr{I}$t seems that just about everywhere you go—in the United States or abroad—you'll find historical societies and museums that display costumes from the past. Here are a few places you can go, online and off, that you'll find especially valuable as resources. Via the Internet, there is the added bonus of museum-visiting pleasure without standing in line. But then again, standing in line entails dressing up for the show.

American Textile History Museum
www.athm.org
491 Dutton Street, Lowell, MA 01854 (978-441-0400)
Recent exhibitions have included "Dressed for the Part: Costumes from the Silver Screen" and "Threads of Light: Chinese Embroidery from Suzhou."

The Bata Shoe Museum
www.batashoemuseum.ca
327 Bloor Street West, Toronto, Ontario, Canada (416-979-7799)

This marvelous website opens with animated shoes cascading into buttons that direct you to their collection. The website includes historical footwear from the ancients to today, the shoes of stars (their Walk of Fame features some wild boots: John Lennon's Beatle boot, Elton John's silver-and-red platform boot, and Pablo Picasso's pony-skin ankle boots from the 1960's). North American Indian footwear by region, descriptions of their current exhibitions, a gift shop, and a fun facts quiz make this an enjoyable virtual museum trip.

The Fabric Workshop and Museum
www.fabricworkshopandmuseum.com
1315 Cherry Street, Philadelphia, PA 19107 (215-568-1111)

This atelier and exhibition space features collaborative experimental works in fabric and new materials by artists of diverse backgrounds.

Museum at the Fashion Institute of Technology
www.fitnyc.suny.edu/museum
27 Street at 7 Avenue, New York, NY 10001-5992

The Museum at the Fashion Institute of Technology boasts the world's largest collection of costumes and textiles with particular strength in twentieth-century fashion. Changing exhibitions have presented contemporary Belgian and Latin American designers, a retrospective of the avant-garde magazine *Visionaire*, and "John Rawlings: Thirty Years in *Vogue*."

Fondation Cartier pour l'Art Contemporain
www.fondation.cartier.fr
261 Boulevard Raspail, Paris, France 75014

Fondation Cartier pour l'Art Contemporain is a modern

building in Paris designed by Jean Nouvel that supports the work of contemporary artists. Their bilingual website provides a peek into their current exhibition. Issey Miyake's "Making Things" was installed here in 1998.

The Glove Museum
www.wegloveyou.com
304 Fifth Avenue, New York, NY 10001 (212-532-1956)

This website is maintained by LaCrasia Gloves, a company that makes new gloves in myriad styles. They maintain a presence on eBay using the seller name glovesla@aol.com. LaCrasia gloves have protected and adorned the hands of Jackie Kennedy, Madonna, Michael Jackson, Sylvester Stallone, and the casts of over 130 Broadway shows, including *Victor/Victoria, Showboat, On the Town,* and *Hello Dolly.* Designers who use their gloves form their own A to Z, including Geoffrey Beene and Vera Wang. The museum is located in their Fifth Avenue showroom and includes a large collection of vintage gloves. Admission to the museum is by appointment. Past exhibitions have included "Celebrities and their Gloves," "Designer Gloves Made in the USA," and "Native American Beaded Gauntlets."

Graceland
www.elvis-presley.com
3764 Elvis Presley Boulevard, Memphis, TN 38116

Here are the King's personal belongings housed in a 1939 mansion occupied by Presley from 1957 until his death in 1977.

The Historic Costume & Textile Collection

http://costume.osu.edu

College of Human Ecology, The Geraldine Schottenstein Wing, 175 Campbell Hall, 1787 Neil Avenue, Columbus, OH 43210-1295 (614-292-3090)

This costume and textile museum is part of the Ohio State University museum system. The collection includes women's garments by American designers of the twentieth century, including James Galanos, Arnold Scaasi, Pauline Trigère, Irene, and Bonnie Cashin.

The Lace Museum

www.thelacemuseum.org

552 South Murphy Avenue, Sunnyvale, CA 94086 (408-730-4695)

Their collection includes lace-trimmed clothing, family heirlooms, and costumes. This website provides information for lacemakers and guild members regarding classes and travel and links to other lacy websites.

Costume Institute of the Metropolitan Museum of Art

www.metmuseum.org

1000 Fifth Avenue, New York, NY 10028 (212-879-5000)

This collection was started in 1946 with the transfer of the holdings of the Museum of Costume Art; the Costume Institute's astounding collection allows only a fraction of their more than 75,000 costumes and accessories on view at any one time. A privileged few are invited to view the drawers, boxes, and racks in the institute's offices and storage areas. Recent exhibitions have included "Jacqueline Kennedy: The White House Years— Selections from the John F. Kennedy Museum and Library" and

"Extreme Beauty: The Body Transformed," an exhibition that examines various zones of the body (neck, hips, feet) that have been bound, padded, and constricted, including one hundred costumes from the sixteenth century to the present featuring Thierry Mugler, Christian Dior, and Madonna's pink satin bustier by Jean Paul Gaultier.

Musée de la Mode et du Costume de la Ville de Paris
www.paris.org/musees/costume/info.html
Palais Galliera, 10 av Pierre I er de Serbie, 75116 Paris, France (47-20-85-23)

The museum presents thematic exhibitions and its permanent collection of French fashion from the eighteenth century to the present day.

Museum of Vintage Fashion, Inc.
www.museumofvintagefashion.org
10 Lacassie Court, Walnut Creek, CA 94596 (925-944-1896)

The museum located in the William Penn Mott, Jr., Memorial Gardens has an extensive collection including 25,000 artifacts, from 1736 to the present day. Seventy-five designers are represented in forty-five accessory subcollections. Recent exhibitions: "A Legacy in Lingerie & Lace" and "Decades: Designer Closet Tour."

The Rock and Roll Hall of Fame and Museum
www.rockhall.com
1 Key Plaza, Cleveland, OH 44114 (216-781-1832)

Costumes, personal artifacts, and other media from and about your favorite rock musicians are displayed in a building designed by I. M. Pei.

The Textile Museum
www.textilemuseum.org

2320 S Street, N.W., Washington, DC 20008 (202-667-0441)

Located in a historic neighborhood of Washington, DC, the museum's collection of textile traditions of non-Western cultures include more than 16,000 objects spanning 5,000 years and a library of more than 15,000 books.

Victoria and Albert Museum
www.vam.ac.uk

Cromwell Road, South Kensington, London SW7 2RL (44-0-20 7942 2000)

The Victoria and Albert Museum in London is the world's largest museum devoted to the decorative arts. It includes collections of vintage as well as contemporary fashion. "Fashion in Motion" is the V&A's innovative way to show the latest collections by leading designers. Models walk through the galleries wearing the clothing on selected Fridays followed by a Fashion Forum with the designer. Recent participants include Clements Ribiero, Catherine Walker, and Robert Cary-Williams.

REELING IN THE YEARS:
MOVIES WITH STYLE INSPIRATION

*But of course that was the day the Germans marched into Paris.
Not an easy day to forget. I remember every detail. The
Germans wore gray; you wore blue.*
  —Ingrid Bergman and Humphrey Bogart in *Casablanca* (1942)

American Gigolo (1980) The definitive menswear movie; watch
the handsome Richard Gere compete for screen time with his
own wardrobe of amazing Armanis.

Annie Hall (1977) Diane Keaton's personal wardrobe is an over-
the-top display of thrift store chic. One of the costume designers
was Ralph Lauren.

Barry Lyndon (1975) Stanley Kubrick's eighteenth-century costume drama, in which the exquisite Marisa Berenson wears one
unforgettable gown after another—even in the bathtub.

Big Night (1996) A cinematic gallery of 1950's style icons, from
the bombshell dresses worn by Isabella Rossellini to the Cadillac

convertible to the casual men's shirts. Beware the inevitable hunger this movie will stir up: You'll never fit into those tight dresses if you indulge in meals like this.

The Birds (1963) Features the sophisticated society girl, played by Tippi Hedren, in this classic Hitchcock horror film of nature run amok in Bodega Bay. Best scene: In stiletto heels and a fur coat, Hedren maneuvers a small motorboat across the bay to surreptitiously deliver some lovebirds.

Blowup (1966) Starring David Hemmings, Vanessa Redgrave, and the fashion model Veruschka, this film exemplifies the style of the swinging 1960's in London.

Bonnie and Clyde (1967) With designs by Theadora Van Runkle, the clothes of Warren Beatty and Faye Dunaway can inspire an immediate visit to the thrift shop.

Boogie Nights (1997) The dark side of the 1970's disco era, with tight Qiana shirts and dresses, oversized platform shoes, and flared pants seen both on and off the actors.

Breakfast at Tiffany's (1961) The supreme Hepburn film, of course, is the inspiration for the thousands of keyworded "little black dresses" on eBay. Everything in this movie is a keyword on a vintage fashion list, from "Givenchy" to "Burberry." A must-see!

Charade (1963) Highlights include Audrey Hepburn's Givenchy-designed orange coat with large black buttons. Cary Grant wears his suit in the shower, proclaiming it, "Drip dry, the manufacturer recommends it!"

Crouching Tiger, Hidden Dragon (2000) Admire the wealth of exquisite Asian costumes—from the traditional and ceremonial to the uniforms of the ninja—in this wonderful film, the era of which appears indefinable.

Dial M for Murder (1954) Grace Kelly has earned herself the position of having her name on the one of the most coveted vintage items of all: the Hermès Kelly bag. This is not *the* exact bag, but one, however, that figures prominently in this Hitchcock film.

The English Patient (1996) Set partly in the Sahara Desert during the 1930's, this movie will make you long for white linen dresses—like the ones worn by Kristin Scott Thomas—and strong, silent men. Notice how Ralph Fiennes's blue buttondown shirt matches his eyes.

Eyes of Laura Mars (1978) Faye Dunaway plays a fashion photographer who has premonitions about the violent deaths of her colleagues. This very stylish 1970's thriller is instilled with the style of fashion photographers Helmut Newton, Sarah Moon, and Deborah Turbeville.

Flashdance (1983) Jennifer Beals gets the guy while wearing leg warmers and a sweatshirt with a torn neck. A style is born, and a nation's mothers are summarily horrified.

Funny Face (1957) Fred Astaire plays a photographer—based on the film's consultant, Richard Avedon—who discovers a young woman in the Greenwich Village bookstore that a fashion magazine commandeers for a shoot. He is determined to turn this "funny face" into the *Quality Woman* for a prominent fashion magazine of the same name. *Funny Face,* the ultimate film about clothes, features an extraordinary blue silk taffeta gown and shawl, Paris, and songs by George and Ira Gershwin.

Gentlemen Prefer Blondes (1953) Marilyn in *that* gown. With *those* gloves. And *that* jewelry.

Gigi (1958) Another Oscar went to Cecil Beaton for his costumes in this film starring Leslie Caron and Louis Jourdan. Maurice Chevalier sings "Thank Heaven for Little Girls."

Gilda (1946) The debut of Christian Dior's New Look in the winter of 1946–1947 caught the eye of Rita Hayworth, who bought a marine-blue taffeta dress called Soirée to wear to the premier of this classic film.

Gone With the Wind (1939) Be inspired by Vivien Leigh's magnificent green gown, which she fashions out of velvet curtains, and her valiant postpartum waist-management campaign.

Goodfellas (1990) Strong-willed gangster-wife, played by Lorraine Bracco, toughs it out in style over three decades—the 1960's through the 1980's. Her fabulous outfits include an eye-popping Pucci ensemble.

The Great Gatsby (1974) Mia Farrow practically floats across the screen in ethereal 1920's dresses; Robert Redford's suits are not to be missed.

High Society (1956) Grace Kelly's dresses are brilliant, of course, but she and Frank Sinatra even manage to make terry cloth robes look glamorous.

How to Steal a Million (1966) Givenchy-clad Audrey Hepburn tools around Paris in vintage sports cars. Fabulous hats, mini-skirted suits with little jackets, and a wicked black cocktail dress with a veil share the screen with gorgeous Audrey, dressed in a nightgown and a pair of wellies; a museum caper movie that is among the best ever made.

James Bond movies (1962–present day) When it comes to over-the-top glamour and hands-on-hips demonstrations of the power of great clothes, the Bond movies are in a class by themselves, whether we're discussing *Dr. No* (1962), in which Ursula Andress *owned* that bikini, or *A View to a Kill* (1985), in which the fabulous Grace Jones personified the fierce 1980's woman of the designers' catwalks. Modern Bond flicks continue to dazzle us. Never mind the gadgets and the explosions—give us leather, sequins, and stilettos.

The King and I (1956) Irene Sharaff won an Academy Award for the exquisite costumes in this classic film starring Deborah Kerr.

Klute (1971) This is a superb and moody suspense piece; Jane Fonda is brilliant as a stylishly costumed call girl whose hairdo launched countless imitations.

Lady Sings the Blues (1972) This was the movie debut of the incomparable Diana Ross, one of greatest divas of our time. Her performance dresses are astounding, as you'd expect—Oscar-nominated costume design is by Bob Mackie, Ray Aghayan, and Norma Koch.

La Femme Nikita (1990) A waiflike Parisian street criminal, played by ex-ballerina Anne Parillaud, is transformed into a sophisticated hit woman who demonstrates the lethal power of high heels and a little black dress.

Les Girls (1957) This Cole Porter musical directed by George Cukor stars the fabulous trio of Mitzi Gaynor, Kay Kendall, and Taina Elg as three gorgeous showgirls, and Gene Kelly as their dancer/boyfriend. Orry-Kelly won an Oscar for best costume designer, as he did for *Some Like It Hot* and *An American in Paris*.

Less Than Zero (1987) Watch Robert Downey Jr. wearing 1980's Japanese avant-garde fashion as he sinks into the twin tar pits of decadence and drug dependency. The other spoiled Hollywood youngsters are equally stylish.

My Fair Lady (1964) Cecil Beaton won an Oscar for costume design for his work on this classic. His dresses are largely black and white. Check out those hats at Ascot.

Network (1976) This Sidney Lumet film from a Paddy Chayefsky screenplay foreshadows the current craze for reality TV. Faye Dunaway, dressed in Theoni V. Aldredge designs, plays an ambitious TV executive with an eye toward the ratings.

North by Northwest (1959) Eva Marie Saint wears a New Look suit in this thriller from Alfred Hitchcock. Dressed in the same gray business suit throughout, Cary Grant, an advertising executive mistaken for a spy, is pursued across the country. Catch Eva Marie hanging around Mount Rushmore!

Notebook on Cities and Clothes: A Film by Wim Wenders with Yohji Yamamoto (1989) Commissioned by the Pompidou Center in Paris, this film is actually an extended conversation with Yohji Yamamoto that was written and directed by the German filmmaker Wim Wenders. Yohji considers his clothes and living in Tokyo, and Wenders reflects on the relationship of two art forms, cinema and fashion. The film contains intriguing predigital film and video techniques and cutting—both cinematic and of the cloth.

A Perfect Murder (1998) Spare, expensive, and elegant 1990's fashion perfectly shown by its wearer, Gwyneth Paltrow.

The Philadelphia Story (1940) An ever-elegant Katharine Hepburn wears gowns designed by Gilbert Adrian. Adrian designed the costumes and gowns for over 230 Hollywood films from 1925 to 1952.

Pretty in Pink (1986) Beautiful, underprivileged Molly Ringwald can't afford to buy her prom gown from a ritzy boutique. Her thirty-something girlfriend helps her refashion a vintage dress, and, of course, she gets the guy. What a wonderful movie.

Quadrophenia (1979) Witness the culture clash between the hip, stylish, scooter-riding mods, who love pop music and American soul, and the leather-jacket-wearing rockers, who zoom around on big motorcycles. The theme of clothing as identity is explored to exhilarating effect.

Qui êtes-vous, Polly Magoo? (1966) If you can possibly get to see this French-language cult classic about Paris in the 1960's by American fashion photographer William Klein, run, don't walk! The 1967 Prix Jean Vigo award-winning film features Grayson Hill as a Diana Vreeland–type fashion editor and model Peggy Moffitt sporting her signature Vidal Sassoon haircut.

The Railway Children (1970) Victorian fashion—at both ends of the economic spectrum—is lavishly depicted in this charming British film about a well-to-do family that falls on hard times and must temporarily relocate to the country.

Rear Window (1954) Alfred Hitchcock's fabulous thriller stars Grace Kelly, who is characteristically lovely in her charm bracelets, pearl necklaces, and elegant dresses. And, of course, she's sporting that Mark Cross overnight case.

The Remains of the Day (1993) Set in pre–World War II Britain, and starring Anthony Hopkins and Emma Thompson, this film is brimming with elegant menswear. The acting is gorgeous, too.

Roman Holiday (1953) Who can forget the image of Audrey as the reluctant princess on the back of a Vespa tooling through the streets of Rome with Gregory Peck? A belted full skirt; a crisp white cotton blouse with the collar turned up, short sleeves rolled up; and a small kerchief tied around her neck evoked the style of a delightful young woman on a carefree spree before accepting the responsibilities of her life.

Sabrina (1954) In this movie, filmed on the Glen Cove estate of the then-president of Paramount Pictures, Audrey Hepburn plays a chauffeur's daughter who is sent off to a cooking school in Paris to get over her crush on the younger son of an industrial tycoon. Hepburn returns from Paris sophisticated and elegant in a black suit, perfectly accessorized with a toy French poodle. She describes the dress that she will wear to her welcome-home party as having "yards of skirt," and it is indeed the strapless dress of all strapless dresses, designed for her by her lifelong friend and personal couturier, Givenchy (though Edith Head won the Oscar). In a timeless and sophisticated fashion, Hepburn wears mid-calf leggings and flat shoes with a long black slim coat when she tells Linus Larrabee (Humphrey Bogart) she is returning to Paris.

Saturday Night Fever (1977) The disco movie that launched a thousand looks, the most memorable of which include John Travolta's half-unbuttoned black shirt, worn with a white jacket, vest, and pants.

Shaft (1971) Richard Roundtree, as Detective John Shaft, shows how to accessorize a black turtleneck: with wicked sideburns, good posture, and attitude to spare.

Six Degrees of Separation (1993) Stockard Channing and her New York society friends wear brilliant 1990's suits and ball gowns in this must-see movie that presents a complex study of Manhattan life featuring numerous hot spots: fashionable restaurants, art museums, and high-rise apartments.

Some Like It Hot (1959) Imagine putting on an evening dress and trying to compete with Marilyn Monroe. Now imagine that you're a man attempting this. Somehow, Jack Lemmon and Tony Curtis are able to hold their own in high heels while cavorting with the immortal blond bombshell. It's a hilarious, timeless masterpiece that's packed with inspiring outfits.

Summer of '42 (1971) Jennifer O'Neill is the quintessential New England beauty in white cotton and breezy 1940's florals.

The Talented Mr. Ripley (1999) This stylish thriller is set in the 1950's, mostly in southern Italy. Gwyneth Paltrow and Cate Blanchett wear some of the prettiest, most elegant mid-century fashions imaginable, and the scenery and music are just as wonderful.

That Touch of Mink (1962) Doris Day is wearing Norman Norell's beige raincoat with a black leather collar and buttons when splashed by Cary Grant's limo in the opening moments of this sophisticated comedy. Grant, as a suave, handsome business tycoon, woos Ms. Day in this elegant-looking New York–based film filled with 1960's sexual and social mores. Watch for a clever cameo appearance by those guys in pinstripes—Mickey Mantle, Roger Maris, and Yogi Berra.

The Thomas Crown Affair (1968) Faye Dunaway and Steve McQueen are ultrachic in this sophisticated 1960's caper about a Boston millionaire planning a bank heist.

Titanic (1997) Many souls were lost in the actual 1912 disaster on which the movie was based, and, at least according to this over-the-top version, another tragedy occurred—*far* smaller, but troubling, all the same: Kate Winslet's amazing beaded gowns, as well as her numerous original paintings and the ship's countless place settings of exquisite china, all ended up on the ocean floor.

To Catch a Thief (1955) In the opening sequence, Cary Grant (the most likely suspect as the jewel thief, John Robie) is dressed in an outfit consisting of a striped shirt with a red neckerchief and gray flannel pleated pants with the most incredible drape. Grace Kelly looks outrageous in fabulous 1950's gowns, jewels, and a sensational black-and-white beach ensemble of bathing suit, capri pants, a half skirt, and large brimmed hat that steals a scene as she walks through the hotel lobby with Grant. This is a great and stylish film that also features a fantastic costume ball with a Louis XIV theme.

Two for the Road (1967) Albert Finney and Audrey Hepburn star in this story of the courtship and marriage of an architect and his wife over a period of approximately ten years. Hepburn wears some marvelous psychedelic prints and Givenchy knits.

Valley of the Dolls (1967) See this movie and immerse yourself in the glamorous, superficial world of 1960's Hollywood, complete with big hair, heavy makeup, and wild clothes.

Vertigo (1958) Alfred Hitchcock certainly knew how to dress his female blond leads. If you are into suits, don't miss the one designed by Edith Head and worn by Kim Novak. And check out Carlotta's necklace.

Witch Hunt (1994) Set in 1950's Hollywood, this murder-mystery TV film stars Dennis Hopper and Penelope Ann Miller.

It's a cinematic picture book of period fashion and, therefore, a must-see for the vintage lover. There are full-skirted dresses, breathtaking gowns, and wonderful wool jackets to spare, as well as plenty of too-cool cars.

The Women (1939) Directed by George Cukor, this is another tour de force for Gilbert Adrian. As was his custom, he created trendsetting looks for glamorous women, and this cast was no exception: Norma Shearer, Rosalind Russell, Joan Fontaine, and, of course, Joan Crawford. It was Adrian who gave Crawford her signature silhouette: the wide, padded shoulders, narrow waist, and slim skirt.

WHERE TO FIND THESE FABULOUS FILMS AND MORE

Best Video
www.bestvideo.com

Hank Paper's extensive inventory of 35,000 cult, foreign, independent, and hard-to-find videos is one of the largest mail-order video rental sites online. You can rent four or more videos for seven nights, including shipping, for under $35.

Dover Publications
www.doverpublications.com

If your interest in vintage fashion from 1970's films is a bit more two-dimensional, you may want to buy *Glamorous Movie Stars of the 70's,* a book of paper dolls dressed in their underwear with two outfits each for Liza Minelli, Diane Keaton, Faye Dunaway, and others.

Internet Movie Database

www.IMDb.com

This oft-visited website is extraordinary in its depth. You can search by title, director, actor, award winners, quotes, biographies, and plots. It's an excellent place to build your own movie database on any subject, like fashion.

BIBLIOGRAPHY

Baker, Patricia. *Fashions of a Decade: The 1950s.* New York: Facts on File, 1991.

Baudot, François. *Fashion: Twentieth Century.* New York: Universe Publishing, 1999.

————. *Chanel.* New York: Universe/Vendome, 1996.

Benstock, Shari, and Suzanne Ferriss, eds. *On Fashion.* New Brunswick, NJ: Rutgers University Press, 1994.

Bowles, Hamish, ed. *Jacqueline Kennedy: The White House Years: Selections from the John F. Kennedy Library and Museum.* New York: Metropolitan Museum of Art; Boston: Bulfinch Press, 2001.

Callan, Georgina O'Hara. *The Thames and Hudson Dictionary of Fashion and Fashion Designers.* London: Thames and Hudson, 1998.

Cawthorne, Nigel. *The New Look: The Dior Revolution.* Edison, NJ: Wellfleet Press, 1996.

Colton, Virginia, ed. *Reader's Digest Complete Guide to Sewing.* Pleasantville, NY: The Reader's Digest Association, Inc., 1976.

Crane, Diana. *Fashion and Its Social Agendas: Class, Gender, and Identity in Clothing.* Chicago: University of Chicago Press, 2000.

Derycke, Luc, and Sandra van de Veire, eds. *Belgian Fashion Design.* Ghent: Ludion, 1999.

Fraser, Kennedy. *The Fashionable Mind: Reflections on Fashion 1970–1981.* New York: Knopf, 1981.

———. *On the Edge: Images from 100 Years of Vogue.* New York: Random House, 1992.

Grand, France. *Comme des Garçons.* New York: Universe, 1998.

Greenbaum, Toni. *Messengers of Modernism: American Studio Jewelry, 1940–1960.* New York: Montreal Museum of Decorative Arts in association with Flammarion, 1996.

Hawthorne, Rosemary. *The Costume Collector's Companion 1890–1990.* London: Aurum Press, 1998.

Hollander, Anne. *Seeing Through Clothes.* Berkeley: University of California Press, 1993.

Keogh, Pamela Clarke. *Audrey Style.* New York: HarperCollins, 1999.

Lehmann, Ulrich. *Tigersprung: Fashion in Modernity.* Cambridge: MIT Press, 2000.

Lurie, Alison. *The Language of Clothes.* New York: Random House, 1981.

Martin, Richard. *Fashion and Surrealism.* New York: Rizzoli, 1987.

———. *Gianni Versace.* New York: Metropolitan Museum of Art, 1997.

Martin, Richard, and Harold Koda. *Jocks and Nerds: Men's Style in the Twentieth Century.* New York: Rizzoli, 1989.

———. *Flair: Fashion Collected by Tina Chow.* New York: Rizzoli, 1992.

———. *Christian Dior.* New York: Metropolitan Museum of Art, 1996.

Mendes, Valerie. *Dressed in Black.* New York: Abrams; London: V & A Publications, 1999.

Michael, Paul. *The American Movies: The History, Films, Awards.* New York: Galahad Books, 1969.

Morrill, Penny Chittim, and Carole A. Berk. *Mexican Silver: 20th Century Handwrought Jewelry and Metalwork.* Atglen, PA: Schiffer, 1994.

Musheno, Elizabeth J., ed. *The Vogue Sewing Book.* New York: Vogue Patterns, 1975.

Saint Laurent, Yves, Diana Vreeland, et al. *Yves Saint Laurent.* New York: Metropolitan Museum of Art/Clarkson N. Potter, 1983.

Sato, Kazuko. *Issey Miyake Making Things.* Paris: Fondation Cartier pour l'Art Contemporain, 1998.

Tolkein, Tracy. *Dressing Up Vintage.* New York: Rizzoli, 2000.

AUCTION CATALOGS

The Couture Collection of Tina Chow. New York: Christie's East, 1993.
The Estate of Jacqueline Kennedy Onassis. New York: Sotheby's 1996.
Rago, David, et al. *Bakelite, Designer Costume, Modernist & Mexican Silver Jewelry.* Lambertville, NJ: David Rago Modern Auctions, 2000.

INDEX

ABOUT THE AUTHORS

LINDA LINDROTH has exhibited her photographs and mixed media artwork in over one hundred solo and group shows. Her work is represented in numerous public and private collections including the Museum of Modern Art and the Metropolitan Museum of Art in New York. She earned a master of fine arts in art from Rutgers University and is an assistant professor of fine art at Quinnipiac University. She lives with her family in Connecticut.

DEBORAH NEWELL TORNELLO was educated in England, Barbados, Honduras, and the United States. She earned a bachelor of science in advertising from the University of Florida. She lives with her family in the Tampa Bay area, where she is working on assorted fiction projects.